Fragile Freedoms

Fragile Freedoms

Human Rights and Dissent in Canada

Thomas R. Berger

Clarke, Irwin & Company Limited
Toronto/Vancouver

Canadian Cataloguing in Publication Data

Berger, Thomas R.
  Fragile Freedoms

Includes index.
ISBN 0-7720-1358-6

1. Civil liberties – Canada – History.   2. Minorities –
Canada – History.   3. Dissenters – Canada – History.
I. Title.

JC599.C2B47   323.4'0971   C81-094871-0

1 2 3 4 5   JD   85 84 83 82 81

Printed in Canada

Acknowledgements

Fragile Freedoms had its origins in lectures I prepared for a seminar on civil liberties I conducted, together with Professor Robin Elliot, in the Faculty of Law, University of British Columbia, in 1980 and 1981. The materials were enlarged for purposes of lectures I delivered in Canadian Studies at Simon Fraser University. The reception given to the lectures by the students at both universities led me to believe that the materials might find a wider audience. My secretary, Mrs. Amber Halliday, typed the lectures with her usual unfailing competence. Mrs. Esther Horswill and my daughter, Erin Berger, have typed the manuscript that evolved from the lecture materials. Both have been patient and painstaking, as the manuscript went through one revision after another. I wish to express my thanks to Mrs. Halliday, Mrs. Horswill and Erin.

Judge Harry Boyle read the manuscript at an early stage and urged me to continue. Alan Cooke, of the Centre for Northern Studies at McGill University, did much work on the manuscript and greatly improved its style. To both of them, and to numerous friends and colleagues who commented on individual chapters, I am most grateful.

Contents

"If human rights and harmonious relations between cultures are forms of the beautiful, then the state is a work of art that is never finished."

F. R. SCOTT

Introduction

Freedom is a fragile commodity in the world today. Everywhere human rights are beset by ideology and orthodoxy, diversity is rejected, and dissent is stifled.

Alexander Solzhenitsyn, Steve Biko, Lech Walesa, Jacobo Timerman—their names have made human rights one of the great issues of our time. They have given form and substance to the contest between freedom and repression. They and other brave men and women have been imprisoned and tortured, and some have been executed, for wanting to be free, and for believing that their countrymen should be free. They have claimed the right to question—and to challenge—the political ideas undergirding the regimes in their own countries. They speak for all mankind.

Mass deportations, terror and torture, racial prejudice, political and religious persecution, and the destruction of institutions from which people derive their sense of identity are assaults upon human dignity and the human condition that are odious to men and women everywhere. In the Western democracies, we especially cherish representative institutions and the rule of law, democracy and due process. These traditions affirm the right to dissent: in politics, in religion, in science and in the arts. We conceive of these rights as individual rights, but they are much more than that. They are the means whereby diversity is maintained, and whereby minorities can thrive.

The questions that minorities raise are not always easy to answer, and they are not always the same. Some minorities wish to integrate, some even to assimilate, and they fear that cultural distinctions will be used to exclude them from equal opportunities in political, social and economic life. Others seek to defend and protect such distinctions, fearing that their erasure will lead to assimilation and the surrender of their identity. Diversity is anathema to the rulers of many modern nation-states. The government of such a state can be an instrument of repression, denying a minority the right to speak its own language, to practise its own religion, or to pursue a way of life that differs from that of the majority—in short, denying the members of a minority the freedom to be themselves.

Canadian history has not been free of these injustices, although there is no reason to flagellate ourselves. We respect human rights and the rule of law. An intellectual tradition founded on the advantages of free inquiry and a long experience of the institutions of liberal democracy have equipped us to learn from our history. Canadians have, however, no justification for being smug. Sometimes we have upheld human rights, but sometimes we have succumbed to the temptations of intolerance. Sometimes we have listened to the voices of protest; at other times we have tried to stifle them. By examining our history, we can understand better what kind of world must be created to foster human rights and fundamental freedoms.

In many nations the struggle for daily existence completely occupies the government and the people. Perhaps in some of these nations the development of democratic institutions and the rule of law must wait. But some nations that are well endowed with natural resources, that possess the advantages of industry, high technology and an educated populace, still deny human rights to their people. Tyrants of the left and of the right make use of the vocabulary of democracy: they hold sham elections, make promises to respect human rights, and promulgate hollow constitutions that guarantee equality to all races, languages, and religions.

The peoples of all of these nations share a deep longing to be free, to live under a government that is accountable to the governed, to know that public order is not purchased at the price of human dignity. The Western democracies have stable governments that rule by consent; their citizens have the means of participating in decisions that govern their own lives; their governments are removed from office without violence and death. All people seek a measure of self-determination in their own lives, and they should be able to seek it in their own way, according to their own traditions; in this search, many seek to emulate the institutions of the Western democracies.

The freedom we enjoy in the Western democracies is a precious commodity, as well as a fragile one, and it represents Western man's idea, evolving since classical times, of the just society. Yet, because our concepts of self-government acquired their present form in the nation-states of Great Britain and France, states that have traditionally been ethnically defined, we have not fully realized or developed institutional guarantees for racial, cultural, religious, and linguistic minorities.

In fact, our ideas of human rights have only recently expanded to include the rights of minorities. Governments are usually opposed to the devolution of power, to the entrenchment of diversity, to what they see as the weakening of the nation-state, This is especially so when a single, dominant people regards the state as its own political instrument. The government of such a state may regard minority languages and cultures as anomalous or transitional. In Canada, however, we have found that such diversity is the essence of the Canadian experience.

Questions of human rights and dissent in Canada are linked to questions of human rights and dissent around the world. Our own successes and failures, our own attempts to accommodate minorities, are important not only to ourselves. If people of differing races, religions, cultures, and languages can live together harmoniously within a great federal state, perhaps they may learn to live together harmoniously in the wider world.

And what of the Canadian experience? What does our history say to us and to the world? Canada is adopting a new Constitution and a Charter of Rights and Freedoms. In doing so, we will sever the last formal link to colonial dependency. Far more important, however, is the fact that

this exercise in constitution-making has forced us to articulate our idea of Canada. For a Constitution does not
merely provide the means of settling present disputes, it
is a legal garment that reveals the values that we hold. It
is a document expressing that decent respect which the
present owes to the past; it is, at the same time, a document
addressed to future generations.

A Constitution is not intended simply to divide up revenue and resources between the federal government and
the provinces. Canada's new Constitution, like the British
North America Act before it, will divide legislative powers
between Parliament and the provinces. This division is
precisely that, a division of powers, powers exercised by
a majority through the federal government or by a majority
within each of the provincial governments. But every
thoughtful person realizes that limits must be set to these
powers: there must be guarantees for the rights of minorities and dissenters; there must be protection for those who
would otherwise be powerless.

Although our notions of democracy and due process
evolved in the ethnically defined nation-states of Europe,
Canada is not such a nation-state. We have two founding
peoples, English and French, within a single state; we have
aboriginal peoples with an historic claim to special status;
and we have a variety of ethnic groups and races who have
immigrated to Canada. Thus, we have many linguistic,
racial, cultural, and ethnic minorities. Each of them will
have a claim to collective as well as to individual guarantees
under the new Constitution and the Charter of Rights and
Freedoms, and each of them has a claim on the goodwill
of the majority. For all of these minorities the right to
dissent is the mainstay of their freedom.

In Canada, we have two great societies, one English-
speaking, one French-speaking, joined by history and cir-
cumstance. When we look to our past, we can see that the
central issue of our history has been the working out of
relations between these two societies. No discussion of
Canadian institutions can proceed except as a discussion
of the evolution of relations between the English and the

French on this continent. The dominant theme of the constitutional discussions that led to Confederation in 1867 was the accommodation of these two communities in Canada. This theme, though sometimes it recedes, still overshadows the continuing constitutional debate of our own time.

These two societies, today, have much in common. Both are urban, industrial and bureaucratic. Although their linguistic and cultural differences are still significant, and they are responsible for the creative tension that is the distinctive characteristic of the Canadian political scene, these differences no longer threaten either side. As Pierre Trudeau has remarked, "The die is cast in Canada. Neither of our two language groups can force assimilation on the other."

It was not always so. The conquest of New France by the British in 1759 led to a series of attempts to assimilate the people of Quebec. These attempts were stoutly resisted by Quebecers, and their population of 60,000 has grown to some six million, and their culture flourishes as never before. The history of the French Canadians of Quebec epitomizes the struggle of minorities everywhere.

Today, in every Canadian province, there is a minority that speaks either English or French, and this fundamental duality places the condition of minorities at the very centre of our institutional arrangements. At the same time, the diversity of our huge nation has given rise to many forms of dissent.

This book is not, therefore, about Laval and Frontenac, Wolfe and Montcalm. It is not about Confederation, the Canadian Pacific Railway, and the North-West Mounted Police; nor is it about Canadian achievements in the First World War and the Second World War. Instead, *Fragile Freedoms* is about the expulsion and return of the Acadians; it is about the destruction of the Metis as a nation and the loss of their homeland on the plains; it is about the school crisis in Manitoba, when French Canadians were denied the right to separate schools, and the school crisis in Ontario, when the French Canadians were denied the right to speak their own language in their own schools; it is about the internment of the Japanese Canadians during the Second World War and their banishment after the war; it is about measures taken against Communists to curb their freedom of speech and of association; it is about the persecution of the Witnesses of Jehovah in Quebec; it is about the internment in 1970 of hundreds of dissidents in Quebec during the October Crisis; and it is about Native rights and the land claims movement of today.

This is a book, then, about minorities and dissenters, about their struggles, their victories, their defeats. But this book is also about Canada and Canadians, for the victories and defeats of our minorities and dissenters are, in their own way, the history of the successes and failures of our institutions: of our Parliament, our legislatures and our courts; and of our politicians, our judges, and ourselves.

Of course, the struggles of Canada's minorities and dissenters do not by any means represent the whole Canadian experience. But they throw into relief the true extent of the Canadian capacity for tolerance and of our belief in diversity. They sharpen our perception of ourselves. Although many of these struggles began long ago, they still continue, and may have a contemporary denouement.

Some Canadians regard our history as a burden and consider that here are only tiresome tales of events long past. How can we progress, encumbered with this historical baggage? Why should we be reminded of these dark passages in the Canadian journey? Is there no end to our *mea culpas*? Today, we are a prosperous and peaceful nation, we have stable institutions, we admit to full citizenship persons of all races, of any religion, of every language. What is past is past. Our only obligation, as President John F. Kennedy said, is to be just in our own time.

But to be just in our own time often requires an understanding of earlier times. The world was not invented this morning, and we cannot comprehend what measures will supply justice in our own time unless we understand the history of times past.

The Canadian Constitution has always recognized that

we are a plural, not a monolithic, nation. This is one of the finest Canadian traditions. Refugees from every continent, immigrants of every race, peoples of all faiths, and persons seeking political asylum have all found their place in Canadian life. It is our good fortune not to be of one common descent, not to speak one language only. We are not cursed with a triumphant ideology; we are not given to mindless patriotism. For these reasons Canada is a difficult nation to govern; there is never an easy consensus. Yet, our diversity shouldn't terrify us: it should be our strength, not our weakness.

Along every seam in the Canadian mosaic unravelled by conflict, a binding thread of tolerance can be seen. I speak of tolerance not as mere indifference, but in its most positive aspect, as the expression of a profound belief in the virtues of diversity and in the right to dissent.

Many Canadians have championed the ideal of tolerance throughout our history. Who can forget the tortured figure of Louis Riel, who died insisting upon the rights of his people? Or the great Laurier, pleading the cause of the Franco-Ontarians during the First World War? Or Angus MacInnis, who insisted upon the rights of the Japanese Canadians during the Second World War when the whole of British Columbia—in fact, the whole nation—stood against them? Or John Diefenbaker, calling for an end to the persecution of the Jehovah's Witnesses during the Second World War; Pierre Trudeau, defender of civil liberties in Quebec during the 1950s under the Duplessis regime; Ivan Rand, a great judge and legal philosopher, who affirmed the rights of political and religious dissenters during the 1950s; and Emmett Hall, whose humane judgement in the Nishga Indians' case in 1973 opened up the whole question of Native claims in Canada?

I am not urging that we set up a national waxworks. But the Canadian imagination is still peopled almost exclusively by the heroes and heroines of other nations, and our knowledge of who we are has suffered as a result. The crises of times past have thrown into prominence many men and women who have articulated and defended an idea of Canada that has illuminated the Canadian journey.

These Canadians—men and women of courage and compassion—were committed to an idea of Canada that we can all share today, an idea that goes deeper than the division of powers, an idea more eloquent than any set of constitutional proposals, an idea that took root long before the present crisis and which will endure beyond it—a faith in fundamental freedoms and in tolerance for all people. This idea of Canada represents the highest aspiration of any nation, and it evokes the best in our Canadian traditions.

Fragile Freedoms

ONE

The Acadians: Expulsion and Return

FOUR EUROPEAN NATIONS colonized the New World: Spain and Portugal have left their cultural and linguistic imprint on Mexico, Central America and South America; England and France have left theirs on North America. France sent colonists to North America before England, and it was on the Bay of Fundy, not along the St. Lawrence River, that the French established their first settlement in the New World. This was Acadia, which soon became and, for a century and a half, remained a focus of conflict between England and France. That conflict reached its climax in 1755 with the expulsion of the Acadians from their homes and their farms on the Bay of Fundy. Canadians are familiar with the poignant story of that painful year, but know little of the history of the Acadians before the expulsion, or of the drama of their return.

The history of the Acadians provides a parable for our own time, for, as Professor Naomi Griffiths has said in *The Acadians: Creation of a People*, that history is "a statement of the rights of small settlements against the claims of large empires." The Acadians wished to be free to till the soil, to speak their own language, to practise their religion, and to pass their values on to their children. This they did, despite the hardships of pioneering, the afflictions of war, and the loss of their homeland.

The rival claims of the English and the French kings began long before the establishment of Acadia. John Cabot, a Venetian in English service, had sailed around Newfoundland in 1497, and English claims in North America were based on his discoveries. Forty years later, after a reconnaissance of the Gulf in 1534, Jacques Cartier, in 1535, sailed up the St. Lawrence River to the then impassable rapids near present-day Montreal. He and his men wintered near present-day Quebec City. There they suffered severely from scurvy, and from the winter's cold, which they had not expected—Quebec City is actually just a little south of the latitude of Paris.

Of course, Cabot and Cartier had not been the first Europeans to see North America since the time of the Norse expeditions to Vinland around AD 1000. Even before Columbus sailed in 1492, fishermen from western Europe had found their way to the Grand Banks off the coast of Newfoundland. Throughout the sixteenth century hundreds of vessels sailed across the Atlantic every year from Spain, Portugal, England and France to fish on the Banks. The North Atlantic cod fishery became one of the great industries of western Europe, and English and French fishermen dominated it. The English established shore bases for the summer season along the east coast of Newfoundland, especially on the Avalon Peninsula. The French established their shore bases around the Gulf of St. Lawrence, along the south coast of Newfoundland, and as far west as Cape Breton Island. In Newfoundland, the English made the harbour of St. John's their headquarters; the French were concentrated in Placentia Bay.

These fishermen regarded the coasts of North America as little more than convenient beaches on which to dry their catches. They might return to the same beaches summer after summer, but they did not establish permanent settlements. Only toward the end of the sixteenth century, when beaver hats became fashionable in Europe, did the growing demand for beaver pelts encourage fishermen to sail along the shores of the Gulf of St. Lawrence and up the great river itself to trade with Indians for furs. With the advent of the fur trade came the first permanent European settlements in present-day Canada.

Pierre Du Gua, Sieur de Monts, had already made several voyages up the St. Lawrence River when, in 1604, he sailed from France to the Bay of Fundy. The king of France had granted de Monts a ten-year monopoly of the fur trade between the 40th and 46th parallels on condition that he establish a colony there. Jean-Baptiste Colbert, the king's principal adviser, believed that a permanent French presence in North America was necessary to exploit the riches of the new continent. Jean de Biencourt de Poutrincourt, a young French nobleman, sailed with de Monts to win new lands for France, and Samuel de Champlain accompanied him as geographer and cartographer.

The de Monts expedition established its first settlement on an island at the mouth of the St. Croix River on the north shore of the Bay of Fundy, and there 80 men spent the winter of 1604-5. But there was no fresh water on the island and little wood. The settlers had a miserable time, and almost half the men died of scurvy. When de Monts' ships returned from France in 1605, they transported the survivors to the site of a new settlement, Port Royal, on the Annapolis River on the south shore of the Bay of Fundy. New recruits helped to dismantle the buildings at St. Croix and to transport the timber to the new location. Forty men spent the winter of 1605-6 at Port Royal. A log habitation provided living quarters for the governor, a priest, tradesmen and soldiers. They traded for furs with the Indians around the Bay. Champlain cultivated a little garden. He dammed a brook to make a trout pond, and constructed a saltwater reservoir in which he kept cod alive. The settlers established the Order of Good Cheer; once a fortnight, each of its members in turn became chief steward and organized a grand dinner, "no meat so tender as moose or so delicate as beavers' tail, at times a half dozen sturgeons."

In 1606, de Monts sent out supplies and more men to Port Royal. The new men included Louis Hébert, an apothecary, and Marc Lescarbot, a lawyer and man of letters, who wanted "to know the land with his own eyes and flee a corrupt world." Ever since Cortez' conquest of Mexico and Pizarro's conquest of Peru, the potentates of Europe had been excited by the prospect of finding more gold and silver in the Americas. Was there another Montezuma to be captured? Another Atahualpa to be held to ransom? Although Champlain carried on a desultory search for a silver mine, the French in Acadia regarded themselves, not as conquistadors, but as settlers in a new land. Lescarbot wrote in his diary,

> ...farming must be our goal. This is the first mine for which we must search, and it is better worth than the treasures of Atahualpa for whoso has corn, wine, cattle, linen, cloth, leather, iron and lastly, codfish, need have naught to do with treasure.

Here is the Port Royal and the heroes of that time—Champlain, Poutrincourt, Lescarbot, and Hébert—that we read about in school, the birthplace of Acadia, the first permanent European settlement in North America north of Florida.

But de Monts could not enforce his monopoly of the fur trade, and many ships poached on his domain. In 1607, the king terminated de Monts' monopoly. Champlain and the others, after harvesting their wheat, sailed back to France, leaving the habitation at Port Royal in the care of the Micmac Indians. In 1608, Champlain crossed the Atlantic again to establish a trading-post at Quebec. He never returned to Acadia.

With the founding of Quebec, the centre of French activities in North America moved from the Bay of Fundy to the St. Lawrence River, and there Champlain, the navigator, explorer, geographer, and colonizer, had ample scope for his great talents. He is rightly called the Father of New France. Champlain saw that from Quebec the St. Lawrence River offered access to a vast hinterland of fur; from Quebec, a network of canoe routes soon covered thousands of miles, reaching into the heart of the continent. Quebec was to be the principal seat of the French empire in North America until its fall in 1759.

Acadia had been abandoned in 1607, but it was not left for long. Three years after de Monts, Champlain and their comrades sailed away, Jean de Biencourt de Poutrincourt returned with his son, Charles de Biencourt; a priest, Father Fléché; and more settlers. At Port Royal they were met by the local Micmac chief. The habitation abandoned in 1607 was intact. There they re-established the settlement. Poutrincourt divided the cleared land among the settlers, and they cleared and ploughed more land. Young Biencourt returned to France at the end of the summer, but he was back at Port Royal in 1611, this time with two Jesuit missionaries, to establish another settlement on the north shore of the Bay of Fundy at the mouth of the Penobscot River. This settlement was named St. Sauveur.

Even in those early times, when the French and English settlements in the New World were only tiny groups clinging to the coast and living precariously on meagre resources, conflicts between them were continual. It seems incredible that the English in Virginia, separated from the French by hundreds of miles of wilderness, should have felt threatened, but the English claimed that the 45th parallel, which crosses the Bay of Fundy, was the northern boundary of Virginia. In 1613, the governor of Virginia commissioned Captain Samuel Argall to destroy the French settlements in Acadia, even though France and England were not then at war.

In July, 1613, Argall sailed north and seized St. Sauveur, taking the settlers prisoner. In October of the same year, he sailed north again, and looted and burned the buildings at Port Royal. But many of the settlers were in the fields or the woods, and thus escaped. Poutrincourt was in France when the raid occurred. He discovered the ruins of his hopeful enterprise when he arrived in 1614 with more colonists. Most of the colonists returned to France with Poutrincourt. Before leaving, he turned over to his son, Biencourt, all of his rights and holdings in Acadia. Biencourt and the settlers who had avoided capture stayed behind and rebuilt Port Royal.

In 1621, disregarding French claims to Acadia, King James 1 of England granted the whole of Acadia to a fellow Scot, Sir William Alexander, Earl of Stirling. Alexander decided, following the examples of New France, New England and New Amsterdam, to call his new domain New Scotland, or Nova Scotia. In 1627, he sent 70 colonists in four ships to Nova Scotia. They seized the small French settlement at Port Royal. In 1629, Champlain was forced to surrender Quebec to an English fleet under Thomas Kirke. In 1632, however, by the terms of the Treaty of St. Germain-en-Laye, England agreed to evacuate "all places occupied in New France, La Cadie and Canada." The Scots returned home.

In the decade that followed, between 200 and 300 French settlers came to Acadia, of whom probably no more than 60 were women. From this stock, the population of Acadia steadily increased. These settlers built a new fort. They replanted Poutrincourt's fields. They started a school. As the colony grew, they cleared new farms along the shores of the river and they built dikes to protect their fields from the Bay of Fundy's tides. The colony sent furs and fish and timber to France, and it began to prosper in a small way.

At this time there was a dispute, lasting more than a decade, between two Frenchmen, Charles de la Tour and Charles d'Aulnay, as to which was entitled to rule Acadia in the name of the king. The dispute between them was bloody and bizarre (de la Tour, having killed d'Aulnay, married Madame d'Aulnay to consolidate his claim). Despite these alarums and excursions, the settlers continued to bring more land under cultivation, quietly extending the agricultural domain for which the two frantic nobles contended.

Not long after de la Tour had triumphed in his struggle with d'Aulnay, the real contest for Acadia, that is, between England and France, was renewed. The boundaries of Acadia had never been clearly defined, but it lay as a wedge between the expanding empires of New France on the St. Lawrence and of New England on the Atlantic seaboard farther to the south. France and England were in constant conflict over Acadia. In just over a century, Port Royal changed hands nine times: six times by force of arms, three times by treaty.

The historian John Bartlet Brebner said, "There were, in effect, two Acadias, each important; one the scene of international conflict, the other the land settled and developed by the Acadians." In 1654, the English took Port

Royal again, but it was returned to the French in 1670. By that date, some 350 or 400 French-speaking settlers, the great majority of them Acadians by birth, lived along the shores of the Annapolis valley. In 1671, some Acadians left Port Royal to establish a settlement at Beaubassin at the head of Chignecto Bay, and a decade later others began to settle the marshes around Minas Basin. In a few years, there were several Acadian settlements around the head of the Bay of Fundy, and soon the population at the head of the bay was larger than that at Port Royal.

The Acadians' principal crop was wheat, but every farm had a vegetable garden and a small orchard. They raised cattle, and they also kept sheep and pigs. The Acadians reclaimed their farms from the salt marshes around the Bay of Fundy. They built dikes to regulate the flow of water through the marshes and devised sluice gates that would let the fresh water of the marshes out into the sea while at the same time preventing the sea water from flowing in.

With persistence and hard work, the Acadian communities around the Bay of Fundy prospered. The ordinary household contained three or even four generations. The farmers were also fishermen, and there were blacksmiths, wheelwrights, carpenters and coopers. They had saw mills and grist mills. France forbade them to trade with New England, but was powerless to stop them from doing so, and they exchanged furs, wheat and livestock for molasses, sugar, axes, and ironware. In fact, the Acadians had little to do with the French garrison at Port Royal, less to do with Versailles, and still less to do with New France (the French colonists on the St. Lawrence).

By 1701, when the Acadians had been living around the Bay of Fundy for almost a century, they numbered 1,134. No longer were they an outpost of the French empire; they were native to Acadia, where they had developed a way of life enviable in their time, and, indeed, in any time. For the most part, they governed themselves. They had no garrisons, for their relations with the Indians were harmonious. There was land enough for an expanding population. A priest in every settlement drew up marriage contracts, made wills, oversaw the division of property, adjudicated disputes among the farmers, and taught some of the children to read and write. Daniel Auger, Sieur de Subercase, the last French governor of Acadia, said, "The more I see of these people, the more I think that they are the happiest people in the world."

Meantime, conflict between Great Britain and France continued. After the outbreak of the Thirty Years' War in Europe in 1618, Britain and France were almost continuously at war for nearly a century. Every clash between the two powers was carried into North America. Indeed, relations between the French and the English in North America before 1759 often seem to have been a history of meaningless wars with confusing names and obscure European origins. King William's War lasted from 1689 until 1697. In 1690 Port Royal was taken by the English again, but it was returned to France once more by the Treaty of Ryswick.

Queen Anne's War, or the War of the Spanish Succession, followed in 1702 and lasted until 1713. In 1710, a combined force of British regulars and New England militia, more than 1,900 men, sailed up the Bay of Fundy to attack Port Royal by sea. The invaders landed and, after a week of seige and bombardment, Subercase, the French commander, with a garrison of only 258 officers and men, surrendered the fort. Port Royal never returned to French rule. The British, in honour of their Queen, renamed the garrison Fort Anne, and the town Annapolis Royal. This time the peace treaty did not restore Acadia to the French. In 1713, by the Treaty of Utrecht, the colony passed permanently into the hands of the British. France agreed to recognize Britain's claims to Hudson Bay and Newfoundland and ceded Acadia "with the ancient boundaries," although she retained Ile Royale (Cape Breton Island) and Ile St. Jean (Prince Edward Island). France also retained fishing rights on the Grand Banks and along the north coast of Newfoundland.

There were by now 2,500 Acadians, and their numbers

were growing rapidly, primarily owing to natural increase. What was to become of them now that Acadia was a British colony? The Treaty of Utrecht provided that they might immigrate to French soil. The Acadians were, however, unwilling to give up their fertile farms on the Bay of Fundy to settle on Ile Royale or Ile St. Jean. They stayed where they were, a French and Catholic population under British rule—Britain's first attempt to rule a people whose language, religion and cultural heritage were different from and, in some respects, opposed to her own. The venture began well. The treaty had provided that if the Acadians chose to remain they would become British subjects, but they would have the right to the free exercise of their own religion. But the venture did not continue well.

The conflict between Britain and France in North America was not over. The French had not surrendered their ambition to become masters of the continent. They moved their garrison at Placentia to Ile Royale and, almost immediately, they began to build the greatest fortress in North America at Louisbourg to dominate the entrance to the St. Lawrence River. The cession of Acadia was limited to its "ancient boundaries." These boundaries had never been defined, and the French contended that they had ceded only the Nova Scotian peninsula (as we know it today) and that they still held what is now New Brunswick. The Acadians were, therefore, still caught up in the rivalry of the two colonial powers.

At first, the British were as little disposed as France had been to rule the Acadians with a heavy hand. The new garrison at Annapolis Royal was as removed from the life of the Acadians' farms as the French garrison had been. The British writ hardly ran at Minas and at Beaubassin, and not at all in the scattered hamlets established by the Acadians on the disputed north side of the bay. One thing, however, the British did insist upon. The Treaty of Utrecht had stipulated that the Acadians should take an oath of allegiance to the king of England. The Acadians were prepared to pledge their loyalty to the British Crown, but they wanted an assurance that this pledge would not commit them to military service against France. The British would not allow such an exception, so the Acadians refused to take the oath. Again and again the British insisted on their taking it and, for 40 years, the Acadians temporized. They feared that they would again be ensnared in the unceasing conflict between France and England.

The British regarded the Acadians doubtfully as a suspect population. The French regarded them hopefully as the means of recapturing the peninsula. No doubt the Acadians would have preferred to live under the French flag, but they had no desire to serve the French as a Trojan horse. The truth was that, although the Acadians did not want to fight against the French, neither did they want to fight for them. They were far more concerned about their own families and farms than they were about the claims made by British or French kings on their allegiance. They would not take the British oath, although some of the villages returned an oath of their own composition to the British, which contained a proviso that they should never be required to bear arms against the French or the Indians.

In 1730, Governor Phillips persuaded the Acadians to make their submission to the British Crown, and he exempted them, in writing, from having to bear arms on the king's behalf. The Acadians regarded this arrangement as a treaty that gave them the status of neutrals. Indeed, the British often referred to them thereafter as "the French neutrals," but they remained concerned about the prospects of defending a colony of French-speaking Catholics in a war with France.

Some of the French priests among the Acadians were no more inclined than the British to permit the Acadians to remain neutral. Abbé Jean Louis Le Loutre, missionary to the Micmacs, kept the Acadians in a continuous state of apprehension. He organized Indian raids against the English, and he urged the Acadians to leave their farms in British territory to relocate on Ile St. Jean and Ile Royale or at Fort Beauséjour, which the French had established on the isthmus at the head of the Bay of Fundy.

In 1743, the interminable struggle between Britain and

France resumed with the War of the Austrian Succession. In 1745, after a siege of seven weeks, Louisbourg fell to an expedition under the command of Governor William Shirley of Massachusetts. By the Treaty of Aix-la-Chapelle in 1748, Britain agreed to return Louisbourg to France, to the disgust and dismay of New Englanders. But the continuing warfare was still not over: one or other of the great powers must ultimately prevail in North America. There could be no question of peaceful co-existence between the French and British colonies and there could be no peace for the 10,000 Acadians (for that was how their numbers had grown by mid-century).

The struggle between the British and the French in North America was moving toward its climax in the St. Lawrence basin, in the Ohio valley, and in Acadia. In 1749, the British established Halifax to counter the French strength at Louisbourg, and new fortifications were established on both sides of the Chignecto isthmus. In 1755, a British force composed largely of New England militia attacked Fort Beauséjour, the French fortification on the isthmus, and when the fort fell, they found that 200 Acadians were there serving under arms. The Acadians claimed that they served only under pain of death, but the British did not believe them. The governor and officer commanding in Nova Scotia, Colonel Charles Lawrence, was fearful of having to fight the French with 10,000 Acadians at his back. So, apparently believing that he had no choice, he decided to expel them from the colony.

The expulsion of the Acadians was not, however, simply a question of securing Nova Scotia against French attack. It was also a question of land. In 1740, Jean-Paul Mascarene, a French Huguenot in British service, had warned the Acadians that, should they continue to refuse to take the oath of allegiance, "the people of New England would ask nothing better than to take possession of lands cleared and ready to receive them." Three of the five members of the Council of Nova Scotia were New Englanders. Soldiers from New England had been campaigning in Acadia since the beginning of the century, and had seen the fertile farms around the Annapolis valley. Why should these rich acres continue to be held by a people who were waiting for a French victory in the war that was certain to come soon? If the Acadians were expelled, their farms would become available to land-hungry New England. Colonel John Winslow, a British officer, wrote in his journal:

> We are now hatching the noble and great project of banishing the French neutrals from the Province....If we accomplish this expulsion, it will have been one of the greatest deeds the English in America have ever achieved, for among other considerations, the part of the country which they occupy is one of the best soil in the world, and, in this event, we might place some good farmers on their homesteads.

In July, 1755, the governor and council of Nova Scotia summoned deputies from the Acadian villages to Halifax and ordered them to take an oath of allegiance to the king. They refused. On July 25, 1755, the governor and council passed a formal resolution to deport them.

> That the inhabitants may not have it in their power to return to this Province, nor to join in strengthening the French of Canada or Louisbourg it is resolved that they shall be dispersed among His Majesty's Colonies upon the Continent of America....

The Acadians had no chance to change their minds; they were treated as French subjects whose presence was an active threat to British security. Charles Morris, surveyor-general of Nova Scotia and a New Englander, recommended that the dikes built by the Acadians be broken and their crops burned to remove any inducement to them to return. Governor Lawrence ordered his troops to clear the country of Acadians.

> And if you find that fair means will not do with them, you must proceed by the most vigorous means possible not only in compelling them to embark but in depriving those who shall escape of all means of shelter or support by burning their houses and destroying everything that may afford them the means of subsistence in the country.

During September and October, 1755, British regulars and New England militia rounded up the Acadians and embarked them on transports provided by the Royal Navy. Annapolis, Minas and Chignecto were the three main points of embarkation. Winslow supervised the operation at Minas, where he bivouacked 400 New Englanders in the church-yard at Grand Pré. He ordered the Acadian men to assemble in the church where he locked them up under guard. Then he read out the governor's order of expulsion.

> Gentlemen, I have received from His Excellency, Governor Lawrence, the King's instructions, which I hold in my hand. By his orders you are called together to hear His Majesty's resolution....His Majesty's instructions and commands...are, that your lands and tenements and cattle and live stock of all kinds are forfeited to the Crown, with all your other effects except money and household goods, and that you yourselves are to be removed from this Province....

He then allowed the women and children to visit their husbands and sons and to bring them provisions while they waited for the transports to arrive. Winslow recorded in his journal the events of the day on which the transports arrived.

> I sent for Father Landrey, their principal speaker, who talks English, and told him the time was come for part of the inhabitants to embark and that the number concluded for this day was 250 and that we should begin with the young men, and desired he would inform his brethren of it. He was greatly surprised. I told him it must be done and that I should order the whole prisoners to be drawn up six deep, their young men on the left, and as the tide in a very little time favoured my design, could not give them above an hour to prepare for going on board, and ordered our whole party to be under arms and post themselves between the two gates and the church in the rear of my quarters, which was obeyed, and agreeable to my directions the whole of the French inhabitants were drawn together in one body, their young men as directed on the left. I then ordered Capt. Adams with a lieutenant, eighty non-commissioned officers, and private men, to draw off from the main body

to guard the young men of the French amounting to 141 men to the transports and order the prisoners to march. They all answered that they would not go without their fathers. I told them that was a word I did not understand for that the King's command was to me absolute and should be absolutely obeyed and that I did not love to use harsh means but that the time did not admit of parlies or delays, and then ordered the whole troops to fix their bayonets and advance towards the French, and bid the four right-hand files of the prisoners, consisting of twenty-four men which I told off myself, to divide from the rest, one of whom, I took hold on (who opposed the marching) and bid march. He obeyed and the rest followed, though slowly, and went off praying, singing and crying, being met by the women and children all the way (which is 1 1/2 miles) with great lamentations upon their knees, praying etc....

There were not enough ships to evacuate the whole population at once, so the men were taken away on the ships that were available, leaving their families behind to be transported later. Because the ships had different destinations, many families were dispersed, never to be reunited. It was, Winslow wrote, "a Scene of Woe and Distress."

The British then burned houses and barns and turned cattle loose. The fields and marshes that had been cleared, diked and drained were left in desolation. Within hours, the work of 150 years of patient toil was turned to ashes.

Altogether, the British forcibly removed and transported around 6,000 Acadians in 1755, and perhaps 2,000 more in the following years, out of a total population of about 10,000. Some of the Acadians took refuge in the forests, just as their ancestors had when Argall destroyed Port Royal a century and a half before. From Chignecto, many of them made their way along the valleys of the St. John and Miramichi rivers. Others went to the settlements along the St. Lawrence. Still others fled to Ile St. Jean, which was still in French hands. Acadian prisoners on one of the transports on the way to South Carolina captured the ship and sailed it back to Saint John. There was resistance elsewhere to the deportation. At Chignecto, the French, the Acadians and the Indians harassed the British forces engaged in destroying the Acadian settlements on the north shore. Farther north, along the shores of Baie des Chaleurs, sporadic fighting went on for many years.

The deportations of Acadians from Nova Scotia occurred a year before the beginning of the Seven Years' War between England and France, and the war itself led to a second deportation of Acadians from Ile St. Jean. Acadians had been migrating from the Bay of Fundy to Ile St. Jean even before 1755. In that year many who had escaped Governor Lawrence's troops fled to the island. They had, within a very few years, cleared several thousand acres and had built homes and churches. In 1758, the British occupied Ile St. Jean and, in October and November, while ships waited at anchor in Port La Joye, soldiers were dispatched from them to round up the Acadians on the island, and 2,000 captives were loaded on the ships to be transported to Europe. Three of these ships were lost at sea and some 700 prisoners were drowned. Those who could escaped from the island. Some 300 Acadians at Malpaque Bay fled into the woods, returning to their farms when the ships had left. Many of the Acadians who live on Prince Edward Island today are descended from these survivors.

When Louisbourg fell in 1758, the British had made themselves masters of Acadia and of the whole region of the Gulf of St. Lawrence. In 1759, the British and French fought the decisive battle on the Plains of Abraham, and Quebec was taken. With the French cession of Canada in the Treaty of Paris in 1763, all that remained of France's empire in North America were the small islands of St. Pierre and Miquelon and the French shore of Newfoundland.

The deportation of the Acadians had denuded the settlements of Acadia and the Gulf of St. Lawrence. Nova Scotia was now a British province in fact as well as name, and it fell into the possession of the New Englanders. Owing to overpopulation and erosion, the New Englanders needed more agricultural land, but the Appalachian

Mountains and unfriendly Indians still constituted a barrier to agricultural settlement farther west. New Englanders had participated in the capture of Port Royal in 1710. New England militia had carried out the expulsion. Agents of the Nova Scotia government went to Massachusetts, Connecticut, Rhode Island—indeed, throughout all of Britain's colonies in New England—to offer prospective settlers free transport and provisions. The prospect of obtaining good farmland that was already cleared elicited a healthy response. New Englanders arrived to claim the Acadian farms in the Annapolis valley, around Minas Basin, and along Nova Scotia's southern shore. Others took up land in the St. John valley. Between 1760 and 1770, about 7,000 New Englanders immigrated to Nova Scotia. Few New Englanders arrived after 1770, but the flow of English-speaking immigrants to Nova Scotia—Yorkshiremen, Scottish Highlanders, and Irishmen—continued.

What of the Acadians, the forlorn cargo of the transports that arrived in Massachusetts, New York, the Carolinas and Georgia? Although dispossessed and dispersed, the Acadians now began the most amazing chapter in their history. They began to make their way back. Those who had taken refuge in the St. John valley or on the islands of the Gulf were among the first to return. Those who had been scattered along the Atlantic seaboard soon followed. Three thousand of them returned, some overland, some by sea. They journeyed on foot, by canoe, and by cart, some of them from as far away as Louisiana. In time, these weary travellers would reconstitute the Acadian people.

With the end of the Seven Years' War in 1763, the deportations came to an end. After 1764, Acadians were once again allowed to own land in Nova Scotia. Of course, those who came back were not allowed to return to their old farms—they had been taken over by New Englanders. The government was, however, prepared to let them settle on the colony's vacant lands. The best vacant lands available to the Acadians were in present-day New Brunswick, especially along its east coast. If Nova Scotia had been the

Acadians' land of deportation, New Brunswick was the land of their return.

The dispersal of this pastoral people did not destroy them. They survived. The expulsion became the unifying fact of Acadian experience. Wherever Acadians re-established themselves, they found comfort in their extended families and in their common language, religion and experience of hardship. Antonine Maillet, Acadia's great novelist, in *Pélagie-la-Charette* (for which she won the 1979 Prix Goncourt) has told the story of an indomitable woman, Pélagie, who, after *le Grande Dérangement*, spent ten years travelling by cow-cart, with others she found along the way, from Georgia back home to Acadia. "When they built their carts," Maillet has said, "they were just families. By the time they returned to Acadia they were a people."

After the end of the American Revolution (1775-83), some 60,000 United Empire Loyalists decided to leave their homes in the triumphant Thirteen Colonies. Half of them went to Nova Scotia. The Loyalists included civil and military officials, lawyers, doctors, landowners and merchants. Some brought their servants with them. Arable land was becoming scarce on the Nova Scotia peninsula, so many of the newcomers took up land along the St. John River. In fact, some 5,000 Loyalists arrived in the St. John valley within 12 months, and they immediately acquired a political and economic ascendancy over their Acadian neighbours. Soon the Loyalists wished to be free of control from Halifax and, in 1784, Nova Scotia was divided at its isthmus to establish the province of New Brunswick. The Acadians living in New Brunswick were not consulted.

With the arrival of the Loyalists, the Acadians were driven from the St. John River valley. They retreated north along the coast of New Brunswick and around to the shores of the Gulf of St. Lawrence, establishing settlements along the way. Finally, left to themselves again, the Acadians resumed the measured existence of previous generations. They were situated on the periphery of the institutional life of New Brunswick, clinging to their own language and customs in tightly knit parishes. Their remoteness and a life based on agriculture and the sea sustained and strengthened their traditions. There was little intercourse between the Acadians and the Protestant and class-conscious Loyalists.

Until the mid-nineteenth century, most Acadians were illiterate, except for a few whom Catholic priests had taught to read and write. Parish schools began to emerge in the 1850s in New Brunswick. Each denomination had its own schools. Acadian children, of course, went to Catholic schools. In 1864 the Church established the College of St. Joseph. In 1867, *Le Moniteur Acadien,* the first Acadian newspaper, appeared: its motto was *Notre langue, notre réligion et nos coutumes.* For the Acadians, oral tradition had been the means of passing on, from one generation to another, "notre langue, notre réligion et nos coutumes." Now, with parish schools and a newspaper, literacy became the means of preserving their language, their religion and their customs. But to read and write in French depended on schooling, and the future of the Catholic schools of the Acadians would be greatly affected by political developments over which they had no control.

In the old colony of Nova Scotia, political power had belonged to the English in Halifax; in the new province of New Brunswick it belonged to the Loyalists of the St. John River valley. When, in 1864, the Fathers of Confederation had their famous photograph taken in Charlottetown, they were there because the representatives from Canada wished the Maritime provinces to join in the proposed federal union. But they did not consult the Acadians. Although Acadians were a minority in each of the Maritime provinces, there were about 45,000 of them altogether living in the Maritimes. They were, however, virtually without political influence, and they took no part in the discussions in Charlottetown nor in later meetings held in Quebec and London. George-Etienne Cartier defended the interests of his fellow French Canadians in Quebec; no one spoke for the Acadians.

Out of the conferences at Charlottetown, Quebec and

London came, in 1867, a new country, and a new Constitution. Canada's Constitution, the British North America Act, was a British statute passed to provide for the government of the new country. Both English and French were to be official languages in Parliament and the federal courts. Although English and French were also to be the official languages of the Legislative Assembly and the courts of Quebec, the Act made no provision for two official languages in New Brunswick, even though Acadians constituted as large, indeed, a larger, proportion of that province's population than Anglophones did of Quebec's population, for whose benefit provision had been made for two official languages in that province.

What the BNA Act said about schools was even more important than what it said about official languages because in the parish schools of the Acadians French was the language of education. Section 93 of the BNA Act declared that education was to come under provincial jurisdiction, but it provided guarantees for denominational schools. Although the provinces were to have exclusive power to make laws in relation to education, no law could be passed that would "prejudicially affect any Right or Privilege with respect to Denominational Schools, which any Class or Persons have by Law in the Province at the Union." Thus the denominational schools of a minority would not be at the mercy of the provinces: if they were receiving public funds under provincial law at the time of Confederation, these could not be cut off.

Here Acadian history began to merge with that of French-Canadian minorities elsewhere in Canada. Roman Catholic denominational schools were, throughout Canada, the vessels of French culture and language, and Section 93 was supposed to protect these schools from measures which the English-speaking provinces might take to diminish their functions in this regard, just as it was supposed to protect the denominational schools of the English-speaking minority in Quebec. Section 93 proved to be a feeble defence for the denominational schools of the French-Canadian minorities. Its first test came in New Brunswick.

The Parish Schools Act of 1858 had established a system of public schools in New Brunswick. These schools had become denominational in localities where the population was of one religion, and they continued to receive public funds. New Brunswick, therefore, had denominational schools in practice, although the law provided for public schools. In 1871, just four years after Confederation, New Brunswick passed the Common Schools Act, which denied funds to denominational schools: all tax-supported schools had by law to be non-denominational. The informal arrangements whereby public funds were made available to denominational schools were no longer to be countenanced.

The Acadians challenged the law in the courts. They argued that Section 93 guaranteed that no provincial statute could take away rights or privileges they had had at the time of Confederation with respect to denominational schools. But Section 93 applied only to denominational schools that had been established *by law*. The provision of public funds to denominational schools in New Brunswick had not been established by law before 1867; it was merely a matter of practice. This fact was an insuperable obstacle to the Acadians' case. In 1873, the Supreme Court of New Brunswick held that no right or privilege with respect to denominational schools had been prejudicially affected by the legislation of 1871 because, as Chief Justice William J. Ritchie said, " . . . the rights contemplated must have been legal rights: in other words, rights secured by law, or which they had under the law at the time of the Union." The Privy Council in Britain, the highest court to which Canadians could go, agreed.

This decision was plainly against the spirit, although not a narrow interpretation of the letter, of the British North America Act: "Disappointing—even if legally sound," as Pierre Trudeau was to put it in 1964. The Acadians urged the federal government to intervene on their behalf. The federal government had the power under the BNA Act to disallow provincial legislation, but it was unwilling to use it in this instance. (The power of disallowance was exercised often in the early years of Confederation, although today it has fallen into desuetude.) In 1872, the House of Commons did pass a resolution urging New Brunswick to restore denominational schools, but the government of New Brunswick was not prepared to comply. English-speaking Protestants, who outnumbered the Catholics, supported their government in refusing to provide funds for separate schools. In 1874, the government that had passed the Common Schools Act of 1871 was returned with a large majority. The Acadians protested. In 1875, at Caraquet on the Baie des Chaleurs, troops were used to subdue Acadian rioting against the Common Schools Act. That same year, Parliament again discussed the New Brunswick school question, and the House of Commons passed a motion of regret that the province had not acted on the resolution the House had passed in 1872. This gesture was as futile as the earlier one. The province remained intransigent. There would be no funds for separate schools.

The refusal of the courts to interfere with this kind of legislation in the Maritimes presaged what was going to happen in Manitoba when, in 1890, the question of separate schools reached a crisis there. Of the Manitoba school question, Canada's greatest constitutional lawyer, F.R. Scott, has remarked that "French Canada felt that on the first great test of her rights the B.N.A. Act had failed her." It was a failure that had been limned in New Brunswick.

Supporters of separate schools had to pay for them as well as to pay taxes for the support of public schools. In time, however, the authorities in New Brunswick (and the other Maritime provinces) began to allow religious instruction in public schools in which the pupils were predominantly Catholic, and French continued to be the language of instruction in these schools. These concessions obviated the full rigour of the Common Schools Act. But the Acadians were, nevertheless, without any constitutional guarantees for even these limited privileges.

The Acadians believed themselves to be a distinct people—not French, although descended from France, and not Québécois, because of their quite separate history. This collective consciousness began to manifest itself in a formal way in the late nineteenth century, when the Acadians held their first convention in 1881 at Memramcook. At that time, they declared, "The Acadian has no other national history than his own and that of France. At Confederation, in 1867, they knew nothing of Lower Canada, except that there were, at Quebec and at Montreal, Frenchmen who called themselves Canadians."

That collective consciousness, that shared language and experience, persists to this day. It is the heritage of all Acadians. But is it of any consequence to other Canadians?

The eminent Canadian historian, Arthur Lower, has argued in *Colony to Nation* that the Acadian experience has had no lasting significance for Canada. He believes that, before 1755, their history was little more than a prelude to the real history of Nova Scotia, which began in earnest when the New Englanders arrived to take over the Acadian farms. And he considers that, for all practical purposes, the history of New Brunswick began with the coming of the Loyalists. Is the story of the Acadians, then, nothing more than a story of survival, the record of a people imprisoned by their own past, living with their collective memories? Many have thought so, and have been ready to believe that the Acadians had no art, no literature— nothing to say to the contemporary world. In 1949, Professor Alfred G. Bailey of the University of New Brunswick, in an address given at Halifax to the Canadian Humanities Research Council, Maritime Regional Conference, spoke of the expulsion of the Acadians as "...the blow from which they have never entirely recovered, at least in a psychological sense." He also said:

> Those who managed to evade expulsion, together with those who returned, have, for all their fine qualities, made no contribution to French-Canadian culture....As a peasant people they were quite different from the enterprising Yankee with his enquiring mind, his political acumen, and his cultivation of the intellectual virtues, and it is therefore doubtful whether the Acadians would have developed the kind of social dynamic that was necessary to high accom-

plishment in the field of literature, had they been allowed
to remain in possession of their lands.

There is a familiar ring to Bailey's dismissal of Acadian
culture. Lord Durham's Report of 1837 had described the
French Canadians of Lower Canada as "a people with no
history and no literature." Durham searched in vain for
a single French-Canadian book. Better to assimilate the
French Canadians, since they had no intellectual contribution to make to Canadian life. So the political structures
of the Act of Union of 1841 were designed to achieve that
very thing. How poor a country would Canada be today
if Lord Durham had succeeded! And how poor if the flow-
ering of Acadian letters today, which has revealed the
limitations of Bailey's view of the world, had never come
to pass!

But, even acknowledging the awakening consciousness
of Acadians, and its expression in plays, novels, and songs,
aren't we still inclined to dismiss the history of the Acadians as somehow quaint, one of the back eddies of the
Canadian experience? I suggest that a moment's reflection
will show that Acadian history can provide a profound
insight for us in Canada and for many other countries. Can
a people, locked into a nation-state, condemned forever
to minority status, survive, or is assimilation inevitable?
The Acadians have retained their consciousness of who
they are even though they are a people without official
institutions. There has never been a sovereign state of
Acadia. Confederation did not guarantee that the Acadians
would be protected as a people. They had no province of
their own, or schools of their own. Yet they survived.

The Acadians refused to accept the idea that they were
simply an outpost of the French empire in North America
and, later, merely vassals of the English king. The tragedy
of their diaspora did not defeat them. Their triumph is the
triumph of a people, not of a charismatic leader. Their saga
illustrates the difference between history as a collection of
battles, dates and parliaments, and history as the cultivation of the land, the establishment of communities, the
sense of place, and the strength of bonds that, although

they may seem fragile, have held a people together through centuries of adversity.

Acadian communities now share the industrial ethos that predominates in the Atlantic provinces, as it does in the other provinces. The drive towards industrialization often results in a loss of a sense of community, an increasing reliance on consumer goods and electronic participation in community life. Increasing numbers of Acadians are moving to the cities. There is television in Acadian homes. What will become of Acadian culture, preserved so long in the face of so many challenges? Will the consumer culture of North America succeed where Governor Lawrence failed? The answer to that question is, of course, up to the Acadians.

Simple justice, however, demands that the Acadians be given the means to ensure that their language and their culture can be strengthened and enhanced. The New Brunswick legislature passed an act in 1969 designating French as one of the official languages of New Brunswick. The Charter of Rights and Freedoms entrenches official bilingualism for New Brunswick in the Constitution. Neither Nova Scotia nor Prince Edward Island have made any provision for official bilingualism; and the Charter contains no provision for French to be one of the official languages of these two provinces. Thus official bilingualism for the Acadians will be limited to New Brunswick.

But, under the Charter, Acadians throughout the Atlantic provinces, together with French-Canadian minorities in every province, will have the right to have their children receive their primary and secondary school instruction in French, out of public funds. This latter provision should not be regarded as a concession made to a minority who have refused to be otherwise appeased. Rather, it should be looked upon as a manifestation of the central idea of Canada, a means whereby we acknowledge the virtues of diversity within our own nation and in the larger world. The Acadians are a people with a common history, a common experience, and a common language that give meaning to their lives today. To attempt to efface that history, to ignore that experience, to fail to protect that language, would be out of keeping with emerging notions of human rights.

For it is not just a question of minority rights, it is as well a question of the health of the body politic. Minorities make a positive contribution, indeed an indispensable contribution to the life of the nation. The United States has struggled to erect a political nationality that overwhelms all differences; but Canada has been less ambitious than the United States in this regard. It is to our advantage that in Canada we have minorities that regard the world in different ways. Their presence within the nation is a stimulus to creativity. Nothing can be more stultifying than a bland conformity, and nothing is more dangerous to democracy than the animosity which such conformity may engender towards others whose beliefs, whose language, whose colour, may be different from the majority's.

The Acadians have thus far waged their struggle alone. Now, given the encroachment of industry and technology and the pervasiveness of mass communications, the time has come for Canadian institutions to recognize the distinct contributions that the Acadians have made to Canadian life, and to provide the means for their culture to flourish. Everywhere, and within every nation-state, there are peoples who will not be assimilated, and whose fierce wish to retain their common identity is intensifying as industry, technology and communications forge a larger and larger mass culture, extruding diversity. Diversity in Canada may help to ensure the permanence of diversity in the world.

TWO

Louis Riel and the New Nation

THE PASSION OF Louis Riel has obscured the fate of the people he led. They were the Metis, the New Nation that arose on the plains. In the contest between Canada and the New Nation, Riel perished and the New Nation was destroyed. The people of the New Nation still survive, however, in a hundred cities and towns on the prairies. They remember that they were once masters of the plains, and they remember Riel.

Riel is a mythic figure in our history, but there is no single myth. There is Riel, the rebel; Riel, the founder of Manitoba; Riel, the centre of the conflict between French and English in Canada; Riel, the mystic and prophet. But it is Riel, the symbol of a people's history, who is more important than any of these. Riel remains an heroic and compelling figure to the Metis in their search to rediscover their own past, and to find a place for themselves in Canadian life today.

Today, the Metis make hardly any impression on the Canadian consciousness. Riel, however, continues to fascinate us. The Metis were half-Indian buffalo hunters of the plains, but Riel—he had studied for the priesthood, he inspired two uprisings, and he was hanged amid a din of controversy between English and French. Riel's achievements were many and remarkable. In 1869, he led an uprising at Red River and organized a provisional government that for a whole winter effectively ruled a colony of more than 10,000 persons. He negotiated the terms upon which Manitoba entered Confederation. In 1885, he launched another rebellion: it challenged the capacity of the North-

West Mounted Police to maintain law and order in the Canadian west, indeed, it called into question, for a time, Canada's ability to rule its vast hinterland.

Riel's uprisings failed because neither in 1869 nor in 1885 could the Metis effectively resist or even check, except for a few weeks or months, the advance of the agricultural frontier and the occupation of the prairies by the Canadians. Riel's insurrections were made possible by the Metis riflemen, and his career is etched against the history of the Metis. To understand the meaning of his career, we must look into that history: the appearance of the Metis on the plains, their emergence as a people, their dependence on the buffalo, and their sad retreat—all occurring in just over a century. Where did this people, this New Nation, come from?

During the eighteenth century, the French had extended the fur trade far into the west and had built a chain of trading posts from the Great Lakes to the Rocky Mountains. La Vérendrye, born in Trois-Rivières, was the first White man to explore the Canadian plains west of Lake Winnipeg, and his sons sighted the foothills of the Rocky Mountains in the 1740s. The British had reached the prairies by ascending the rivers that flow into Hudson Bay. For a long time after the Hudson's Bay Company's incorporation in 1670, British traders waited at their posts "at the bottom of the Bay" for the Indians to bring their furs down to them to trade. Only after French traders began to intercept these Indians northwest of the Great Lakes did the British traders explore canoe routes to the interior and establish posts there.

Because of the long canoe journey from Montreal to points west of the Great Lakes, many of the French traders, the *voyageurs*, wintered among the Indians and returned home with their furs during the next summer. As the trade expanded, some traders spent years at a time among the Indians, supplied each summer by canoe brigades from Montreal. These traders, living among the Indians, often took Indian wives. The issue of these unions began to form a new race, neither wholly White nor wholly Indian. They were known as Half-breeds, *Bois-brûlés* or Metis. By 1775, a Metis population had emerged.

Why should a new nation, a new culture, have appeared on the plains, when nothing like it had appeared on the shores of the St. Lawrence, where there was also a numerous progeny of White and Indian unions? The answer is the buffalo hunt; it lay at the heart of the Metis culture.

At first, the traders at the western fur-trading posts regularly hunted buffalo in summer, not only for meat but, much more important, to make pemmican, the staple food of the canoe brigades. Indian women dried lean buffalo meat, pounded it into shreds, then mixed it with melted suet to make a light, imperishable, nourishing food. The French-Canadian canoe brigades travelled swiftly; the *voyageurs* had no time to hunt or fish, and the canoes had no room for bulky supplies of food. The Montreal-based fur trade depended absolutely on a good supply of pemmican. As the fur trade expanded, more and more pemmican was needed and, as the demand grew, the Metis began to organize elaborate expeditions on horseback to hunt buffalo. These hunts became the basis of a distinctive culture and of a Metis consciousness. Captains of the hunt conducted these expeditions on almost military lines, with close supervision and discipline. While the men hunted, the women skinned the buffalo, then cut the meat to dry in the sun.

It was to the French-Canadian traders, not the Hudson's Bay Company, that the Metis were linked, by blood ties and by the fur trade. By the Treaty of Paris in 1763, France relinquished to Great Britain her claims west and north of the Great Lakes. But this did not mean that the Hudson's Bay Company was now without competition. With Canada now securely in British hands, many English and Scottish entrepreneurs flocked to Canada and they quickly became associated with the Montreal merchants and fur traders who had been exploring west of the Great Lakes. In 1779, several of them formed the North West Company which, pushing westward both north and south of the Great Lakes, offered a vigorous challenge to the Hudson's Bay Company throughout its domain. The North West Company used large numbers of French-Canadian *voyageurs* in the canoe brigades that served their western posts, and links between the Montreal-based company and the increasing number of Metis were, therefore, close.

The Metis, like the Acadians before them, developed a sense of collective identity with surprising speed. Because they had Indian mothers, they regarded the plains as their homeland. Both the Hudson's Bay Company and the North West Company discouraged settlement in Indian territory, so there was no one else there—yet—to contest their claim. However, settlers were not long in coming.

The Canadian northwest—the great hinterland lying to the north and to the west of the population centres of Canada on the St. Lawrence and the Great Lakes—was a fur-trading empire. A vast part of it, called Rupert's Land, consisting of all of the land draining into Hudson Bay, had been granted to the Hudson's Bay Company in 1670. To the west of Rupert's Land, extending to the Rockies and to the Pacific, and northwards to the Arctic, lay the Northwestern Territory. In 1811, the Hudson's Bay Company granted 116,000 square miles of its territory, centred on the junction of the Red and Assiniboine rivers, to Thomas Douglas, the young Earl of Selkirk.

Selkirk's motive in asking for land was primarily altruistic. He wanted to establish an agricultural colony for impoverished Scots settlers on the banks of the Red River. The first of the Scots arrived in 1812. The Hudson's Bay Company's motive in granting Selkirk the land was commercial. An agricultural settlement located precisely at the confluence of the Red and Assiniboine rivers, athwart the canoe route linking Canada and Rupert's Land, would interrupt not only the Nor'Westers' line of communication with the fur trade country, but it would control their access to pemmican. The struggle that followed has often been called the Pemmican War.

In January, 1814, Miles Macdonnell, governor of the Selkirk colony, prohibited the export of pemmican and forbade the North West Company to occupy forts within the new District of Assiniboia, as the lands granted to Selkirk were called. In June, 1815, the Nor'Westers and the Metis arrested Macdonnell and ran the settlers out of Red River—although they returned in the fall. In 1816, the conflict intensified. Robert Semple, the new governor, led a series of raids against the Nor'Westers and burned Fort Gibraltar, their post at Red River. In June, 1816, near a grove of oak trees, Semple and a party of settlers intercepted 50 Metis. In the battle that ensued, Semple and 20 settlers died, while only one Metis was killed. The Battle of Seven Oaks revealed the growing strength of the New Nation.

The two pre-eminent historians of western Canada, W.L. Morton and G.F.G. Stanley, have suggested that the idea of a "new nation" did not occur to the Metis by themselves. They argue that the Nor'Westers persuaded the Metis that, through their Indian mothers, they had aboriginal rights, and that Nor'Westers urged the Metis to assert these rights against the Hudson's Bay Company. These historians believe that the Metis were in fact the "loyal dupes" of the Nor'Westers in their struggle with the Hudson's Bay Company, and that the Battle of Seven Oaks was the result of these machinations.

What did aboriginal rights—what did aboriginal title— mean to these unlettered people of the plains? The Metis believed that they were entitled by virtue of their long-established use and occupation of the land—use and occupation which, through their Indian mothers, extended even farther back than the Metis themselves—to claim an interest in the land over which they hunted, and to insist that no one could take the land from them. In fact, the Metis, as the result of their Indian heritage, were well acquainted with the idea of aboriginal title before Selkirk received his grant. The Indians had always had aboriginal title to the lands they occupied. Each of the tribes had the right to the use and occupation of its hunting grounds, and this was acknowledged by the other tribes. It is not surprising that the Metis, the New Nation, should have regarded the buffalo range they hunted as their own.

If the Nor'Westers had called forth the New Nation only as a counter in their struggle with Hudson's Bay Company, it should have disintegrated when the two companies amalgamated in 1821 under the name and charter of the older company. No new fur trade company appeared on the plains to compete with the Hudson's Bay Company, nor had the Nor'Westers any further interest in stirring up national feeling among the Metis. If the New Nation was an artificial creation, then it should have vanished. But, instead, it flourished, and the Metis' consciousness of themselves as a distinct people—the people of the plains—was enhanced by the events of passing years.

The Battle of Seven Oaks helps us to understand the Red River Rebellion and the Northwest Rebellion. At Seven Oaks the Metis were defending their homeland, just as they did later in 1869-70 and 1885. The confrontation at Seven Oaks had nothing to do with religion, Protestant against Catholic, nor with language, French against English. The Metis were trying to impede White agricultural settlement of their territory. They sought, even then, to affirm their aboriginal rights and, though circumstances have altered, they are seeking today, as one of the aboriginal peoples of Canada, to reaffirm these rights.

In 1817, Selkirk himself came out to Red River with a party of Swiss officers and men to re-establish the colony. He accomplished this with the aid of the Roman Catholic Church. Catholic missionaries had come out to minister to the French Canadians engaged in the fur trade, to convert the Indians, and to baptize their Metis children. Selkirk and the priests persuaded the Metis that the settlers on the Red River were no threat to them.

In fact, the Metis soon made the Settlement their own. When, in 1821, the two fur-trading companies amalgamated, both companies discharged employees, many of whom retired with their half-Indian families to the Red River Settlement. By 1831, the Settlement's population stood at

2,314; by 1871, it had increased to more than 11,000, chiefly owing to unions between the Nor'Westers and Indian women and to natural increases among the Metis themselves. Though there were Metis settlements as far west as St. Albert, northwest of Edmonton, the majority of the Metis lived in the Red River Settlement.

Selkirk's philanthropic attempt to found an agricultural settlement for dispossessed Scottish crofters was regarded as quixotic in its time. The land west of the Great Lakes was then regarded as an inhospitable wilderness suited only to the fur trade. Indeed, the settlers could not at first grow enough to feed themselves, and for half a century the Metis supplied the Red River Settlement with buffalo meat. For the Metis, the establishment of the Settlement in their midst had opened a new era, for Red River was predominantly Metis—and, surviving by the buffalo hunt rather than by farming, not at all what Selkirk had intended.

From 1821 until 1869, the Metis were at home equally in the Settlement and on the plains. They served as canoemen and boatmen for the Hudson's Bay Company. They hauled freight by cart from St. Paul in present-day Minnesota, for there was no road to Red River from Upper Canada. They continued the traditional life of hunting, fishing and trapping. Despite these varied activities, the buffalo hunt continued to be the foundation of the Metis economy and culture.

To expand the fur trade, the Hudson's Bay Company had to establish trading posts in remote areas and to supply both these posts and the canoe brigades serving them. The Metis provided buffalo meat for these remote posts and for the canoe brigades. It is hard for us today to imagine the scale of the great buffalo hunts that the Metis organized. In 1820, 540 carts left Red River to carry buffalo meat back from the plains. The expedition of 1840 included 403 horses, 536 draught oxen, 1,240 carts and horses, 740 guns and 1,600 men, women and children. When they returned, they had killed 2,500 buffalo and loaded 800 carts with pemmican, dried meat and buffalo hide.

The buffalo hunt was a sophisticated, well-regulated undertaking. A president of the hunt was elected together with 12 councillors, a public crier, and guides. Captains, each of whom had ten hunters under his command, maintained order. When this army was on the move, the guides were in charge, and the captains and hunters were under their direction until they had reached the hunting grounds and set up camp. All members of the hunt worked in concert; no one was allowed to run the buffalo before the general order was given. This kind of organization and discipline made the Metis the strongest military force in the west.

For 50 years the Metis prospered at Red River. Some had cabins on river lots, where they grew potatoes and other vegetables, and some of them raised a few cattle. But every spring and fall, they took their horses and carts back to the plains seeking the buffalo. Others spent winter as well as summer on the plains or in the forest, living among the Indians. This way of life lasted until the last buffalo herds were destroyed.

The Metis were not the only people of mixed blood at Red River. There were also English-speaking Half-breeds, the offspring of English-speaking traders employed by the Hudson's Bay Company and Indian women, known as the "country-born." One of them, Cuthbert Grant, had led the Metis at Seven Oaks. But the Metis and the "country-born" were by no means a single group with common views and interests. The Metis spoke French, the "country-born" English. The Metis were Roman Catholic, the "country-born" Protestant. Whereas the "country-born" inclined to agriculture and their fathers' way of life, the Metis were inclined to follow the life of their mothers' people. Indeed, Protestant clergymen taught the "country-born" to regard themselves as Protestant and British. They could not, therefore, be taken for granted as allies of Riel during the winter of 1869-70 or in 1885.

During the 1850s and 1860s, the first agricultural immigrants in half a century reached Red River. By the 1850s, good agricultural land in Upper Canada was becoming scarce, and attitudes toward the west and northwest had begun to change. No longer were the prairies regarded as a wilderness. Now they were potential agricultural land. The Canadians who settled at Red River began to call for the annexation of the Settlement, together with all of Rupert's Land and the Northwestern Territory, to Canada.

The Fathers of Confederation had the annexation of Rupert's Land and the Northwestern Territory in mind from the beginning. In 1864, at the meeting of the Fathers of Confederation in Charlottetown, the draft constitution that they prepared included provision for the admission of these territories into the proposed union. In 1867, a new federal state was created that stretched from the Atlantic to Lake Superior. The Fathers intended that Canada should extend across the western plains, and across the Rocky Mountains to the Pacific Ocean. In 1868, the British Parliament passed a statute to provide for the surrender of Rupert's Land to the British Crown and for Rupert's Land and the Northwestern Territory to be admitted to Confederation. Prime Minister John A. Macdonald introduced a bill in the House of Commons on June 4, 1869, to provide for the government of these new lands, which were to be called the Northwest Territories. Canada began work on a wagon road westward from Fort William, to link Canada to Red River, 650 miles away.

From 1857 onwards, the Canadians who had settled at Red River got up petition after petition in favour of annexation of Red River to Canada. They formed an organization they called Canada First to promote annexation. To these men from Upper Canada annexation meant that the northwest would be English-speaking and Protestant. They established their own paper, *The Nor'Wester*, and they achieved an influence at Red River out of all proportion to their numbers. A census taken at Red River in 1871 showed the presence there of 5,720 French-speaking Half-breeds or Metis, 4,080 English-speaking Half-breeds or "country-born," and only 1,600 White settlers. But the Canada Firsters had a program: nobody else did. By 1868 the Hudson's Bay Company was preparing to turn over its administrative responsibilities to Canada.

The Canadians at Red River welcomed annexation, but the Metis did not. No one had consulted them. They were buffalo hunters, guides, and fur traders. What would be their future under Canadian rule? They realized that an influx of agricultural settlers under a Canadian regime would make doubtful the continuance of their way of life. In August, 1869, the Canadian government sent surveyors to Red River to conduct a general land survey even before the land had been transferred to Canada. The surveyors, working on the basis of the American system of square townships, completely disregarded the river-strip holdings of the Metis. On October 11, Louis Riel and a party of armed horsemen broke up a survey party on Metis land. The Metis had found a leader and Riel had found his cause.

Louis Riel was born at St. Boniface, one of the communities comprising the Red River Settlement, on October 22, 1844. His French-Canadian mother was a daughter of the first White woman in western Canada. His father, a Metis leader, was ambitious for his son, and he had arranged with Bishop Taché, the Bishop of St. Boniface, who wished to develop a Native clergy, to send Louis to Montreal in 1858 to study for the priesthood. Louis's sister, Sara, became the first Metisse missionary nun. But Louis left the seminary, before he had completed his classical studies with the Sulpician Fathers at the Collège de Montréal, returning to Red River in 1868.

After breaking up the survey party, Riel convened a Council of the Metis. Metis riflemen were sent to guard the trail from Minnesota (because there was, as yet, no road or railway from Ontario through Canadian territory to Red River, settlers travelled through the United States to reach the Settlement). Macdonald had already dispatched William McDougall, his choice as lieutenant-governor of the Northwest Territories, to Red River. McDougall, travelling north from Minnesota with his party of officials and his baggage in 60 wagons, tried to enter the country on November 2, but was turned back by the Metis at the United States' border. On the same day, Riel seized Fort Garry, the Settlement's principal fortification, gained control of the fort's cannon, rifles and ammunition, and detained the officials of the Hudson's Bay Company, the erstwhile rulers of the Settlement. On November 24, the Metis established a provisional government for the Settlement.

McDougall, though rebuffed, was nevertheless eager to claim his new territory. The Red River Settlement was part of Rupert's Land. Macdonald had told McDougall that the Hudson's Bay Company would formally transfer Rupert's Land to Canada on December 1, 1869. McDougall was, however, instructed not to proceed until informed of the completion of the transfer. The Canadians at Red River had promised him that, as soon as the transfer had taken place, he would be welcomed at the Settlement. So, without waiting to hear from Ottawa, McDougall issued a proclamation in which he claimed legal authority over Rupert's Land, including the Red River Settlement, as of December 1, and he dispatched one of his retinue to the Settlement with it. But all did not go well at Red River. The Canadians, under the leadership of Dr. John Shultz, tried to overthrow Riel, but their attempt failed, and Schultz and the leaders of the Canadian party were imprisoned at Fort Garry. In January, one of them, Thomas Scott, escaped to Portage la Prairie, where the Canadians opposed to Riel had their headquarters. Scott's fate was one of the hinges on which events were to turn during that winter and thereafter.

Riel, although only 25, was a natural leader. Within three months, he had organized the Metis, prevented the lieutenant-governor designate from entering Assiniboia, seized Fort Garry, and defeated the attempt by the Canadians to overthrow him. On December 29, 1869, Riel assumed the presidency of the provisional government of the Settlement.

In Ottawa, John A. Macdonald regarded Riel and the Metis as "miserable Half-breeds." Yet they were the rulers of a colony of 10,000 and would remain its rulers at least until summer. No armed force could reach Red River except by travelling through the United States. Macdonald did not wish to ask for permission to send troops through the United States. Such a demonstration of the tenuousness of Canada's hold on the northwest was out of the question. So Canada would have to wait until the old canoe route would be open, after the spring break-up, to put down the Metis uprising. In the meantime, Macdonald had to postpone the formal transfer of title to Canada of Rupert's Land and the Northwestern Territory. So there was nothing to be done except to negotiate with Riel during the hiatus. Macdonald sent Donald Smith to Red River with funds "to construct a Golden Bridge over which McDougall can pass into the country." Macdonald intended to bribe Riel to leave the country. So began the curious relation between these two men, which ended in Riel's death, in the loss of Quebec as a stronghold of the Conservative party (for the Roman Catholic hierarchy had since 1867 supported Macdonald and the Conservatives; they regarded the Liberals, *les rouges*, as radicals), and the party's eventual replacement by the Liberals as Canada's party of national unity.

Riel's administration bore many of the aspects of a military dictatorship. Yet he sought to rule with the support of the whole Settlement, not just the Metis. Although their paper, *The Nor'Wester,* was suppressed, the Canada Firsters were free to denounce Riel. They were imprisoned only after they tried to overthrow him. And Macdonald's emissary, Donald Smith, was given the right to address the inhabitants at a public meeting. In fact, to forestall Smith's appeal to those not represented in his government, Riel summoned delegates from all of the parishes, English and French, to a convention which elected officers to the provisional government and adopted a List of Rights to serve as the basis of negotiations with Canada. Three delegates were chosen to go to Ottawa.

On February 14, 1870, the Canadians from Portage la Prairie made a second attempt to unseat Riel. They set out to free the prisoners Riel had taken earlier but Riel, acting

swiftly, released the prisoners, then subdued and imprisoned the members of the Portage party. Thomas Scott,
who had escaped from custody following the first attempt
to overthrow Riel, had been instrumental in organizing the
second attempt. He was imprisoned again and brought to
trial.

The leading figures at Red River were all young men.
Riel was 25, Schultz 29, and Scott 26. Scott appeared before
a court martial presided over by Ambrose Lepine, adjutant-
general in the provisional government. A jury of six Metis
found Scott guilty, and he was sentenced to death. Scott
was contemptuous of his captors. In a letter to a friend he
wrote, "The Metis are a pack of cowards. They will not
dare to shoot me." Riel told his followers, "We must make
Canada respect us." On March 4, 1879, Scott was taken
outside the walls of Fort Garry and shot by a firing squad.

The execution could not have been better timed to dam-
age the Metis' cause. George-Etienne Cartier, Macdonald's
partner in the work of Confederation and in the first post-
Confederation government, had assured Bishop Alexandre
Taché (who had seen Cartier in Ottawa on his way back
to Red River from Rome) that there would be an amnesty
for Riel and his followers if they would submit to the new
Canadian regime. Cartier had complete authority to speak
for Macdonald. In the meantime, however, Thomas Scott
had been tried, and he was executed four days before
Taché reached the Settlement.

Scott's execution caused a political firestorm in Ontario.
Scott was from Ontario, and an Orangeman, and he had
been murdered by Riel, a French-speaking Roman Catholic. The Ontario government arrested Riel's delegates on
their way from Red River to Ottawa, though they were
released soon afterward and allowed to continue their journey. Anger in Ontario against Riel was matched by resentment in Quebec, where Riel came to be regarded as
a victim of Orange bigotry. Lost in the blaze of contention
was any awareness of or concern for the Metis themselves.

Taché, on his return to Red River, assured Riel that he
had Cartier's promise that there would be a complete am-

nesty. Riel, therefore, released his other prisoners and agreed to let the Union Jack fly over Fort Garry. When the delegates from Red River arrived in Ottawa with the Metis' List of Rights, Macdonald and Cartier agreed to many of their demands, and incorporated them into the Manitoba Act, which the House of Commons passed on May 12, 1870. Thus the old District of Assiniboia became the "postage stamp" province.

The transfer of title to Canada of the whole northwest, including the new province of Manitoba, took place on July 15, 1870 and on that day, the new lieutenant-governor of Manitoba and the Northwest Territories, Adams G. Archibald (Macdonald had long since dismissed the egregious McDougall), left Port Arthur for Red River. Archibald was accompanied, however, by a force of 1,200 British and Canadian soldiers under Colonel Garnet Wolseley. Macdonald had sent Wolseley and his men to satisfy public opinion in Ontario, which was eager to see Riel punished. Bishop Taché pleaded with Macdonald to grant the amnesty and to stop the troops, but Macdonald would agree to neither plea.

In the meantime, the provisional government at Red River had continued to function. At the end of March, representatives elected from all parts of the Settlement formed a legislature under Riel's presidency and passed a code of laws. James Ross was sworn in as chief justice. Riel's administration carried on until August 24, 1870, when Archibald arrived at Fort Garry accompanied by Wolseley and his troops. Riel had planned to hand the government over to Archibald himself but, by now unsure of the amnesty and unwilling to confront Wolseley's superior military force, he and the leaders of the provisional government fled, leaving their breakfast unfinished, across the Assiniboine River. Wolseley found Fort Garry empty.

Riel was gone from Red River. All that the Metis could rely on now was the Manitoba Act. The Act provided that both English and French should be the official languages of the new province, and there were explicit guarantees to the denominational schools of both Protestants and

Catholics. More important, however, from the point of view of the Metis, was the provision made for the allotment of 1,400,000 acres of public land to the descendants of Half-breed heads of families.

All this was very well. But how could the Manitoba Act protect the Metis' way of life? They were to get land—but after that, what? How could their desire to retain their way of life be expressed in constitutional and legal terms? This was a question that the statesmen of that time did not consider; indeed, it is a question that Canadian statesmen have ever since been unwilling to address. Macdonald, the nation-builder, never acknowledged that the Metis were anything but an impediment to the development of the transcontinental dominion that he envisioned.

At first, however, it appeared that the Manitoba Act had established the conditions whereby the Metis could survive. Lieutenant-Governor Archibald proposed to divide among the Half-breeds the 1,400,000 acres intended for them under the Manitoba Act. The public lands of the province were not owned by the province, however, but by the federal government—public lands and natural resources were not transferred to the province until 1930. The federal government was dilatory to the point of bad faith with regard to the allocation of land to the Metis and the "country-born." Only about 15 per cent of the occupants of the river lots received patents and remained on their land. Not only were there great delays, the federal government placed stringent limitations on eligibility. In 1874, legislation was brought in entitling each half-breed head of family to 160 acres of land, or scrip. Scrip was simply a certificate that entitled the holder to so many acres of land. But scrip was negotiable. The scrip that the Metis were entitled to under the legislation of 1874 was valued at $160.00. But the Metis were soon submerged in a land rush. Most of them still had no title to their river lots, many of which had been allotted to settlers pouring in from Ontario. Metis who had received scrip were unable to acquire any land. In frustration, Metis sold their scrip to speculators, and made ready to leave Manitoba.

The consequences of Riel's insurrection against Canadian authority had still to be sorted out. Ontario's rage over the death of Scott had not abated. In 1872 the Ontario government offered a reward of $5,000 for Riel's capture. As for the amnesty, promised by Cartier, Macdonald prevaricated. He insisted that he had never promised a complete amnesty covering all of the acts carried out in the name of Riel's provisional government; in particular, he was not prepared to agree to an amnesty that would apply to Scott's execution. Bishop Taché claimed that Macdonald had broken his pledge. As for Schultz and his allies, they regarded the coming of Canadian rule as a new dispensation. The Metis, who had provisioned the colony and defended it for half a century, were relegated to the margins of its political and economic life. There were reprisals against the Metis, and two of them were killed. Armed men invaded Riel's home, although they did not find him.

Riel had not, however, left Manitoba. Indeed, his services would soon be needed by the Crown. Wolseley disbanded his military force in the summer of 1871. That fall, Lieutenant-Governor Archibald had to appeal to Riel and Ambrose Lepine to defend the colony against Fenian raids expected from Minnesota. Riel and Lepine raised a force of 300 Metis riflemen which, under Riel's command, paraded before the lieutenant-governor. When the invasion came, United States troops at the border dispersed the Fenians before they entered Canada; until then, the Metis riflemen were, as they had been for so many years before, the only force ready and able to defend the Settlement.

The people of Ontario never understood the Metis' conviction that they were a nation, and they found it impossible to take seriously these "wretched, half-starved people," who claimed the plains as their own. Neither did Quebec understand the Metis. At first, Quebec had regarded the Metis as Indians, "les sauvages." When the uprising occurred at Red River the French-language newspapers of Quebec voiced the same views as the English-language newspapers of Ontario: these Half-breeds could not stand in the way of Canada's westward advance. But, when

William McDougall returned in January, 1870, to Ontario, after Riel had refused to allow him to enter Assiniboia, he accused the Roman Catholic Church of having instigated the insurrection to establish a French and Catholic province in the northwest. When news came that Riel had had Thomas Scott executed, there were all sorts of wild allegations made by politicians and the newspapers in Ontario against the Catholics and the French. As a result, the French Canadians in Quebec began to believe they must resist this assault on their language and their religion. Quebec was agitated, not by the condition and circumstances of the Metis, but by the refusal of the English to acknowledge the rightful place of the French in western Canada.

Louis Riel was at the centre of this controversy. Ontario wanted him tried for the death of Scott. Quebec insisted that he be granted amnesty. Macdonald knew that to grant amnesty to Riel would further inflame Ontario. To refuse him amnesty would outrage Quebec. Macdonald considered that the best thing to do was to persuade Riel to leave the country, and in 1872 the federal government secretly provided him with $4,000 to go to the United States. Riel took the money, but he returned to Manitoba later in the year to be nominated as the Conservative candidate for Provencher. Riel always thought of himself as a Conservative: it was, after all, Macdonald, a Conservative, who had agreed to the List of Rights and to admit Red River to Confederation as a province, and a Liberal government in Ontario that had offered a reward of $5,000 for his capture. But Cartier had lost his seat in Montreal, so Riel gave up his nomination to allow Cartier to run in his place. Here was a man who had led an uprising against Canada now offering his seat to one of the Fathers of Confederation so that he could re-enter Parliament. Riel's career was replete with such ironies. When Cartier died in mid-1873, Riel was nominated again and elected MP for Provencher, but he did not take his seat.

In December, 1873, Macdonald was defeated in the House of Commons over the Pacific Scandal, and Alexander Mackenzie and the Liberals came to power. Mackenzie called a general election in January, 1874, which the Liberals won. Riel was re-elected MP for Provencher, *in absentia*. He did not take his seat on this occasion either but, in another of the melodramatic episodes that marked his life, he went to Ottawa, took his oath in the Parliament Buildings, was recognized, and left at once.

Canadian militants in Manitoba waited for the federal government to take action against Riel and the Metis leaders. Finally they persuaded a justice of the peace to issue a warrant against Riel, charging him with the murder of Thomas Scott, and on February 10, 1875, the Manitoba Court of Queen's Bench convicted him *in absentia* and pronounced a sentence of outlawry against him. Lepine, who had been adjutant-general in the provisional government and had presided at Scott's trial, was arrested, tried, and condemned to death. Now the question of amnesty could be avoided no longer.

Prime Minister Mackenzie was paralyzed by indecision. Like Macdonald before him, he felt he could do neither the one thing nor the other. Finally, in 1875, Lord Dufferin, the governor-general, a man who did not regard himself as a mere figurehead, intervened. Influenced by the fact that Riel and Lepine had come to the aid of the Crown in the Fenian crisis, he commuted Lepine's sentence to two years' imprisonment and the permanent loss of his civil rights. (Lepine lived until 1923; his civil rights were restored a few years before his death.) Mackenzie then moved in the House that a general amnesty be granted covering those who had participated in the insurrection, except for Riel, who was banished to the United States for five years. (Riel was the last Canadian to be banished until 1946, when Mackenzie King banished 4,000 Japanese Canadians.) Riel spent the next decade moving back and forth between Canada and the United States. His mind began to suffer, and he had spells of insanity. In 1878, in the United States once again, he married a Metisse, became an American citizen, and settled down as a teacher in a missionary school in Montana.

The insurrection of the Metis had been a failure. Their leaders were in jail or in exile, their lots along the Red River had been taken, and now the buffalo were disappearing. The new society at Red River was wholly dedicated to commerce and agriculture. It had no need of and no place for the Metis. The Manitoba Act guaranteed the rights of the French and the Catholics, but these rights were not basic issues for the Metis. Basic to them was their way of life on the plains, and clearly it was not going to survive long. Settlers were moving onto the plains, driving the buffalo before them. In 1874, the last Metis buffalo hunt left Red River. Nothing held the Metis at Red River now, so most of them piled their belongings on their carts and moved on. Farther west, there were still buffalo, and the Metis (including Lepine, on his release from prison in 1876) migrated to the valleys of the Saskatchewan River, where they could hunt buffalo for a while longer, and await their next rendezvous with the Canadians.

The Metis camps on the Saskatchewan gradually became permanent settlements among which Catholic missionaries built their churches. St. Laurent, originally a winter camp on the South Saskatchewan, was the most important of these new settlements. The Metis of St. Laurent established their own government based on the rules of the buffalo hunt. They elected a council and a president, Gabriel Dumont; they enacted laws and collected taxes; and a commission settled disputes over land ownership. Along the Saskatchewan they re-established the stable society they had known at Red River.

But even as the Metis began to settle along the Saskatchewan, events were in train that would overtake them there. In 1871, the year after Manitoba entered Confederation, the Canadian Pacific Railway was incorporated and, between 1871 and 1877, the federal government signed seven treaties with the Indians on the plains. These treaties confined the Indians to reserves and opened up western Canada to the railway and to settlement. During 1882 and 1883 the CPR laid track across the prairies. The settlers who followed the railway soon spread out across the hunting grounds of the Indians who, demoralized and disease-ridden, watched, silent and angry, as their lands were divided and ploughed.

Soon the surveyors were measuring the land along the Saskatchewan into great squares, ignoring again the Metis' traditional narrow strips that fronted on the river. The federal government's land grants to the CPR included some of the lands the Metis occupied. Promoters appeared who claimed to hold title to Metis farms. Land speculation was rampant, and friends of the federal government made enormous profits. The Metis had no Crown grants or land titles. If they could not buy their land back from the speculators, they had no choice but to give it up.

Naturally, the Metis on the Saskatchewan wished to have their title to their holdings ratified. In fact, they had been petitioning the federal government since 1873 for this purpose, but they had been largely ignored. In 1879, Parliament had passed legislation that enabled the cabinet to settle the claims of the Metis in the Northwest Territories, but the cabinet was not prepared at this time to implement this legislation—indeed, no lands were allotted to any of the Metis outside Manitoba, and no scrip reached the Metis on the Saskatchewan until after the outbreak of rebellion in 1885. The Metis wanted Ottawa to provide them with patents to the land they already occupied. Despite official entreaties by Inspector Crozier of the North-West Mounted Police in which he urged that Metis claims be settled immediately, John A. Macdonald, who was again prime minister, would not act. Only then, in June, 1884, did the Metis send Gabriel Dumont 700 miles south to Sun River in Montana to fetch Louis Riel.

Not only the Metis were discontented. The Indians of the plains were destitute. And the White settlers at Prince Albert had their own litany of grievances. First, there was the question of the distance from authority. Then, as now, officials in far-off Ottawa governed the Northwest Territories: a Northwest Council sat at Regina, but it was powerless. Crops were bad and prices were low. The CPR was not, as the government had promised, being built along the North Saskatchewan River. So when Dumont went to Riel in Montana to urge him to return, he carried with him letters from White settlers in Prince Albert, together with funds they had given him to bring Riel back.

The historian W. L. Morton has argued that western protest against the policies of Ottawa runs in a direct line from Riel to the present day. I don't agree. The White settlers at Prince Albert are at the beginning of that line of protest. They are the true precursors of the western protest movements of the 1920s and the 1930s. The Metis are no more the progenitors of the Progressives, the CCF, and Social Credit than they are of those powerful interests in the west today who say they are alienated; it is the Metis who have become strangers in their own homeland. Of course, there could be no long-term identity of interest between Riel's Metis and the White settlers. As soon as the first shot was fired, the settlers at Prince Albert took their stand with Canada and the Mounted Police. They had used Riel to bring events to a head, but they had no wish to join him in rebellion.

Riel arrived on the Saskatchewan on July 11, 1884. He made his headquarters at Batoche across the river from St. Laurent, where he and his followers drew up a Bill of Rights that demanded more liberal treatment for the Indians, scrip for the Metis, and responsible government for the settlers. In February, 1885, Macdonald's government agreed to investigate their claims, but this was a promise that was meaningless, for Macdonald had promised as much in the past. The truth was that Macdonald had no intention of acceding to the Metis' demand for scrip: he believed that nine-tenths of them had received it already. After the rebellion of 1885 was over, Macdonald, defending the course he had taken before it broke out, told the House:

The Half-breed was not cultivating the land he had. Giving him more land was giving him nothing. The nomadic half-breed, who had been brought up to hunt, having had merely his shanty to repair in the dead season, when there was no game—what advantage was it to him to give him 160 or 240 acres more? It was of no use to him whatever, but it would have been of great use to the speculators who were working on him and telling him he was suffering. Oh! how awfully he was suffering, ruined, destroyed, starving, because he did not get 240 acres somewhere else, or the scrip for it, that he might sell it for $50. No, sir, the whole thing is a farce.

Macdonald was both right and wrong. What he told the House was true, but it was not the whole truth. Many Metis had received scrip in Manitoba, but then they had sold it and moved on to hunt buffalo on the plains of Saskatchewan. Now the herds of buffalo were gone, and farmers were sowing wheat and raising cattle where the herds had once ranged. And these same Metis, who had received scrip in Manitoba in settlement of their claims, were making demands for scrip all over again. But what else could the Metis ask for? That agricultural settlement on the plains be stopped? That they be left alone to hunt the remaining buffalo, as of old? They decided to ask for scrip, because there seemed to be no other way they could articulate their plea. It was a plea made in desperation, and perhaps made without any conviction that, if it were granted, it would make any difference to them. Even if the problems of scrip, of surveys, and of land grants had been sorted out, probably the Metis would still have been un-satisfied. In truth, Macdonald and the Metis were at cross purposes. The Metis sought a settlement of their aboriginal claims, but they could not foresee what measures were needed to enable them to remain a distinct people on the plains. They had no political vocabulary except that of Riel and of 1869-70, and Macdonald was determined to reject any claims expressed in such a vocabulary. Only in our own time have the Metis developed a political vocabulary that truly expresses their dilemma and their proposals for a contemporary resolution of it.

As for Riel, he proposed to re-enact the drama of 1869-70. But the drama could not be repeated. Riel had, by this time, left the Catholic Church and, to the bemusement of his followers and the chagrin of the Church, he had proclaimed himself the Prophet of the New World. The Church would not be his ally this time. The political situation was also quite different: there was no constitutional hiatus, no basis for questioning Canadian authority. Riel had his captain-general, Gabriel Dumont, and 500 buffalo hunters, who were crack shots and used to living off the land. But Riel and his men were now pitted against the forces of a great Dominion stretching from sea to sea. Their defeat was not only inevitable, it could not be postponed even for a season.

When Macdonald rejected the last Metis petition, Dumont insisted that the time had come. On March 18, 1885, Riel seized the church at Batoche. On March 19, he formed a provisional government. At once, Inspector Crozier sent for reinforcements and moved his headquarters up the river from Prince Albert to Fort Carleton. There Riel and his riflemen confronted him. Riel told Crozier that he must surrender or face a war of extermination—but Crozier would not give up the fort. Five days later, Crozier set out with 100 men from Fort Carleton to Duck Lake for supplies. Half of his men were Mounted Police, the other half were volunteers from Prince Albert. On their way, they met Riel and his men. Within 15 minutes, 12 of Crozier's men lay dead and 11 were wounded; only five of the Metis were killed. Riel stopped his men from pursuing Crozier's force, an action that enabled Crozier and his men to retire to Prince Albert—otherwise they might well have been exterminated.

Riel had been trying to enlist the Indians in his cause. When the Indians learned of the Metis' victory over the Mounted Police at Duck Lake, they rose to join Riel. Chief Poundmaker's Indians seized the stores at Battleford, forcing the population of that settlement to take refuge in the Mounted Police barracks across the river. Another Indian attack obliged the Mounted Police and the settlers of Fort Pitt to evacuate the post. Chief Big Bear's Indians took possession of Frog Lake, killing nine persons.

News of these events created a frenzy of excitement in eastern Canada, not only because of the rebellion by the Metis, but also because Riel had incited an Indian uprising, which Canada, mindful of the bloodshed in the Indian wars in the United States, deeply wished to avoid. The government sent a force of regular troops and militia, more than 3,000 men altogether, to crush the Metis and the Indians. Within ten days, the CPR had transported the Canadian forces to Fort Qu'Appelle. There, under General Middleton's command, the army prepared to march to the North Saskatchewan, where Riel, for the moment, prevailed. But he would not prevail for long. Among the Indians, Poundmaker and Big Bear were Riel's only allies. The government had begun, belatedly, to send flour, bacon, tea and tobacco to the Indians in the Qu'Appelle valley, and they did not rise. The English-speaking Halfbreeds had already refused to follow Riel, and the Whites were against him. Even the Metis were not united in his support. On April 16, after having ignored the Metis' petitions for years, the government authorized the issue of scrip, thereby preventing some of the Metis from joining Riel.

In May, General Middleton's forces, a mixed body of cavalry and militia, marched north from Qu'Appelle across the plains in three columns. Dumont wanted to harass Middleton, to use to advantage the Metis' knowledge of the terrain, their ability to live off the land, and their capacity to hit and run. But Riel refused. The Canadians first met the Metis at Fish Creek. The Metis held their position, and Middleton lost eight men, with 40 wounded. On the day of this battle, another Canadian column, under Colonel Otter, reached Battleford to relieve the police and settlers in the barracks there. Otter was rebuffed when he attacked Poundmaker's encampment at Cut Knife Creek. The Indians killed eight and wounded 14 of his men, but Poundmaker, seeking to avoid further bloodshed in a conflict that he now knew was hopeless, would not allow his warriors to pursue the fleeing troops.

By May 9, Middleton and his main column had reached Batoche. The Metis were well entrenched in rifle pits there, but they were badly outnumbered. They soon ran out of ammunition and, on the third day of battle, the Canadians overran the Metis and took the town. Dumont escaped across the United States border. Riel fled into the woods, but gave himself up on May 15. Poundmaker surrendered on May 26, and Big Bear gave himself up on July 2. Riel's second rebellion had lasted less than two months.

With Riel, the Canadians had taken 129 prisoners altogether: 46 were Metis and English-speaking Half-breeds, 81 were Indians, and two were Whites. They were tried. Forty-four of the Indians were convicted, eight of them for murder, and these were executed at Battleford. Riel was charged with treason. His lawyers argued that he was insane. Riel insisted that he was not. He was convicted on July 31; the jury recommended mercy. Poundmaker and Big Bear, the Cree chieftains, were each sentenced to three years imprisonment, but their sentences were commuted.

Would Macdonald allow Riel to be hanged? An appeal to the Manitoba Court of Queen's Bench and then an application for leave to appeal to the Privy Council in London both failed. Macdonald appointed three doctors to report on the question of Riel's sanity: they found him sane. Amid a rising clamour, Macdonald's lieutenants in Quebec urged him to intercede, and the expectation in Quebec was that Riel's sentence would be commuted. Supported by Ontario, Macdonald was, however, determined to see the matter through. Riel was hanged on November 15, 1885, nine days after Donald Smith, now Lord Strathcona, had driven the last spike of the CPR at Craigellachie.

Riel is generally believed to have led the Metis to disaster in 1885. Why would he not listen to Dumont, who had urged the tactics of guerilla warfare? But the outcome would have been the same, whatever tactics had been adopted. The occupation of the plains by White settlers could not be halted. The Metis had no chance of winning their struggle. Canada had the technological sinew and the military strength to hold the west, and it had the will to hang Riel. Dumont had been prepared to see Riel safely across the United States border, but Riel refused to join him. Riel knew that his tragedy had to be played out to the end.

Macdonald had seriously misjudged the impact that Riel's death would have. After Riel had been hanged, a motion was brought before the House of Commons to express regret that Riel had been executed. It was defeated, but 25 of the French-Canadian Conservatives from Quebec had voted for it. On November 22, 1885, Wilfrid Laurier, leader of the Opposition, addressed a great meeting of 40,000 persons on the Champs de Mars in Montreal: "Had I been born on the banks of the Saskatchewan I would myself have shouldered a musket to fight against the neglect of the government and the shameless greed of speculators." Honoré Mercier, hitherto a Conservative, used the occasion to launch a Quebec nationalist party, a concept that has frequently recurred in Quebec political life ever since and is today realized in the Parti Québécois.

But there were no Metis on the Champs de Mars that day. What had these speeches to do with the plight of the remnants of the New Nation far away on the plains? Mercier's opening words were "Our poor brother is dead. He has been sacrificed to the fanaticism of the Orangemen." He had put the matter well. The response of Quebec was as much a reaction to the Ontario Orangemen's hatred of Roman Catholics as it was of grievance over the death of Riel. As for the Metis, they were scattered now. Some of them fled to the United States, some to the Mackenzie River basin. Some took up life among the Indians on the reserves. Some decided to assimilate. Some still clung to their identity as Metis, but they were destitute, without land, without capital, and unable to follow a way of life that had vanished with the herds of buffalo.

The Metis today still suffer from the legacy of 1885. Macdonald insisted that the Metis could not, as a people, assert any claim to aboriginal title. Only the Indians could claim aboriginal title. The Metis were not a distinct people. They had to choose between becoming Indians or White men. Macdonald refused to recognize in them the people of a New Nation. "If they are Indians," Macdonald said, "they go with the tribe; if they are Half-breeds, they are White." There could be, in his opinion, nothing in between, no race that partook of both cultures, yet was unique in itself.

Still today, the Metis refuse to assimilate; they still contend that they are neither Indian nor White. Of course, in a sense they are both, yet they are neither. Riel, in his own person, epitomized this conflict. A student, a teacher, an agitator, a politician, and a religious mystic he may have been, yet he was a product of the plains—a Metis. To the end, Riel remained maddeningly ambiguous.

Many attempts have been made to improve Riel's image, but the cosmeticians' efforts should be resisted. Did he accept a bribe from Macdonald in 1872 to go to the United States? All right, he did. Was he prepared to accept a bribe in 1885 (although none was forthcoming)? Perhaps. But should we regard that action as heinous in Riel, when at the same time we think of Macdonald's offering bribes as an aspect of his roguish charm: it was a flaw, like his drinking, in Macdonald that endears him to us. If Macdonald bribed Riel, it was a canny thing to do, the sort of thing expected of a nineteenth-century statesman who had to deal with a half-mad, half-savage rebel. As for Riel, there he stands, in all his fervent and perplexed humanity. Crucifix in hand, he called Dumont back when he had the North-West Mounted Police on the run at Duck Lake. A rebel, a man of charismatic personality, he saw himself as a prophet and martyr. Was he obsessed by injustice both to himself and to his people? Why shouldn't he have been? Can anyone deny that Riel and the Metis were badly used? Driven from the plains, they were offered no place in the agricultural society established on what they believed was their land. Macdonald had promised them an amnesty, then he betrayed them. The Metis had raised a force of their own men to protect the new province of Manitoba against the Fenians, yet they were still treated as criminals and fugitives by the very government that had enlisted their help. Riel had agreed to let Cartier stand in his stead in Provencher, an act that would have earned him a seat in the Senate today, but then it went unacknowledged; and when he was elected to Parliament in his own right, he was not allowed to take his seat.

Was Riel a martyr? I think the answer is yes. He lived dangerously for his beliefs, and he died on the scaffold. Today, even though he led them to defeat at Batoche, Riel is a hero to the Metis.

Both English-speaking and French-speaking Canadians think of Riel as a symbol of their struggle for hegemony in the Canadian west. Yet the Riel uprisings on the Red River in 1869-70 and on the Saskatchewan in 1885 are really episodes in the Metis' resistance to the advance of the Canadian agricultural frontier. Not only have the English and French taken the Metis' homeland from them, but they have also appropriated the symbol of the Metis' struggle: to the English, Riel was a murderer; to the French, he was a defender of the French fact in the Northwest. But all that is in the past. Riel lives today, not in the grateful memory of French Canadians, but in the hearts of the Metis.

The new Constitution provides that the aboriginal rights of the aboriginal peoples of Canada will be recognized and affirmed. It goes on to define the Indians, the Inuit and the Metis as the aboriginal peoples of Canada. Thus, express recognition will be given to the Metis as one of the aboriginal peoples of Canada. With this recognition there should be an acknowledgement that the Metis are a people whose lives are woven into the fabric of Canadian life, and whose history entitles them to assert their claims today.

But is it now too late? How can there be a settlement of Metis claims today? How can the aboriginal rights of the Metis be acknowledged in a country that has, for a century, pretended that—in a constitutional sense—the Metis did not exist? The Metis are caught up in a tangled skein of history, constitutional law, and sociology that leaves unanswered many difficult questions. Who is a Metis? What form should a settlement of their claims take today? How can we deal collectively with a people many of whose ancestors individually received scrip a century ago? It may take years to unravel such questions. But Canada has undertaken to address these issues.

In this tangle, one fact is certain. The Metis who vanished over the prairie horizon in their carts, retreating before the westward advance of agriculture, did not disappear, and they will not disappear. For a time they dwindled. The 1941 census, the last census to identify Metis separately, listed only 8,692 of them. But now, many more persons claim to be Metis. Their long journey has brought them back to the banks of the Red River, to the site of the settlement they defended for so many years, and back to the city where Riel was hanged. Today they may be found in Winnipeg and Regina, and all across the prairies. They share a common idea of who they are: descendants of the people who constituted *la nation métisse*. Although few of them now speak French, their sense of a common past draws them together, and provides them with a contemporary identity.

The legal and historical arguments over whether or not the federal government is bound to negotiate with the Metis may be inconclusive. No doubt the ancestors of many, perhaps of most, present-day Metis took scrip at one time or another. Representatives of the federal government were dispensing scrip across the plains until 1908. But a wise and just federal policy will reject the notion that the provision of scrip to the Metis in the past extinguished their aboriginal rights. Federal insistence, a century ago, that the Metis should take scrip was an official rejection of the idea that they constituted a society that was—and is—distinct from Indian society and the dominant White society. To persist in such a policy today would be to repudiate the high promise of the new Constitution.

Some may suggest that all we should gain by opening

such negotiations would be another round of problems to plague us during the next century. But these so-called problems will be waiting for us, no matter what we do. Macdonald believed that he had disposed of these problems in 1885 when he declared that the Metis must become Indians or White men. His government denied their very existence, but the Metis persisted, refusing to assimilate. They still refuse to assimilate, they still refuse to surrender their heritage as one of the aboriginal peoples of Canada.

The history of the Metis is not simply a curiosity, a footnote to the drama of White occupation and settlement of the plains. The Metis share a common past and a common pride. Like the Indians, they are advancing claims based on their aboriginal rights. In this the Metis have made common cause with the non-status Indians (those Indians who, because of marriage to non-Indians, or for some other reason, are no longer eligible to claim Indian status under the Indian Act).

A settlement of aboriginal claims is not a matter of theoretical justice, a merely abstract question of minority rights. How are the prairie provinces, and their cities and towns, going to cope with their swelling Native population? There have been many programs designed to alleviate the condition of Native people. Has the "problem" been solved? No one can be unaware of the poverty, violence and degradation that disfigure life in many Native communities. The problems have not gone away: if anything, they have been aggravated. Why? Because the problems of Native people are not simply problems of poverty, but of a people trying desperately to preserve their cultural identity. Their search for a contemporary expression of that identity has given rise to Native land claims and the call for Native self-determination.

The 1981 Report of the Metis and Non-Status Indian Constitutional Review Commission, established by the Native Council of Canada, has presented the views of the Metis and the non-status Indians. They seek "collective integration into the political, economic, social and cultural life of the country." They seek "the right to integrate as *lectivity,''* not one by one. They reject the notion that access to the mainstream can only be achieved by assimilation. They have provided an agenda and they have identified the institutions that bear most heavily on their lives:

> ...the laws and administrative structures governing the definition of Native; the education systems responsible for the teaching and the socialization of Native children; and the family law and child welfare systems which often govern the fates of Native families. Native people believe that these institutions have worked towards the fragmentation of the Native collectivities and the assimilation of their members.

In working out a settlement with the Metis, it would be a mistake to seek a narrow interpretation of the new Constitution, to try to limit the numbers of persons who qualify as Metis and the rights that, as Metis, they may assert under the Constitution. For it is not now, nor was it ever, merely a question of land or scrip. As Riel said at his trial:

> I suppose the Half-breeds in Manitoba, in 1870, did not fight for two hundred and forty acres of land, but it is to be understood that there were two societies who treated together. One was small, but in its smallness had its rights. The other was great, but in its greatness had no greater rights than the rights of the small, because the right is the same for everyone.

The experience of the Metis reveals how fragile minority rights can be in the face of social, political, and demographic change. Of course, minorities must change, too. The question is whether they must, in the course of such change, abandon their sense of collective identity. Is there a way in which, in a modern, industrial country, a minority such as the Metis can be themselves? If there is no such way in Canada, then it is unlikely that a way will be found in any other country.

Can this small people claim its rights today? Does Canada have another rendezvous with the New Nation? The new Constitution will oblige Canada to treat once more with the Metis. Will we offer the Metis merely another opportunity to assimilate? Or can we rather provide the Metis with the means whereby they may regain their past and secure their future? The Metis cannot become buffalo hunters again, but they can become once more a proud, resourceful people.

THREE

Laurier and the Separate Schools

> Francophones outside Quebec are like a family whose home
> has been destroyed by fire. We are without shelter, our
> eyes fixed on odd belongings scattered here and there. But
> we are still alive.

FRENCH CANADIANS, IN every province except Quebec, are
a minority—often a beleaguered minority. Ever since Confederation, they have sought constitutional guarantees for
their religion and their language, but these guarantees,
when they have mattered most, have been denied them.
Without such guarantees, the French Canadians have been,
and they remain, vulnerable to assimilation.

French Canadians are, of course, a majority in the province of Quebec. There can be no doubt that the French-
speaking majority of that province have established a permanent place for themselves in North American society.
Lord Durham in 1839 foresaw their assimilation; in fact,
he sought to establish the conditions by which it might be
accomplished. Yet the attempt was abandoned within a
decade. In 1867 they acquired a province of their own,
together with constitutional safeguards, which—given their
numbers—have ever since provided the means to preserve
them in the Anglophone sea of North America. But the
history of French-speaking minorities in the other provinces has been one of continuing assaults on their language, their religion, and their culture, and of continuous
retreat before these assaults.

The difficulty goes back to Confederation. By the 1850s,
English-speaking Canadians outnumbered French-speaking Canadians in the Union of the Canadas (the old Province of Canada). Confederation made the French Canadians

predominant in the new province comprising their ancestral home. George-Etienne Cartier had insisted upon that point. If he had not succeeded, Quebec would not have agreed to enter Confederation. After 1867, therefore, the French-speaking people of Quebec could speak their own language and practise their own religion, free from any interference from the national capital in Ottawa, where English-speaking Canadians were in the majority.

It was provided in Section 133 of the British North America Act that English and French should be the official languages of the federal Parliament and of the federal courts. In the same way, English and French were to be the official languages of the legislature and the courts of Quebec. These were the only provisions in the BNA Act relating specifically to language rights.

The real mainstay of the French-Canadian language and identity in the BNA Act was thought to be Section 93. In Section 93, the Fathers of Confederation agreed that education should be exclusively a provincial matter. This meant that there could be no federal interference with the schools run by the Roman Catholic Church in Quebec. What about Catholics outside Quebec? Section 93 provided that the provinces could not interfere with or abrogate rights to denominational schools already established by law, by the Catholic Church or by the Protestant churches at the time of Confederation. This provision protected the schools of both the Protestant minority in Quebec and of the Catholic minority in Ontario. Everyone regarded it as an effective instrument as well to protect Catholic education and, therefore, French-Canadian identity in the other provinces. Not only did Section 93 forbid provincial interference with separate schools (the Catholic schools were referred to in the BNA Act as separate schools), it went on to provide that, if any province abrogated rights to separate schools, the federal cabinet was authorized to intervene and to require, if need be, that remedial action be taken by the province, and Parliament was authorized, if need be, to pass remedial legislation.

How did Section 93 protect French-speaking minorities

when it had nothing to do with language rights? Section 93 is concerned with denominational schools. The schools operated by the Catholic Church were, in the provinces outside Quebec, the place where French-Canadian children were taught to read and write in their mother tongue. These schools were to be maintained out of public funds. The disputes that arose between the English and the French over Section 93 were in the beginning disputes—at least superficially—over whether or not separate schools should be supported by public funds. In reality, they were disputes about a fundamental issue: were the French-Canadian minorities outside Quebec to preserve their language, their religion, and their culture, not as a matter of private choice but as a matter of constitutional right? Was Canada to be truly a bilingual, bicultural country?

The first test of Section 93, in New Brunswick, turned out badly for the Acadians. It was tested again in Manitoba, then in Ontario, and the outcome in each instance was devastating for the French-Canadian minorities in those provinces. Moreover, the political structure of Confederation drove a wedge between the French Canadians of Quebec and those in the other provinces. In Quebec, the majority could rely on provincial powers to preserve their language, religion, and culture. In the other provinces, English-speaking majorities used provincial powers to diminish French language, religion, and culture. The struggle can be best understood through the life and political career of Wilfrid Laurier.

Laurier's career spanned the three great crises of the French-Canadian minorities in Canada. He was a back-bencher in the House of Commons in the 1870s when the Acadians lost their claim to constitutional guarantees for their schools; thereafter they had to rely upon the goodwill of the provincial governments of the Maritimes. Laurier was leader of the Opposition in the 1890s when the government of Manitoba denied the Roman Catholics of that province the right to their own schools supported by provincial funds. As prime minister he negotiated the Laurier-Greenway agreement in 1896, which gave to the Catholics in Manitoba the right to conduct religious teaching in the public schools after regular school hours. He was in opposition again when the Ontario government sought to limit the use of French in the Catholic schools of Ontario in 1912, through the implementation of Regulation 17.

Laurier entered Parliament in 1870. Throughout his career, he was acutely concerned by how best to defend Quebec's position within Confederation; he was concerned as well by how to protect French Canadians outside Quebec. He deeply believed that the federal government must never be allowed to trespass upon provincial rights. But the assertion of provincial rights by the provinces with English-speaking majorities inevitably led to the erosion or loss of French-Canadian rights in those provinces. When New Brunswick abolished public funding for separate schools in 1871, politicians from Quebec tried to persuade the federal government to intervene. Laurier saw the dilemma clearly. He knew that the interests of Quebec, the heartland of French-Canadian culture and identity, must come first, even if consideration of Quebec's interests led to the defeat of French-Canadian rights elsewhere. Quebec federalists have faced this dilemma ever since Confederation. Today Quebec *Indépendantistes* simply say that French-Canadian minorities in the other provinces cannot survive; as the position of these minorities is undermined, so is the case for federalism undermined.

Each time the school question came up, the courts held that Section 93 did not mean what French Canadians had thought it meant. Repeatedly, Laurier had to ask himself, should the federal government intervene to uphold the rights of French Canadians in the English-speaking provinces? But how could he urge such a course? If the federal government exercised such power, then the day would surely come when that power would be used against Quebec. Throughout the crises over separate schools, Laurier never wavered in his understanding of what had been agreed at Confederation, and he never wavered in what he thought he must do. With unfailing clarity and eloquence, he tried to protect the French Canadians outside

Quebec. Yet never did he urge the federal government to intervene on their behalf in provincial matters. All that he could do was to plead for tolerance, compromise, and understanding: invariably, his pleas were not enough.

Tolerance, compromise and understanding, on the other hand, had always been in evidence in Quebec. The schools of the Protestant minority there had never been threatened. Consider the words of John Rose, who represented Montreal Centre in the Legislative Assembly of the Province of Canada in 1865:

> Now, we, the English Protestant minority of Lower Canada, cannot forget, that whatever right of separate education we have, was accorded to us in the most unrestricted way before the Union of the provinces, when we were in a minority, and entirely in the hands of the French population. We cannot forget that in no way was there any attempt to prevent us educating our children in the manner we saw fit, and deemed best; and I would be untrue to what is fact, if I forgot to state that the distribution of State funds for educational purposes was made in such a way as to cause no complaint on the part of the minority.

After Confederation, the French-Canadian authorities in Quebec continued to show the same tolerance to the English-speaking minority. Not until the 1970s did the government of Quebec attempt to limit the enrolment of certain pupils in the province's English-language schools. Even then, the government made no attempt to deny public funds to these schools or to limit the teaching of English in them.

The great disputes over separate schools in Manitoba and Ontario were the most divisive issues bearing on relations between the English and the French in Canadian politics between 1890 and 1920. In Manitoba, the dispute centred on religion. In Ontario, it centred on language. But in each case the issue was identical: were French Canadians to have a distinct place, guaranteed by the Constitution, in the society of the English-speaking majority outside Quebec?

Schools are the institutions whereby a language and a

cultural tradition are transmitted from one generation to the next. A minority can preserve its culture and identity only if its children are taught about their own people and their own past. This is true of every ethnic group. Without constitutional guarantees, such groups would, in the ordinary course, be expected to assimilate. The hallmark of assimilation is language. Thus the importance of schools where the language of a minority can be preserved and passed on.

Why shouldn't the French Canadians assimilate, just like any other minority ethnic group in the English-speaking provinces? You might equally as well ask, why shouldn't the English-speaking minority in Quebec assimilate? The case for the French Canadians rests on quite a different footing from other ethnic groups in Canada. Until the eighteenth century France (and her Indian allies) dominated North America, from the Atlantic coast to the Rockies, from the sub-Arctic to the Gulf of Mexico, while the English held their colonies on the Atlantic seaboard and their posts on Hudson Bay. The French were the first Europeans to settle in the Maritimes and on the St. Lawrence, and the first to explore the west. They did not arrive in Canada expecting to assimilate, as immigrants from other countries do. They have been here all along. They are one of the two founding peoples of Canada, and entitled to retain their own language and their own culture anywhere in Canada.

The Charter of Rights provides guarantees for minority language education, out of public funds. For the first time in Canadian history, the right to be educated in a minority language will be entrenched in the Constitution. So the descendants of the two peoples, the French and the English, who were the principal architects of Canadian history and institutions, will be guaranteed the right to educate their children in their own language. This has become necessary because the Fathers of Confederation failed to provide effective guarantees for minority language education rights, and because the courts refused to give a liberal interpretation to the measures that were included in the BNA Act to protect the separate schools of Catholics outside Quebec.

Until the mid-nineteenth century, what schools there were in Canada were denominational: schools established by the churches. In New France, education had always been a monopoly of the Roman Catholic Church, and the Church has always believed that religion must permeate education. Protestants also believed that their children should be given Christian instruction in their schools. During the nineteenth century, however, the idea grew that every child had a right to at least an elementary education: education should no longer be the privilege of the few. This movement occurred throughout the Western world, and led to the establishment in many nations of non-denominational, or public schools. How these schools should be financed, together with the questions of religious instruction and of the language of instruction, became controversial issues. The Catholic Church resisted secularization of education. So, at first, did the Protestant churches. Even today the schools in Quebec and Newfoundland are operated by denominational schoolboards. As the number of non-denominational, or public schools, grew, so did clashes between Church and State. In Canada that clash centred on the question of whether or not the provinces would provide public funds to support separate schools for Catholics, and the related question of what language would be used to instruct the children in these schools.

Quebec supported two school systems, Catholic and Protestant, but none of the English-speaking provinces acknowledged a need for two systems. Rather, they saw the Catholic schools as an anomaly—they were seen as exceptions to the rule, and attempts were made to diminish their functions or even to abolish them outright. With the expansion of education, and the coming of public schools supported by public funds, the English-speaking provinces began to deny public funding to separate schools. The struggle that ensued was a struggle over separate schools, but the outcome of this struggle would also determine the fate of the French-Canadian minorities in these provinces.

The battle over schools in Manitoba engaged the attention of the whole nation. By the Manitoba Act of 1870, the province had become officially bilingual. English and French were made the official languages of the legislature and the courts. Section 22 of the Act, modelled on Section 93 of the British North America Act, guaranteed the right of both Protestants and Catholics to public funds for denominational schools. Indeed, Section 22 of the Manitoba Act went further than Section 93 of the British North America Act: it provided that no law on education made by the province should prejudicially affect "any Right or Privilege with respect to Denominational Schools which any class of persons have by Law *or Practice* in the Province at the Union" of Manitoba with Canada. These words were deliberately chosen. When Manitoba was admitted to Confederation, it had no laws or ordinances respecting education. It was the absence in New Brunswick prior to Confederation of legal provision for public funds for Catholic schools that had led the courts to say that the Acadians could not claim the protection of Section 93. So Riel's delegates to Ottawa in 1870 had the words "or practice" included in Section 22 of the Manitoba Act precisely to avoid the kind of dispute that was then raging in New Brunswick prior to the passage of the Common Schools Act.

In 1871, the Manitoba legislature adopted a dual system of tax-supported denominational schools. This was the system that had existed as a matter of practice in the Red River Settlement before Manitoba became a province. It was this arrangement that Riel's delegates to Ottawa had sought to safeguard.

Under the Manitoba school legislation of 1871, two superintendents, one Protestant and one Roman Catholic, oversaw the work of the dual system of schools. This was entirely in keeping with the spirit of the Manitoba Act. Yet before the century was out, these provisions had been overturned. Manitoba was not to become a new Quebec in the west, as Cartier had hoped—and as others had feared. Indeed, there had never been a chance of it. In 1871, when the dual system of schools was adopted, the population of Manitoba was about evenly divided between Anglophones and Francophones. But the two populations ceased to be equal soon after the passage of the Manitoba Act. Ontario lay between Manitoba and Quebec. During the late nineteenth century, Ontario's economy was dynamic and expanding. After 1870, waves of English-speaking settlers emigrated from Ontario to Manitoba. While the Anglophone proportion of Manitoba's population steadily rose, the Francophone proportion declined.

With the tremendous increase in the number of Protestant, English-speaking settlers from Ontario, as well as from the British Isles and the United States, the dual system of schools was bound to come under attack. Archbishop Taché sent emissaries to the rural parishes of Quebec to recruit French-Canadian settlers, but the immigrants from Ontario outnumbered those from Quebec by about six to one. Quebec's population was increasing rapidly, too, but rural Quebecers were moving to Montreal or to work in the mill towns of New England. Still others moved into eastern Ontario. Relatively few migrated farther west. The French Canadians who did migrate to Manitoba found themselves exposed to assimilative forces that grew ever stronger as the movement of Ontarians to the west continued. John A. Macdonald recognized what was happening. The people of Quebec, he said,

> ...will not migrate in that direction. They, wisely, I think, desire to settle in the lands yet unoccupied in their province and to add to their influence in eastern Ontario. The consequence is that Manitoba and the Northwest Territories are becoming what British Columbia now is, wholly English—with English laws, English, or rather British immigration, and, I may add, English prejudices.

How long would an English-speaking majority accept an institutional framework that gave equal status to the language and religion of a French-Canadian minority? When the day came that the English no longer supported the dual system, the French Canadians would have no protection for their rights except the Manitoba Act, because they did not have the political battalions to defend themselves.

By 1890, the Manitoba government had for a decade or more been controlled by English-speaking Protestants. In that year, it passed legislation that put an end both to official bilingualism and to separate schools. The struggle that ensued is known as the Manitoba school question. It revealed the determination of the English-speaking Protestant majority to dominate western Canada. At the same time, it demonstrated how limited was the scope of Section 93 and of its counterpart, Section 22 of the Manitoba Act, which was supposed to protect the interests of the Franco-Manitobans.

English-speaking Canadians were deeply convinced that the Roman Catholic Church, which they regarded as dogmatic, hierarchical and controlled by a foreign pope, should not be allowed to become influential in the life of western Canada. At the same time, many of them felt the use of the French language to be an anomaly in North America, an anomaly that ought to be confined to Quebec. But it was not simply a question of religion or even of language. It was as well a matter of conflicting views about industrialization and modernization and about the kind of citizenry necessary to uphold the institutions of democracy. Protestants wanted state schools, in which the government, not the church, would appoint the teachers and prescribe the curriculum. They regarded state schools as the means of inculcating in the rising generation the values of democracy. Separate schools were, to them, an impediment to progress.

The French Canadians, on the other hand, believed that separate schools were essential to their survival as a people. They wanted their own schools, with Catholic schoolboards, Catholic teachers, and textbooks that followed Catholic doctrine. They saw that language and religion are closely allied, and they believed that the use of French was the means of keeping the Catholic faith wherever French Canadians settled, and that its use as the language of instruction would protect them from the contamination of

Protestant heresies and from modern secular tendencies.

But the Ontarians' drive to take possession of the west was prevailing over the French Canadians' claim that the west was the dual heritage of the two nations that founded Canada. Manitoba was important in the calculations of the Orange Lodge, which was immensely powerful in the political life of Ontario. Its membership was widespread, including virtually all those of British descent who believed in the supremacy of Protestantism and the Imperial connection. Separate schools in Ontario were provided for by pre-Confederation legislation, and thus were protected by the BNA Act. But the Orangemen saw no reason why they should not do all in their power to prevent such schools from being maintained or established in Manitoba and the Northwest Territories. The concept of Canada as a union of two founding peoples in which Quebec and Ontario had joined at Confederation, each secure in the possession of its own cultural institutions in every province, was not going to be extended farther west. Indeed, the Orangemen intended to destroy any progress that had been made in that direction.

By 1887, when Laurier had emerged as the leader of the Liberal party, English-speaking settlers from Ontario had pre-empted the agricultural lands of Manitoba and had laid their cultural and political impress upon the region. In 1889, Dr. John Schultz, the leader of the Canadian party whom Riel had imprisoned during the Red River uprising, was named lieutenant-governor of the province.

In that year also, the Orangemen in Ontario formed the Equal Rights Association to establish the supremacy of the English language and of state schools throughout the nation. D'Alton McCarthy, a Conservative and one-time confidant of John A. Macdonald, made a tour of Manitoba and the Northwest Territories to advance these goals. On August 5, 1889, in a speech at Portage la Prairie, he denounced the Catholic Church and the provision of public funds for separate schools. Joseph Martin, the attorney-general of Manitoba, at the same meeting urged the abolition of separate schools.

In 1890, Premier Thomas Greenway brought a bill before the Manitoba legislature to do away with French as an official language and another bill to replace tax-supported denominational schools with a single public school system. The English-speaking Protestant majority in the legislature passed both bills. McCarthy's view was a plain man's view, widely shared in Manitoba: "This is a British country, and the sooner we take up our French Canadians and make them British, the less trouble will we leave for posterity." McCarthy's view still has adherents in Canada.

The French Canadians saw at once which of these measures was the more serious. Without separate schools in which French was the language of instruction, there would be no future generations with the ability to use French as an official or unofficial language. The Franco-Manitobans at once challenged the province's power to compel them to pay taxes for state schools and at the same time to deny them public funds for separate schools. A Catholic rate-payer in Winnipeg, John Barrett, challenged the legislation in the courts, claiming that it violated the Manitoba Act. When *Barrett vs. Winnipeg* reached the Supreme Court of Canada, the judges of that court, Protestant and Catholic alike, English-speaking and French-speaking, unanimously held that the Manitoba School Act of 1890 prejudicially affected the rights and privileges of Catholics with respect to denominational schools, rights and privileges that they had held "by practice" when Manitoba joined Confederation in 1870. Sir William J. Ritchie, now chief justice of Canada, had, when he was chief justice of New Brunswick, held against the Acadians when they had sought to assert their rights under Section 93 of the BNA Act. The rights of the Acadians had not been established by law at Confederation, they merely existed as a matter of practice. So they were not protected by Section 93. But Section 22 of the Manitoba Act explicitly protected the rights of those who sent their children to Catholic schools, even where such rights existed merely as a matter of practice. Now Chief Justice Ritchie and the Supreme Court of Canada upheld the rights guaranteed by the Manitoba Act. Discussing the effect of the Schools Act on the Catholic ratepayers, he asked:

> Does it not prejudicially...affect them when they are taxed to support schools of the benefit of which, by their religious belief and the rules and principles of their church, they cannot conscientiously avail themselves, and at the same time by compelling them to find means to support schools to which they can conscientiously send their children, or in the event of their not being able to find sufficient means to do both to be compelled to allow their children to go without either religious or secular instruction?

The French Canadians of Manitoba seemed to have won. The constitutional guarantees secured by Riel's delegates had saved their schools. But the litigation did not end there: an appeal was taken to the Privy Council in Britain, the highest court to which Canadians could appeal. The Privy Council held that the only right or privilege the Roman Catholics had possessed by law or practice when Manitoba entered Confederation was the right to establish and maintain such schools as they pleased, but that the province was not bound to provide funds for their support. It is impossible to justify the Privy Council's decision on any rational basis in light of the express language of the Manitoba Act. The Privy Council said that because Manitoba had passed no statute providing for separate schools before it entered Confederation, Catholic parents who chose to send their children to separate schools were not exempt from paying taxes for public schools, and had no claim on public funds for the support of separate schools. But, of course, it was for the very reason that there was no such statute that the words "by practice" had been included in Section 22 of the Manitoba Act.

The decision of the Privy Council was a setback to Canadian unity. A small group of peers in far-away Westminster had, without any personal knowledge of Canada and with little or no understanding of Canadian history, found themselves unsympathetic to the idea of state-supported separate schools. For no better reason, so far as we can judge from their opinion, they reversed the Supreme Court of Canada. Now the Franco-Manitobans' only recourse was remedial action provided for by the Manitoba Act, for Section 22 of the Manitoba Act, like Section 93 of the BNA Act, provided that, when a province had taken away rights or privileges pertaining to separate schools, the federal cabinet could direct the province to remedy the situation and if the province refused to comply, Parliament could then enact remedial legislation to enforce compliance. When the Franco-Manitobans requested the cabinet to require Manitoba to restore their right to public funds for their separate schools, the cabinet referred the matter to the Supreme Court of Canada, asking the court whether or not, in view of the opinion of the Privy Council in *Barrett vs. Winnipeg*, the cabinet could exercise its remedial power, that is, could the cabinet, in the face of the Privy Council's opinion in *Barrett vs. Winnipeg*, require Manitoba to restore public funding for separate schools? The Supreme Court, relying upon the Privy Council's decision, held that the cabinet did not have that power. The attorney-general of Canada then appealed to the Privy Council and, in what Professor Donald Schmeiser, in *Civil Liberties in Canada*, calls "an amazing turnabout," the Privy Council held that the Manitoba Schools Act did prejudicially affect the rights of the Catholic minority in respect of education. They now held that, because state-supported denominational schools had been established *after 1870*, the federal government could direct the province to restore such support to the Roman Catholic minority. Once again, the opinion of the Privy Council made little sense, unless it is regarded as a belated acknowledgement by the peers of the wrongheadedness of their opinion in *Barrett vs. Winnipeg*.

The Catholics now looked to the cabinet to intervene. The Conservative government of Prime Minister Mackenzie Bowell (the third of Macdonald's successors after his death in 1891) was prepared to act. The cabinet passed an order-in-council that called upon the Manitoba government to restore to the Catholic minority the right to maintain their own schools, the right to share provincial school grants, and the right to exemption from payment for the support of state schools. By now it was 1895: court proceedings had taken five years and the new Manitoba school system was in place. The Manitoba government defied Ottawa. Premier Greenway called an election, and an overwhelming majority of Manitobans endorsed his refusal to obey the cabinet's order-in-council.

The federal government then brought a remedial bill before the House of Commons to override the Manitoba Schools Act. Viewed through the prism of Canadian politics today, the debate that followed in Parliament has a strange ring. We think of the Liberal party as the champion of French-Canadian interests. But in those days it was the Conservative party, still clinging fast to the alliance Macdonald had forged with the Catholic hierarchy, that was prepared to exercise to the full its constitutional power to dictate to Manitoba. Charles Tupper, the greatest figure in the Conservative party at that time, was brought back from his post as high commissioner in London to lead the battle for the remedial bill in the House of Commons (Bowell was the only Prime Minister to lead the government from the Senate).

The Catholic Church considered that all good Catholics would support the remedial bill. But Laurier, now leader of the Opposition, saw that this bill would create a precedent that could be used, in future, to justify federal interference with provincial legislation in Quebec. So he opposed the bill. To be sure, he also foresaw that he might win the coming election if he appeared to the Orange legions of Ontario to be a lesser evil than Tupper and the Conservatives. The issue was one, however, on which he was guided by conviction. Laurier was thus placed squarely between Church and State, between the instructions of his confessor and his own view of Confederation. Laurier moved, on second reading, that "the Bill be not now read the second time but that it be read the second time this day six months," a parliamentary manoeuvre intended to kill the bill. Laurier was under enormous pressure from the Roman Catholic clergy. Father Albert Lacombe, a famous missionary priest to the west, sent an ultimatum to Laurier: if Laurier did not support the bill, and the Conservatives were beaten, "...the episcopacy, like one man, united with the clergy, will rise to support those who may have fallen in defending us." Yet Laurier insisted that, though a Catholic, he was not bound to support the bill. In a speech that anticipated President John Kennedy's now famous address in 1960 to Protestant clergymen in Houston, Laurier said:

> I am here representing not Roman Catholics alone but Protestants as well, and I must give an account of my stewardship to all classes. Here am I, a Roman Catholic of French extraction, entrusted by the confidence of the men who sit around me with great and important duties under our constitutional system of government. I am here the acknowledged leader of a great party, composed of Roman Catholics and Protestants as well, as Protestants must be in the majority in every party in Canada. Am I to be told, I, occupying such a position, that I am to be dictated the course I am to take in this House, by reasons that can appeal to the consciences of my fellow-Catholic members, but which do not appeal as well to the consciences of my Protestant colleagues? No. So long as I have a seat in this House, so long as I occupy the position I do now, whenever it shall become my duty to take a stand upon any question whatever, that stand I will take not upon grounds of Roman Catholicism, not upon grounds of Protestantism, but upon grounds which can appeal to the conscience of all men, irrespective of their particular faith, upon grounds which can be occupied by all men who love justice, freedom and toleration.

Laurier went forward with his motion to kill the remedial bill. When the vote came on Laurier's motion, there were many defections from Conservative ranks, and it soon became apparent that the government would not be able to get the bill through the House. Parliament was, in any case, near the end of its life. There was a dissolution in 1896. In the election campaign that followed, Tupper, now prime minister, promised to bring the remedial bill before Parliament again after the election. Although Laurier promised to work to redress the grievances of French Canadians in Manitoba, he assured English-speaking Canadians that Manitoba had the right to decide upon its own system of education. He would not, if elected, force the province to restore separate schools, but would instead pursue, he said, "the sunny way" of compromise. The Catholic bishops of Quebec had a pastoral letter read in every diocese in Quebec to declare that Catholics could not vote except for candidates committed to the restoration of separate schools in Manitoba. But Laurier won the election; and he won in Quebec against the opposition of a Catholic hierarchy as powerful as that anywhere in the world, and he won decisively. Quebec had voted to make him the first French-Canadian prime minister.

Upon assuming office, Laurier sent a delegation to see Premier Greenway in Manitoba. The French Canadians did not get their schools back, but Greenway made some concessions. An agreement was reached, which became known as the Laurier-Greenway agreement, by which Manitoba passed an amendment to the Manitoba Schools Act to allow religious instruction in the public schools during the last half-hour of each day. Given sufficient numbers of Catholic pupils (10 children in a rural school, 25 children in a city, town or village school), Catholic parents might petition the school trustees to employ at least one Roman Catholic teacher. The amendment also dealt with the subject of minority language education. It provided that, when 10 or more pupils spoke any language other than English as their first language, they might be taught in that language as well as in English. This provision rejected the notion that French should have an official status as a language of education. The French Canadians were lumped in with all other non-English groups. Not only those who spoke French, but also any other language group could benefit by this provision. French had no greater protection than any other minority language. Within a generation, the broad scope of this concession was to constitute grounds for its nullification.

The Roman Catholic hierarchy in Quebec was far from satisfied with the Laurier-Greenway agreement, and they continued to attack Laurier and his government. Laurier, together with other Catholic members of the House and Senate, petitioned Rome to restrain the Quebec hierarchy from interfering in politics. "If allowed to continue," they said "[it] might be extremely dangerous to the constitutional liberties of this country, as well as to the interest of the Church itself." Pope Leo XIII sent Monsignor Merry del Val to investigate the matter. He persuaded the bishops to mitigate their attacks on Laurier and, after del Val's return to Rome, the Pope issued an encyclical, *Affari vos*, in December, 1897, which informed the angry Quebec clerics that, in seeking justice, "the rules of moderation, of meekness, and of brotherly charity were not to be lost sight of." The Church in Quebec had been rebuked by Rome.

Thus was the Manitoba school question settled, at least for the moment. That left the question of official languages. The Franco-Manitobans had not challenged the 1890 legislation abolishing French as an official language. It was the schools that were fundamental. Having lost the fight over schools, the Franco-Manitobans had no resources with which to undertake another fight, although French-speaking members of the provincial legislature continued to assert what they still considered to be their right to use the French language under the Manitoba Act. Nearly a century was to pass before the Greenway administration's legislation to abolish French as an official language in Manitoba was challenged in the superior courts. In 1979, the Supreme Court of Canada held that the legislation was unconstitutional, that French is still one of the official languages of Manitoba. The restoration of French as an official language, after a lapse of 89 years, is important, but to a great extent this importance is symbolic. What is required now is the restoration of French as a language of instruction where the Franco-Manitobans wish to have it.

The troubled question of separate schools arose again with the creation of the new provinces of Alberta and Saskatchewan in 1905. In the new provinces, English-speaking residents greatly outnumbered French-speaking residents. Laurier argued that there should be guarantees for denominational schools to protect the French-Canadian minorities. But when Clifford Sifton, Laurier's most influential minister from the west, insisted that there should be no guarantees for separate schools in the new provinces and was ready to resign on the issue, Laurier had to give way. He felt that he could not insist upon rights for French Canadians in Alberta and Saskatchewan that he had yielded in Manitoba. The French Canadians in the west therefore found themselves without any of the measures for the protection of their language and their schools that the Anglophones of Quebec had always had.

Laurier's government was defeated in 1911. In 1916, a Liberal government in Manitoba abrogated the Laurier-Greenway agreement of 1896. The Franco-Manitobans had been able to take advantage of the provision of the agreement that allowed them, where 10 pupils in a district spoke French as their mother tongue, to claim the right to have them taught in both English and French. But this exception was made for other languages as well and, as large numbers of immigrants from eastern Europe arrived in the province, they, too, claimed the benefit of this provision. The system became impossible to maintain, and in 1916 Manitoba insisted that English must henceforth be the only language of instruction. Once again, there was a refusal to accept that the claim to the use of French rested on a footing quite different from that of other minority language groups.

Laurier felt that there was little he could do to preserve what had been agreed in 1896. He was no longer in office, but leader of the Opposition. But he did not, in any event, think that the British North America Act offered a constitutional right to bilingual education. Certainly Section 133, the only provision in the British North America Act dealing with language rights, had nothing to do with schools or with education. There was simply no constitutional guarantee for minority language education in French. On July 12, 1916, in a letter to a friend concerning the repudiation by the Manitoba government of the Laurier-Greenway agreement, Laurier wrote,

> ...The [Quebec] Nationalists...maintain that since we have the right to speak French in the federal parliament and before the courts, we have the right to teach French in the schools of every province....
>
> It is an historical fact that without the French population of Quebec the union of the provinces of British North America would have been a legislative union; the French population of Quebec would never have consented to such a form, since that would mean its disappearance as a distinct element. It is Quebec that suggested the federal form, and it must be accepted with all its consequences. For the French population of Quebec the advantages have been immense; outside Quebec, in face of the positive terms of Section 133, the French tongue has nothing to look for aside from whatever sentiments the justice of the cause may arouse and whatever influence may be brought to bear on the majority....
>
> Yet from this comes also the anguish of the present hour. What are the rights of the French language other than those defined in Section 133, and, to come to the question of the moment, what are the rights of the French language in the matter of education?

The answer was that there were none. The French-Canadian minorities have survived, but without constitutional guarantees. Laurier could only plead—in vain—for what he called "the regime of tolerance." Laurier was intellectually consistent; he did not claim any rights for French as a language of education under the Constitution. He could not urge the federal government to disallow Manitoba's repudiation of the Laurier-Greenway agreement.

But by now a new voice was being heard from Quebec. Henri Bourassa had entered the House of Commons as a

Liberal, but had resigned from the Liberal party in 1899 because he opposed Canada's participation in the Boer War. After that he sat as an Independent until he left the House in 1908. Two years later he founded *Le Devoir*. In the years that followed he became a powerful spokesman for Quebec nationalism. In 1911 he had joined with the Conservatives to bring Laurier down. Bourassa was combative and uncompromising when it came to the question of the place of French Canadians in the English-speaking provinces. Only constitutional guarantees, he warned in a speech on March 9, 1912, in Montreal, would suffice.

> If the Canadian constitution is to last, if the Canadian Confederation is to be maintained, the narrow attitude towards minorities which increasingly manifests itself in the English provinces must disappear, and we must return to the original spirit of the alliance.

Bourassa went on to describe his vision of a bilingual, bicultural Canada, an Anglo-French nation from sea to sea:

> ...We deserve better than to be considered like the savages of the old reservations and to be told: "Remain in Quebec, continue to stagnate in ignorance, you are at home there; but elsewhere you must become English."
>
> No, we have the right to be French in language; we have the right to be Catholics in faith; we have the right to be free by the constitution...[and] to enjoy these rights throughout the whole expanse of Confederation.

In our own day, Pierre Trudeau has adopted Bourassa's idea of a bilingual and bicultural Canada. Trudeau is Bourassa's heir, not Laurier's. The Official Languages Act of 1969 enlarged the availability of services in English and French in federal departments and institutions, pursuant to Section 133 of the BNA Act. A further expansion of the scope of these two official languages will take place under the Charter of Rights. It is, however, the Charter guarantees relating to the right to use French and English as minority languages of education that can make truly meaningful Trudeau's implementation of Bourassa's vision. In the Charter, it is education in the French language, not denominational education, that is protected. But what is at stake is the same as in 1890 or 1896: French-Canadian identity. The Charter provides the means of restoring what was lost in the 1890s, the right of Franco-Manitobans to have their children taught in their own language.

Would the French language have found a secure place in western Canada if Laurier had supported the federal government's remedial legislation in 1896? Tupper and the Conservatives had, after all, taken a firm stand on the issue. If Laurier had made the issue bipartisan by offering his support, would the federal position have prevailed? Certainly the remedial bill would have been passed, but no one can say how far the *fait accompli* in Manitoba could have been altered at that stage. Only one thing is certain: if the French Canadians had been able to rely on a constitutional guarantee of their right to separate schools, their position would have been greatly strengthened.

The English-speaking majority in Manitoba wanted to enforce the assimilation of minorities, including the French, and this pressure became more and more irresistible as continued immigration to western Canada from central and eastern Europe reduced the French Canadians to a minority with no political power. It was, ironically, under the Laurier administration that the greatest wave of immigration to the west took place. Many of these immigrants spoke neither English nor French. Given the dominance of the English-speaking population, French-speaking centres assimilated few of these immigrants. In such a milieu a minority without constitutionally entrenched rights was bound to suffer heavy casualties.

In Ontario, when the school crisis came in 1912, it was over the use of French as a language of instruction. The struggle was at first not one between Catholics and Protestants, but between Catholics and Catholics; their dispute was not over religion, it was over language.

Under pre-Confederation statutes, both school systems in Upper Canada, the state schools and the separate schools, were supported by property taxes, and this arrangement was entrenched in the Constitution in 1867. Section 93, whatever else might be said about it, unmistakably protected separate schools that had been established by law before 1867. It was, as French Canadians in New Brunswick and Manitoba had discovered, schools protected only by custom or practice that were not. At any rate, in the case of separate schools established by law, the province of Ontario could not take away the right to public funds.

Local authorities in Ontario determined the language of instruction. Catholic schools in Ontario with French-speaking students were taught in French, though it was understood that French-speaking students should acquire a competence in English. But Ontario's was not a dual system, like that of Quebec. It was a single system, designed with a view to the enforcement of uniform provincial standards. Provincial supervision and control brought the separate schools under close scrutiny, and the province's educational authorities, convinced of the need for every child to be able to speak English, tried to limit the use of the French language in the Catholic schools. By 1890, English was the language of instruction "except so far as this is impracticable by reason of the pupil not understanding English." French-speaking pupils followed the same course of studies as English-speaking pupils, although they were permitted to have additional instruction in French. These regulations were not rigidly enforced, however, and French continued to be the language of instruction in many of the separate schools.

At this time, many French Canadians were emigrating to Ontario from Quebec. In 1890, Franco-Ontarians made up not more than 5% of the province's population. By 1910, they had increased to 10%. They were most numerous in eastern Ontario, especially along the Ottawa River. The Catholic Church provided schools for the French Canadians who were pouring into eastern Ontario from Quebec. These schools were supposed to be bilingual schools, that is, pupils were to receive instruction in English and in French. But there were complaints by Irish Catholics, many of whom also lived along the Ottawa River, that French was being taught to the exclusion of English.

There had been French Canadians who immigrated to Ontario even before the 1890s. They had been the first settlers in Kent and Essex counties in southern Ontario. But in southern Ontario, English was the dominant language, and, as in eastern Ontario, the Catholics were not exclusively French. Indeed, in southern Ontario the Irish Catholics opposed the use of French in the separate schools, on the ground that teaching in these schools was not truly bilingual. In August, 1910, Michael Fallon, newly appointed Bishop of London, repudiated the notion of "La Langue, guardienne de la foi." He and the other bishops of southern Ontario favoured assimilation to English. Bishop Fallon epitomized the split between the French Catholics and the Irish Catholics. He denounced "an alleged bilingual school system which teaches neither English nor French, encourages incompetency, gives a prize to hypocrisy, and breeds ignorance," and he said that he wanted "to wipe out every vestige of bilingual teaching, in the...schools of this Diocese."

The level of achievement in the separate schools was certainly below the provincial average. The Franco-Ontarians were largely rural, and they had lower incomes than the majority of Ontarians. Nor were teachers in the separate schools always properly qualified. F.W. Merchant, chief inspector of public and separate schools of Ontario, reported in 1912 that English was inadequately taught in the Catholic schools because the teachers in them were not qualified to teach English. They were not, he said, bilingual schools in the full sense. He recommended improved training for the teachers in separate schools.

The Ontario government decided to take firm measures because it believed that French-speaking Catholics were trying to eradicate English as a language of instruction in areas where the French were a majority. In 1912, the Ontario department of education passed Regulation 17, which placed French in a distinctly subordinate position in the separate schools. After the third year, English was to be the sole language of instruction, and the study of French as a school subject was to be limited to one hour a day.

In Manitoba, the French Canadians had lost their schools. In Ontario the French Canadians had retained their schools, but they had lost their right to give instruction in French in them.

The French Canadians protested, but both the Conservative and the Liberal parties in Ontario supported Regulation 17. They were eager to assimilate the Franco-Ontarians by denying them the means to educate their children in their mother tongue. The Franco-Ontarians fought back. School trustees, teachers and students refused to comply with Regulation 17. There were marches, demonstrations and school strikes. The Ontario department of education withheld grants to the separate schools in Ottawa, where resistance was fiercest. When the trustees of the separate schools in Ottawa refused to open the schools, the legislature authorized the provincial government to establish a commission to take over the Ottawa Separate School Board, to run the schools, and to enforce Regulation 17. Inevitably, litigation ensued.

The French Canadians claimed that Regulation 17 violated rights guaranteed by Section 93 of the British North America Act. But Section 93, of course, says nothing about language rights. Once again, the litigation reached the Privy Council, which ruled against the French Canadians, holding that Regulation 17 was not unconstitutional and that restrictions on the use of French were a valid exercise of provincial power because Section 93 protects religious minorities, not language rights. Regulation 17 did not take away separate schools or limit the provision of public funds for separate schools, it simply determined what language should be used in them. It was not, therefore, in violation of Section 93. This time the Privy Council's reasoning was sound.

Court proceedings had revealed once again the limited scope of Section 93. In the 1870s, in proceedings in New Brunswick, Section 93 was held not to guarantee public funds to separate schools that had not been established by statute. In the Manitoba proceedings, it was held that its counterpart, Section 22 of the Manitoba Act, did not guarantee public funding to separate schools that had received such funds merely as a matter of practice, even when there was an explicit provision that they should. Now, in the Ontario proceedings, Section 93 was held not to offer any constitutional protection to French as a language of instruction in separate schools. Not only the French Canadians in Ontario were resentful: French Canadians in Quebec and in the west also believed that Regulation 17 was unjust. Among them was Laurier. He wrote to Newton W. Rowell, leader of the Liberal Opposition in Ontario:

> ...it is the duty of the State, you say, [to see] that every child in the Province receives a good English education. To this, I agree completely. You add that where the parents desire that their children should also study the French language, there should be no objection. To this, I also completely agree. But this is exactly what is denied by Regulation 17.

In the midst of this controversy, Canada entered the First World War at Britain's side. The question of French-Canadian participation in the war was inevitably mixed up with the question of Franco-Ontarian rights. Henri Bourassa now emerged as the champion of the Franco-Ontarians. He thundered in *Le Devoir*:

> In the name of religion, liberty, and faithfulness to the British flag, the French Canadians are enjoined to go fight the Prussians of Europe. Shall we let the Prussians of Ontario impose their domination like masters, in the very heart of the Canadian Confederation, under the shelter of the British flag and British institutions?

Canada made a remarkable contribution to the Allied cause in the First World War. For English-speaking Canadians, the war seemed to represent the nation's coming of age. But Quebec felt no similar sense of exhilaration about the war. Bourassa created an uproar among Ontarians, whose indignation at Quebec's failure to support the war affected their view of the Franco-Ontarians' right to use their own language in separate schools. What right had the French to such a claim when they were unwilling to defend the nation from which they claimed the right? On December 16, 1915, when Bourassa was speaking in Ottawa at a tumultuous meeting, a sergeant climbed onto the platform to hand him a Union Jack, and ordered Bourassa to wave it. Although the front rows were filled with soldiers, Bourassa refused. "I am ready to wave the British flag in liberty," he said, "but will not do so under threat."

Laurier had to act. He had always opposed federal intervention in provincial affairs because the precedent might later be turned against Quebec. Still, he had to do something or Bourassa and the Quebec nationalists would appear to be the only champions of the French Canadians. If French Canadians were to be represented exclusively by a French-Canadian nationalist party, they would be perpetually left in a minority position.

In the 1890s, Laurier had declared the Manitoba school question a provincial matter in which Parliament could not interfere. In spite of that position and against the wishes of the Liberals from Ontario and the west, he now brought the Ontario school question before the House of Commons. He told Prime Minister Robert Borden that he must do so because he needed "some sheet anchor with which to fight the Nationalists." He must act, whether or not Parliament had the power to act. In 1896, he had refused to come to the aid of French Canadians in Manitoba. Now, 20 years later, he insisted on coming to the aid of French Canadians in Ontario. True, he was not, he said, trying to coerce Ontario, as Ottawa had sought to coerce Manitoba in 1896. The question did, he said, fall within provincial jurisdiction—just as it had in 1896. But the fact remains that, in 1896 he had declined a role as champion of the rights of French Canadians outside Quebec; in 1916 he embraced it.

The dispute still centred on separate schools, but everything else about it was different. This time the French Canadians were fighting to preserve, not their religion, but their language. Once again, Laurier met opposition from Quebec. This time it was not the Church, it was Bourassa. In 1896, Laurier had been the unchallenged leader of Quebec. Now, 20 years later, Bourassa contested his right to speak for the people of Quebec. In 1896, Laurier had been a mediator, with every reason to believe that his appeal for a "sunny way" of compromise would yield better terms for the French Canadians in Manitoba. In 1916, he was a mendicant, pleading on behalf of his people for consideration, yet knowing that his pleas would secure little or nothing for the Franco-Ontarians. There were no Conservatives urging the policies of Macdonald, no Tupper insisting upon fairness to the French Canadians. Perhaps Laurier had other motives, too. Perhaps he calculated that, if he held Quebec, he might once more be prime minister. He could not allow Bourassa to cut into his strength in Quebec, as he had in 1911, and deny him office again. Perhaps Laurier was looking towards his own place in history, and felt that in the end he must take his stand with the French Canadians.

The differences between Laurier and Bourassa went deeper than personalities and the rivalry for leadership of French Canada. They differed on what had been agreed in 1867. Bourassa believed that Confederation had promised that the whole of Canada would be bilingual and bicultural. Laurier did not believe Confederation had offered that assurance. He believed that French Canadians outside Quebec, to protect their language, must depend, not on constitutional guarantees—for there were none—but on the sympathetic tolerance of the English-speaking majority. Laurier now had to appeal to the majority in Ontario to display that tolerance.

On May 9, 1916, the Liberals in the House of Commons moved a resolution:

> That this House, while fully recognizing the principle of provincial rights and the necessity of every child being given a thorough knowledge of English education, respectfully suggests to the Legislative Assembly of the province

of Ontario the wisdom of making it clear that the privilege of the children of French parentage of being taught in their mother tongue be not interfered with.

Laurier spoke in support of the resolution. He agreed that every child in Ontario should be able to speak English, but he pleaded for the right of children of French-Canadian parentage to a second education in a second language. Laurier, now in his seventies, was still able to summon eloquence and passion.

I want to appeal to the sense of justice and fair play of the people of Ontario, and to their appreciation of British institutions—no more. Even if I am wrong—and I hope I am not—I am sure that a frank understanding between the majority and the minority in Ontario, between the two great elements which compose the Canadian people, may force a solution of this troublesome question. Every man in the province of Ontario, every man in this room who comes from the province of Ontario, whether he sits on that side or on this side, is determined that every child in the province of Ontario shall receive the benefit of an English education. To that, sir, I give my fullest assent. I want every child in the province of Ontario to receive the benefit of an English education. Wherever he may go on this continent I want him to be able to speak the language of the great majority of the people of this continent.

Now I come to the point where I want to speak to my fellow countrymen in the province of Ontario. When I ask that every child of my own race should receive an English education, will you refuse us the privilege of education also in the language of our mothers and fathers? That is all that I ask today; I ask nothing more than that. I simply ask you, my fellow-countrymen, British subjects like myself, if, when we say that we must have an English education, you will say: "You shall have an English education and nothing else." There are men who say that in the schools of Ontario and Manitoba there should be no other language than the English language. But, sir, when I ask that we should have also the benefit of a French education, will you refuse that benefit? Is that an unnatural demand? Is that an obnoxious demand? Will the concession of it do harm to anybody?

And will it be said that in the great province of Ontario there is a disposition to put a bar on knowledge and to stretch every child in the schools of Ontario upon a Procrustean bed and say that they shall all be measured alike, that no one shall have the privilege of a second education in a single language. I do not believe it; and, if we discuss this question with frankness, as between man and man, in my humble opinion, it can yet be settled by an appeal to the people of Ontario. I do not believe that any man will refuse us the benefit of a French education.

The resolution was rejected by the House. Borden's government took the position, as Laurier's had in 1896, that the matter came under provincial jurisdiction, and they opposed the resolution. Laurier, by the exercise of his personal authority, carried the Liberal party with him. Liberal MPs from Ontario remained loyal to their chief, though 11 Liberals from the West would not support him. (During the First World War conscription crisis a year later, Laurier again found himself obliged to give paramount importance to the interests of Quebec; but his personal authority could not then carry his party with him.)

There is nothing more poignant in the turbulent controversies over separate schools than this great man's recognition of the inexorable logic of the form of federal government on which Quebec had insisted in 1867. What finally did Laurier achieve? Was his career only "a great illusion"? He had been unable to restore Manitoba's separate schools. He had had to agree that there should be no guarantees for separate schools in Saskatchewan and Alberta in 1905. He had offered the Franco-Ontarians only a futile gesture of support. In 1916, he saw the Manitoba government repudiate the Laurier-Greenway agreement. His career, in office and out of it, had spanned more than a generation, and it had seen a progressive loss of French-Canadian rights in Ontario and western Canada.

But there is more to be said. Laurier's accession to power was in itself an affirmation of the duality of Canada. He was the first French Canadian to become prime minister,

and Macdonald and he stand as the two foremost pro-
ponents of Canadian unity. Laurier brought his fine in-
tellect, his formidable eloquence, and his compassion to
bear on the central problem of Canada's existence. His life
and thought can stand for us today as a paradigm of tolerance in a plural society.

Indeed, Ontarians did not altogether reject the regime
of tolerance. Once the First World War ended, many
English-speaking Ontarians began to feel that they had
treated Franco-Ontarians badly. And, of course, Franco-
Ontarians themselves continued their protest against Regulation 17. They decided that, if public funds were only
going to be made available to separate schools where French
was placed in a distinctly subordinate position to English,
they would establish and maintain, without public funds,
separate schools in which French was the language of instruction; and they did.

In 1927, F. W. Merchant was asked to report again on
the separate schools of Ontario. Merchant had not suggested the drastic measures that the Ontario government
had taken in 1912. He had approved even then the use of
French as a language of instruction in the separate schools;
he had simply urged that the training of teachers for separate schools be improved. His recommendations in 1927
followed the same lines and, as a result, new courses for
the teaching of French as a subject and French textbooks
for other subjects in the early grades were prepared. The
University of Ottawa opened a Normal School to train
teachers for the separate schools. Legally, English still became the language of instruction after the third grade but,
in practice, French was often used in all of the elementary
grades.

But that was not the end of the school question in Ontario. It has emerged again in our own time. Throughout
the 1970s the establishment of French-language secondary
schools divided Ontarians at the local level, and conster-
nated politicians at the provincial level. For while it is an
issue that goes back many years, it is in every sense a
contemporary issue, particularly in Essex and Kent coun-

ties, where the Franco-Ontarians have lived for a century and a half, in northern Ontario, and in the Ottawa valley.

Many Ontarians continue to refuse to accept that Franco-Ontarians are entitled to public funds for secondary schools where children are taught in French. The desire for uniformity can be seen in other provinces besides Ontario. Indeed, in every province there are those who prefer to see all children educated exclusively in English. They wish even today to turn the clock back to 1839, when Lord Durham said that Canada should be British, that Canadians should speak English and no other language. But there can be no retreat into the past. Canadians must learn to live with diversity, they must accept the fact of pluralism. French Canadians will not give up their right to educate their children in their mother tongue. Their deeply felt desire in this regard is not simply a sentimental attachment to the language of their ancestors. For linguistic minorities, it is by their mother tongue that children understand their own parents, learn about their own people, and know their own past. It is by the mother tongue that a collective imagination and conscience is preserved and by it that a people comes into its own cultural inheritance. The only alternative for French Canadians would be assimilation.

In the constitutional sense Confederation was not a compact between the provinces, nor an agreement between English-speaking and French-speaking peoples. It was rather the creation of an Imperial statute. Nevertheless, a new perception has made its way into our consciousness, an acceptance that, whatever the constitutional lawyers may say, we have two linguistic communities and that their language rights must be entrenched from sea to sea. This is the unfinished business of Confederation.

The French-Canadian minorities in the provinces outside Quebec should not have to depend on the goodwill of their provincial governments. No premier ever lost an election by campaigning against a linguistic minority. Neither should they be obliged to call upon the federal government to intervene on their behalf, for the precedent might endanger their Francophone cousins in Quebec. The Francophones of Quebec have often been ready, as Laurier and Bourassa were, to campaign outside Quebec on behalf of other French Canadians, but equally as often they have been preoccupied at home with their own concerns. The same has been true of English-speaking Canadians. We have seen, in the 1970s, how easy it has been for them, after the first flush of indignation, to overlook the limitation of Anglophone rights in Quebec. Canadians should have a right to educate their children in English or in French in any province or territory. These rights should be entrenched, not only in Quebec, Ontario, Manitoba and New Brunswick, but in all the provinces and territories. It is not simply a question of providing these guarantees in each of the provinces where there is a large linguistic minority; guarantees are most important in provinces where the numbers of French Canadians are least.

Will the Charter of Rights and Freedoms establish Laurier's "regime of tolerance"? The BNA Act and the Manitoba Act make English and French the official languages of Quebec and Manitoba. The Charter provides that English and French are to be the official languages of New Brunswick. It is greatly to be regretted that there is no provision for two official languages in Ontario. Given the necessity of obtaining the agreement of the government of Ontario to the Charter of Rights, such a provision could not be included in the Charter.

Official languages, however, are not vital, but schools are. The Charter entrenches the right of the French-speaking minorities to the use of French as a language of education in primary and secondary schools. The Charter offers similar guarantees for the English-speaking minority in Quebec. The *Indépendantistes* who wish to create a fortress Quebec have opposed the entrenchment of English-speaking minority rights in that province, and their principal allies have been Anglophones from the western provinces who wish to see French expunged from politics, courts and schools outside Quebec.

The Charter addresses the vital questions of our constitutional history. But how well? Under the Charter, the right of Canadians to have their children receive primary and secondary school instruction in the French language applies only where in a province the number of children "is sufficient to warrant the provision to them out of public funds of minority language instruction." Whether or not such instruction is received in minority language schools (as opposed to classrooms in majority language schools) depends on the meaning of "minority language educational facilities." No one can be sure how this language will be interpreted by the courts. Certainly these guarantees go far beyond those provided in Section 93 of the British North America Act. To a great extent, however, the effectiveness of the guarantees for French-Canadian minorities will still depend on provincial willingness to expend public funds. True, the French Canadians are entitled under the Charter to go to court to enforce their rights, but the enjoyment of those rights may still be impeded, if not frustrated, by recalcitrant premiers and provincial legislatures.

Some will argue that separate schools will be divisive. But it has been the denial of the right to separate schools which, again and again, has caused division in Canada. Diversity in a province will not cause national division, but the refusal to acknowledge diversity in a province may. If the safeguards in the Charter are not to be emasculated by political intransigence at the provincial level, Canadians must be aware of the history of Section 93. The Charter must not be allowed to fail as Section 93 did.

Under the Charter, as before under Section 93, for Francophone minorities the object is the same—to maintain their separate identity,

> ...to reverse the process of assimilation which is thinning out our ranks and which, in the foreseeable future, will annihilate the communities which have marked and permeated the history of this country.

The difficulties that face these French-Canadian minorities should not be underestimated. The mass culture of North

...merica is English-speaking. It sometimes impinges irre-
sistibly on isolated French-Canadian communities. The
necessity for speaking English at work and on the street
is ever present. English predominates in television, radio
and films. The church and the family have not by themselves been able to check the advance of English. What
chance, then, do these minority communities have, if the
children do not speak French in school?

The French Canadians' wish to have their own schools
should be respected. It is the essential means to the preservation of the French language. This is important not only
to French Canadians. The preservation of French-language
rights in the English-speaking provinces is in the long run
likely to preserve English-language rights in Quebec.
Moreover, though the French and English languages are
constitutionally protected, and thus stand on a different
footing from the languages of other ethnic groups in Canada, they are in a sense a bulwark for those languages.
Constitutional protection of French and English makes the
way easier for other languages, because it negates the idea
of a monolithic culture. Thus official bilingualism and biculturalism is not a rejection, but an affirmation of multiculturalism, of the idea of Canada as a mosaic, a country
where diversity is cherished. This was Laurier's vision of
Canada. Rejecting the American ideal of the melting pot,
he thought of Canada as a Gothic cathedral.

> ...a harmonious whole, in which granite, marble, oak and
> other materials are blended. This cathedral is the image of
> the nation that I hope to see Canada become. As long as
> I live, as long as I have the power to labour in the service
> of my country, I shall repel the idea of changing the nature
> of its different elements. I want the marble to remain the
> marble; I want the granite to remain the granite; I want the
> oak to remain the oak.

FOUR

The Banished Canadians: Mackenzie King and the Japanese Canadians

DURING THE HEARINGS of the Special Joint Committee on the Constitution, which sat during the winter of 1980-81 to consider amendments to the Charter of Rights, it was generally conceded that the evacuation and internment of the Japanese Canadians during the Second World War represented an evil instance of mass racial hysteria, made worse by the pusillanimity of the federal government. All agreed that it was an event which must never be repeated. It should be remembered, however, that the expulsion of the Japanese Canadians from Canada's west coast in 1942 was not a sudden manifestation of anti-Japanese feeling which occurred as a result of the Japanese attack on Pearl Harbor on December 7, 1941, and was gone as soon as the war with Japan ended. The crisis of 1942 had its origins in racial prejudice against Orientals in British Columbia which began in the nineteenth century, with the founding of British Columbia itself, and persisted into the middle of the twentieth century: indeed, which reached its shameful climax after the Second World War was over.

The story of the Japanese Canadians is not simply the story of a painful episode which may now safely be forgotten. As Gordon Kadota, speaking for the National Association of Japanese Canadians, told the Special Joint Committee on November 26, 1980, "Our history in Canada is a legacy of racism made legitimate by our political institutions." Although our institutions and our laws no longer foster racial prejudice, it still exists in Canada, disfiguring the face of society. A knowledge and understanding of the Japanese Canadians' experience may enable us to isolate the virus of racial prejudice—endemic in history—when it threatens to escape again.

British Columbia had, before the Second World War, a long history of animosity towards and of discriminatory legislation against Orientals. This anti-Oriental feeling lapped near the homes of Japanese Canadians on the west coast many times before the Japanese assault on Pearl Harbor generated a wave of anti-Japanese hysteria which swept them and their homes away, destroyed their communities, and dispersed them as a people.

In 1941, there were some 22,000 Japanese Canadians in British Columbia. They had many enemies and, with the outbreak of war with Japan, there were few to defend them. Thousands of them had chosen to become Canadian citizens, and thousands more had been born in the province. But, when they found themselves under attack and, vulnerable and helpless, looked for protection to those who held the highest political offices, they found none. When they sought redress in the courts, they found none. They were removed from the west coast, interned, their property confiscated, and many of them sent into exile. All because of their race—because they were of Japanese descent. Nothing in our history demonstrates so well the necessity constantly to be aware of our own attitudes towards racial minorities, and the wisdom of entrenching in the Constitution our belief that racist measures are wrong and of providing legal safeguards that will protect racial minorities against such measures.

The Japanese were preceded in British Columbia by the Chinese. It may be said that anti-Oriental feeling in British Columbia began in 1858, the year the Crown Colony of British Columbia was established. That was the year of the Cariboo gold rush, when prospectors, a few of them Chinese, came from California seeking gold. More Chinese came to the colony in the 1860s and 1870s, but virtually all of them came from China, and not as prospectors, but as cheap labour.

No Japanese came to British Columbia until 1877. Japan had kept herself isolated from the rest of the world until

1852, when Admiral Perry of the United States Navy forced his way into Tokyo Bay. In 1867, the Japanese began to look outwards, and undertook a program of rapid industrialization. Population grew and men unable to find employment in the new industrial centres started to go abroad. Thus began the migration of Japanese across the Pacific Ocean to Hawaii, California, and British Columbia.

When the Japanese began to arrive on Canada's west coast in the 1880s, they were hired as cheap labour, as the Chinese had been before them. They found work in railway construction, mining, logging camps and sawmills. Most of the Japanese who came to Canada then were young men. They did not intend to stay; they wanted only to make some money, then return to their villages in Japan. But many of them did not return, and by 1900 concentrations of Japanese population had emerged in a number of British Columbia communities along the coast, as far north as the Skeena River. The most important of these were "Little Tokyo" in Vancouver, whose residents had a Japanese-language newspaper; and Steveston, a fishing port at the mouth of the Fraser River. By 1901, out of a provincial population of 178,657 there were 4,738 Japanese. The Chinese by this time numbered 14,885. Thus, Orientals constituted ten per cent of the province's population.

The presence of Orientals in such numbers caused apprehension, resentment and fear among the White majority of British Columbia. While the railway builders and other industrial magnates insisted upon the advantages of cheap Oriental labour, the White working class feared this influx of workers of a different race and colour who were prepared to accept lower wages than they were. The competition for jobs was felt mainly by the working class, but all classes in British Columbia felt that the burgeoning Oriental population represented a long-term threat to the White character of the province. They regarded the Orientals, few of whom spoke English, as unassimilable. Thus, they endangered the ideal of White homogeneity in British Columbia.

From the late 1870s onwards, there were many attempts

to curb Oriental immigration into British Columbia. Under the BNA Act, however, the provinces have no jurisdiction over immigration: only the federal government could stem this flow. In 1880, at British Columbia's insistence, the federal government imposed a head tax of $50 on Chinese immigrants. Not satisfied with this, the British Columbia legislature passed a series of anti-Chinese statutes in the early 1880s, but the federal government disallowed them. John A. Macdonald, the prime minister, favoured the immigration of Chinese to work on the railway he wanted to build to the Pacific. Macdonald did say, however, as he told the House of Commons in 1882, that he had no desire to see the Chinese remain in Canada when the railway was finished. After that, he said, he would "be quite ready to join to a reasonable extent in preventing a permanent settlement in the country of Mongolian or Chinese emigrants." In the meantime, he had no objection to excluding the Chinese from enjoying elementary rights of citizenship. In 1885, when his government passed the first federal franchise act, it denied Orientals the right to vote. "Person" was defined in the act so that it excluded Chinese and Mongolians.

At the turn of the century the British Columbia legislature attempted to pass what were in effect provincial immigration laws. In 1900 the province tried to impose English-language qualifications as a condition of admittance for persons entering the province. The federal government disallowed the legislation, just as it did when the province passed similar legislation in 1903 and, yet again, in 1905.

Laurier and the Liberals had succeeded the Conservatives in 1896. Laurier, like Macdonald, would not let the province pass its own immigration laws. Laurier was prepared to acknowledge, however, that once Orientals had become naturalized, they should have the right to vote: in 1898, his government granted to naturalized Orientals the right to vote in federal elections. But though legally they now had the right to vote in federal elections, they couldn't exercise their right because the provincial list of voters was used to prepare the federal list. And in 1895, the British Columbia legislature had passed an amendment to the Provincial Elections Act to deny the vote to Orientals, including those who had become naturalized, and including those born in Canada.

In 1900, Tomey Homma, a naturalized Japanese Canadian, applied to enroll his name on the provincial voters' list. When the registrar of voters rejected his application, he asked the Supreme Court of British Columbia to order the registrar to allow him to vote. This court, in a remarkable judgement for the time, upheld Tomey Homma's right to vote. Chief Justice Angus McColl wrote:

> ...the residence within the province of large numbers of persons, [citizens] in name, but doomed to perpetual exclusion from any part in the passage of legislation affecting their property and civil rights would surely not be to the advantage of Canada, and might even become a source of national danger

The court affirmed the right of the Japanese Canadians and the Chinese Canadians to vote in provincial elections, holding that the legislation in question went beyond the powers of the province. In 1902, the case went to the Privy Council, which continued its virtually unbroken record of denying minority rights in Canada. It reversed the decision of the Supreme Court of British Columbia, holding that the legislation was within provincial powers. The editor of the *Victoria Colonist* rejoiced.

> We are relieved from the possibility of having polling booths swamped by a horde of Orientals who are totally unfitted either by custom or education to exercise the ballot, and whose voting would completely demoralize politics....They have not the remotest idea of what a democratic and representative government is, and are quite incapable of taking part in it.

The Japanese Canadians could still theoretically claim the right to vote in federal elections. But even that shadowy claim passed away in 1920, when Parliament passed an act providing that persons disenfranchised by any province

because of their racial origin would be disqualified for federal elections unless they were war veterans.

But it was not only the right to vote that was denied to
Orientals, citizens or not. Though every citizen was eligible
for employment in the public service of British Columbia,
Canadians of Oriental descent were excluded *de facto*. Professor H. F. Angus, of the University of British Columbia,
writing in 1931, said that while such employment would
not be illegal, it "would occasion general amazement."
They were, in the same way, excluded from municipal
employment. Provincial legislation prohibited the employment of Orientals in the construction of public works. If
a contractor violated this provision, he was liable to forfeit
any money that was due under his contract with the government. It was a condition of sales of Crown timber that
Orientals could not be employed. Nor could they enter
certain professions. For example, no person who had not
been on the voters' list at the age of 21 could be enrolled
as an articled clerk with the Law Society of British Columbia. And when the law did not overtly bar Orientals from
professional employment and other callings, discriminatory practices were effective enough to do so. Thus a network of law, regulation, and custom kept Orientals out of
a whole range of occupations. As Angus wrote in 1941,
"You will look in vain in British Columbia for Japanese
lawyers, pharmacists, accountants, teachers, policemen or
civil servants."

These measures were sanctioned by public opinion. By
the turn of the century anti-Orientalism had become entrenched in the political culture of British Columbia. This
antipathy was especially keen in the case of the Japanese.
When, during the late nineteenth century, Japan began to
emerge as an industrial power, the rest of the world began
to look upon the Japanese as very different from the Chinese.
In the Sino-Japanese War, 1894-95, Japan easily defeated
China and established herself as a military power. Then
came the Russo-Japanese War. It was all very well for Japan
to modernize its economy and to crush the Chinese, but

Japan's triumph in 1905 over Russia was greeted with unease, even alarm, by the Western nations. It was the first victory in modern times of an Asiatic nation over a European nation. These events affected the way in which the Japanese in Canada were perceived. They came to be regarded as more enterprising, competitive, and ambitious than the Chinese and, like Japan herself, as a greater threat to British Columbia than China or the Chinese.

Japan was able, through treaties with Great Britain which were binding at that time on Canada, to assure entry into Canada for Japanese immigrants. China, truly a helpless giant, could not assure such access for Chinese immigrants; in fact, the head tax on Chinese immigrants had risen to $500 by 1900. This head tax was to last until 1923. But while Japan could ensure Japanese access to Canada, her reach was limited. Japan could do nothing for the Japanese once they arrived in British Columbia, and mounting hostility toward the Japanese there exploded in 1907. In that year, the legislature had passed yet another statute to limit Japanese entry into British Columbia. The lieutenant-governor, James Dunsmuir, refused to assent to the act. A summer of protest against Oriental immigration culminated in a gathering of 5,000 persons before City Hall in Vancouver. The crowd became a mob, and it stormed through Chinatown, breaking windows and destroying storefronts. The Chinese Canadians did little to resist. But, when the mob reached "Little Tokyo," the Japanese Canadians defended their homes and their property and pelted their attackers from the rooftops with bottles and clubs, until the mob turned back.

Mackenzie King, then deputy minister of labour, was sent to British Columbia to investigate Japanese Canadians' claims for damages and the question of Japanese immigration. King was then only 29 years old. He had come to Ottawa to edit *The Labour Gazette*, the department of labour's monthly publication. Soon he became the department's deputy minister and, before long, he had persuaded Laurier to find him a seat in the House of Commons and a place in cabinet. This visit to British Columbia was the first occasion on which the path of this strange man crossed that of the Japanese Canadians.

King urged that restrictions be placed on Japanese immigration, and Ottawa took the matter up with the Japanese government. Japan agreed to limit emigration by those leaving Japan to enter the Canadian labour force, but there were to be no restrictions on emigration of wives and families. The nature of Japanese immigration to Canada changed at once: young women replaced young men. Japanese workers already in Canada, through an exchange of photographs, arranged for brides to be sent to them from Japan. During the next 20 years, the so-called "picture brides" made up the majority of Japanese immigrants to Canada. Families were formed, new communities were established, and the Japanese-Canadian population rapidly increased; by 1920 there were more than 4,000 children born in Canada of Japanese descent, and the Japanese population in British Columbia had risen to 15,000. By the late 1930s the population of Japanese Canadians exceeded that of the Chinese Canadians in British Columbia. Many of the men still worked in logging camps and sawmills. But now in Vancouver Japanese-Canadian families ran rooming houses, grocery stores, dry-cleaning and dress-making shops. A growing number of Japanese-Canadian fishermen lived in Steveston, at the mouth of the Fraser River. Forbidden by law to acquire Crown lands directly, the Japanese Canadians could buy property privately. In this way they acquired farms in the Fraser valley and in the Okanagan valley.

Attempts to restrict the expansion of the Japanese Canadians over the economic fabric of British Columbia were concentrated on the fishing industry, for it was in the fishing industry that the Japanese Canadians were to be found in greatest numbers. As early as 1893, Japanese Canadians held 20 per cent of the salmon gill-net licences issued in the province. By 1901, they had nearly doubled this percentage. By 1919, Japanese Canadians held half of the salmon gill-net licences issued in the province. That year, at the insistence of White fishermen, the federal department of marine and fisheries promised to "gradually eliminate Orientals from the fishery" and, by 1925, half of the licences held by Japanese Canadians had been cancelled. A variety of other measures were taken, some of them bizarre forms of discrimination. For instance, between 1921 and 1930 Japanese-Canadian fishermen were barred from using gas-powered boats on the Skeena River. The Japanese-Canadian fishermen had to row their boats along the Skeena to the fishing grounds, while White and Indian fishermen sped by under power. These measures achieved their purpose. By 1941, Japanese Canadians held only 12 per cent of the fishing licences in British Columbia. The confiscation of Japanese-Canadian property did not begin after Pearl Harbor: it had been going on for some 20 years.

All of these measures, whether taken by the provincial government or by the federal government, were explicitly racial. There was no constitutional limitation on the power of either government to enact discriminatory legislation against particular racial groups. To be sure, there was a division of legislative power between the federal and provincial governments, but if a particular measure was within the legislative competence of the government which passed it, nothing could be done to challenge it. The Charter of Rights provides that every individual is equal before the law and under the law and has the right to the equal protection and equal benefit of the law without discrimination based on race. This is a guarantee of racial equality, which should, at the very least take from Parliament and the provinces the power to pass legislation which discriminates against any group on account of race, and prevent the federal government and the provinces from erecting in future a network of laws and regulations designed to restrict the opportunities available to any racial group in Canada.

In British Columbia in the 1920s, there was such a network. But these restrictions, designed to deal with the Japanese population the province already had, were not enough to satisfy the militants. They believed no more Japanese should be allowed to come to Canada. In 1922, Premier John Oliver of British Columbia urged Mackenzie King, now prime minister of Canada, to ban further Oriental immigration. The province's attorney-general, A. M. Manson, said, "The Oriental is not possible as a permanent citizen in British Columbia because ethnologically they cannot assimilate with our Anglo-Saxon race." It was true that British Columbians claimed that the Japanese would not or could not assimilate, but at a deeper level there was a fear that, if they were assimilated, the White character of the province would be drowned in a sea of brown-skinned fecundity.

In 1923, Mackenzie King brought in legislation to restrict Chinese immigration; as a result, few Chinese entered Canada until after the end of the Second World War. British Columbia politicians continued to press for legislation against Japanese immigration and for yet stronger measures, including repatriation to Japan. In 1927, Premier Oliver told King that:

> The stopping of Oriental immigration entirely is urgently necessary, but that in itself will not suffice, since it leaves us with our present large Oriental population and their prolific birth rate. Our Government feels that the Dominion Government should go further, and by deportation or other legitimate means, seek to bring about the reduction and final elimination of this menace to the well being of the white population of this province.

King undertook to negotiate a new arrangement with Japan. In May, 1928, Japan agreed to limit the number of emigrants to Canada to 150 persons a year. The Japanese-Canadian population would now depend on natural growth for its increase. King was not prepared to act on Oliver's call for deportation—that would have to wait until 1946.

Of course, the politicians were reflecting popular prejudice. There were few who argued that this prejudice had no rational foundation. Few spoke in defence of the Japanese Canadians. There may be a liberal establishment that speaks for the rights of minorities today, but it did not exist in the days before the Second World War. Newspaper editors inveighed against the Chinese and the Japanese. Nor did the churches preach tolerance. Far from it. The Anglican Bishop of New Westminster told his synod, "We should have a province that will be white; that will be British and that will be Christian." No political party was prepared to urge the enfranchisement of the Japanese Canadians and Chinese Canadians until the advent of the Co-operative Commonwealth Federation (CCF) in 1933. Indeed, during this long period, no more damaging allegation could be made against a political opponent in British Columbia than to suggest that he favoured giving Orientals the vote.

The Regina Manifesto, the party platform adopted by the CCF in 1933, announced that the new party would seek "equal treatment before the law of all residents of Canada, irrespective of race, nationality or religious or political beliefs," J. S. Woodsworth, leader of the CCF, carried this policy to the House of Commons, and the Liberals used it against the CCF in British Columbia in the federal election of 1935. The Liberals opposed giving Orientals the vote, and they ran newspaper advertisements to say, "A vote for any CCF candidate is a vote to give the Chinamen and the Japanese the same voting right as you have." In 1938, the Conservative party in national convention passed a resolution in favour of the complete exclusion of all Orientals from Canada.

Entreaties to reason did no good. In May, 1936, a delegation led by S. I. Hayakawa, a Vancouver-born Nisei who had become a university professor in the United States (and was elected to the United States Senate from California in 1976), appeared before a parliamentary committee in Ottawa with a brief in support of the Japanese Canadians' right to vote. Two British Columbia Members of Parliament, Thomas Reid and A. W. Neill, urged that the franchise should not be extended to them. They advanced the same old reasons: the Japanese were a race that lived apart and would not be assimilated. Nor could assimilation be any kind of answer, for it would lead to the full horrors of miscegenation.

Nevertheless, the social landscape of British Columbia had begun to change. During the 1920s, the growth of the Japanese-Canadian population had slowed, and during the 1930s, with immigration from the old country reduced to a trickle, the population stabilized. The Japanese Canadians were themselves changing, too. Few of the immigrant generation of Japanese, the Issei, spoke English. But the Canadian-born generation, the Nisei, spoke English as well as Japanese. They attended public schools, although many students also attended Japanese-language schools after public school. Many families were converted from Buddhism to Christianity. Between the rising generation and the older generation, there was often distance and tension. In his book *The Enemy That Never Was*, Ken Adachi has written:

> The life of the school and of the street widened the separation between generations. If it did nothing else, the school introduced a rival source of authority, the image of the teacher competing with that of the father. In the process, the child came to believe in a universe divided into two realms, one for school and one for home, each with rules and modes of behaviour of its own. As the children grew up, they felt an increased compulsion to choose between the one way and the other. The immigrants themselves were torn by a conflicting desire to have their sons and daughters be like themselves and yet lead better lives. Still, they rarely saw their children as mediators between the culture of the home and the culture of the wider society. Even if they did, they resented it, for it reversed the "proper" order of things. In their eyes, the second generation was undisciplined and ungrateful

In the 1930s the stereotype held by White Canadians of their Japanese-Canadian neighbours began to crack. In 1931, the Trades and Labour Congress of British Columbia passed a motion calling for the enfranchisement of all native-born Canadians. The CCF urged that all citizens, including those of Oriental descent, be granted the vote, and some academics such as H. F. Angus spoke out in their favour. But any changes that might have come from these stirrings were thwarted by the warlike course of the Japanese Empire on the other side of the Pacific Ocean.

In 1931, Japan invaded Manchuria and, in 1937, she invaded China. Japan's invasion of China crystallized and legitimated anti-Japanese feeling in British Columbia. Even the Chinese Canadians joined in boycotting Japanese-Canadian merchants. The Japanese Canadians were virtually isolated. In case of conflict with Japan, wouldn't the Japanese Canadians constitute a subversive element behind the Canadian lines? The reasons that had led Colonel Lawrence in 1755 to conclude that he could not defend Nova Scotia against the French so long as the Acadians were at his back loomed large in British Columbia. There were demands that Japanese Canadians should carry identification cards; that they should be denied trade licences; that Japanese-language schools should be closed; and that the Japanese Canadians should be removed from the west coast.

On September 10, 1939, Canada declared war on Germany. Many Nisei immediately tried to enlist, and some who signed up east of the Rockies were accepted but, in British Columbia, there was *de facto* exclusion. (During the First World War, 202 Japanese Canadians had enlisted and 59 of them had died overseas.) On January 8, 1941, Mackenzie King announced that Canadian citizens of Japanese ancestry were to be exempted from military service.

Exemption from military service was prompted by King's desire to forestall any claim the Japanese Canadians might make to a right to vote based on military service. It would be difficult to argue that the Japanese Canadians might die for their country, but that they should not have the right to participate in choosing who should govern it. In 1931, the British Columbia legislature had granted (by one vote) the franchise to Japanese veterans of the First World War, and it was a precedent that the province's politicians did not wish to be compelled to follow. Duff Pattullo, the premier of British Columbia from 1933 until 1941, wrote to

King urging him to prevent the recruiting of Nisei. "If they are called up for service, there will be a demand they be given the franchise, which we in the province will never tolerate...."

Japanese Canadians were anxious and apprehensive as war with Japan drew ever closer. Throughout 1941, Members of Parliament from British Columbia urged the federal government to take drastic measures against the Japanese Canadians. Only one MP from the province, Angus MacInnis of the CCF, defended the Japanese Canadians. Here is MacInnis speaking in House on February 25, 1941:

> If we are to have harmonious and friendly relations between the oriental population and the rest of our British Columbia citizens, we must stop discriminating against and abusing the orientals. We must find some common ground on which we can work, and I think it can be found. Is there any reason, if we should get into difficulties with Japan on the Pacific coast, why the Japanese in British Columbia should be interested in helping Canada, after the way in which we are treating them? I am satisfied that if we treat the Japanese and our other oriental citizens aright, we shall get their loyalty, because they are no longer orientals in the accepted sense of that term. They would feel as much out of place in Japan as we would. I know them, speak to them; I visit them and have them in my home, and I have not the slightest doubt that what I say is correct. If we are to avoid the troubles that other countries have had with racial minorities, then we must take a realistic view of the situation in British Columbia and attempt to make these people feel at home among us. We will secure their loyalty by fairness and kindness and by the practice of those other attributes which we exercise in our relations with other people.

But MacInnis was the only parliamentarian to come to the Japanese Canadians' defence. They had no one in high office they could rely upon; and they had no constitutional guarantees. They would have to rely on the "regime of tolerance" to which Laurier had appealed. The Japanese Canadians themselves understood this very well. With war against Japan imminent, an editorial in *The New Canadian*, the weekly newspaper of the Japanese Canadians, on November 14, 1941, said, "We need now to place our assurance in the inherent tolerance, good sense and decency of our Canadian neighbours and the democratic way of life."

Three weeks later, on December 7, 1941, the Japanese attacked Pearl Harbor. Immediately, 38 Japanese Canadians were interned, and 1,200 Japanese-Canadian fishing boats were impounded. Within a month, all persons of Japanese origin, whether they were citizens or not, were banned from the fishing industry, and their fishing boats were sold. At a stroke, the Japanese Canadians had finally been removed from the fishing industry.

Not surprisingly, immigrants who had retained their Japanese citizenship were required to register with the Registrar of Enemy Aliens, in the same way that Germans and Italians in Canada had been obliged to do. That was on December 7. On December 16, however, an order-in-council was passed requiring all persons of Japanese descent, citizens or not, to register. No similar measure had been taken with respect to Canadians of German and Italian origin, although Canada had been at war with Germany and Italy since September, 1939.

After the Japanese attack on Pearl Harbor, the virus of racial antagonism infected the whole province, and virtually all of its politicians, federal and provincial, jostled one another in proposing draconian measures to be taken against the Japanese Canadians. In his book *White Canada Forever*, Professor W. Peter Ward has described the wave of hostility which fell upon the Japanese Canadians. It was one

…in force and amplitude surpassing all previous racial outbursts.…This sudden, dramatic attack roused the racial fears and hostilities of white British Columbians to heights never before attained. In turn, they loosed a torrent of racialism which surged across the province for the next eleven weeks. This outbreak of popular feeling demanded an immediate response from the King government. In attempting to placate white opinion it offered a succession of policies, each one aimed at further restricting the civil liberties of the west coast Japanese. As it proved, nothing short of total evacuation could quiet the public outcry.

Mackenzie King told the nation by radio that the authorities "were confident of the loyal behaviour of Canadian residents of Japanese origin." This was a toothpick in a typhoon. The public clamour for the Japanese Canadians, citizens or not, to be evacuated and interned mounted steadily with each day's news of Japan's stunning victories in the Far East and the South Pacific.

On January 14, 1942, King announced that Japanese nationals between the ages of 18 and 45 would be removed from the west coast. Twenty-two hundred men were placed in road camps in the interior of the province. But this was only a partial evacuation. It did not satisfy the militants. "Take them back to Japan," demanded MP Thomas Reid on January 15, "they do not belong here...." Parliament reconvened on January 22, and its British Columbia members made another round of demands in even more strident language for complete evacuation to locations "east of the Rockies." They asserted, without the least evidence, that the Japanese Canadians constituted a fifth column. Early in 1942, Conservative MP Howard Green told the House:

> We should be protected from treachery, from a stab in the back....There has been treachery elsewhere from Japanese in this war, and we have no reason to hope that there will be none in British Columbia....The only complete protection we can have from this danger is to remove the Japanese population from the province.

There were wild rumours of Japanese subversion, but no evidence at all for the rumours. Many persons were, of course, genuinely afraid of Japanese landings on the west coast of Canada. But, apart from taking some remote islands in the Aleutian chain, the Japanese had not menaced North America. On June 20, 1942 a Japanese submarine shelled the lighthouse at Estevan Point on Vancouver Island, but there were no casualties. In any event the shelling occurred well after King had decided to evacuate the Japanese Canadians. Even if King had feared a Japanese attack on the west coast, he had no reason to believe that the Japanese Canadians were likely to aid and abet such an attack.

Today the apologists for the evacuation say that it was necessary for the protection of the Japanese Canadians themselves, that Canadians might spontaneously have fallen upon their fellow citizens in rage and frustration. An argument can, indeed, be erected on this footing. On Christmas Day, 1941, Japan had taken some 1,600 Canadian troops prisoner in the capture of Hong Kong. Was King thinking of the Vancouver riot of 1907, more than 30 years before? Did he fear that anti-Japanese riots in British Columbia might lead to reprisals against the Canadian prisoners taken in Hong Kong? It seems unlikely: the argument had little currency at the time. Certainly, none of those who were most vociferous in their denunciation of the Japanese Canadians advanced it then.

There was, in fact, no justification for their evacuation. No compelling military advice urged the course that King took. Compare the evacuation of the Japanese Canadians with the expulsion of the Acadians. In 1755, except for the English garrison, the Acadians constituted the whole population of Nova Scotia. The Japanese Canadians were only a small minority of the population of British Columbia and their numbers were of no significance at all in Canada as a whole. The Acadians had refused to swear an oath of loyalty to the British king and they had refused to serve against the French king. The Japanese Canadians had professed and amply proved their loyalty. Far from refusing to serve in the Canadian forces, they tried to enlist—but they were refused.

On February 26, 1942, King gave in to the militants. There would be a complete evacuation. He announced that all persons of Japanese ancestry would be evacuated from the west coast. Orders-in-council established a British Columbia Security Commission, which had the power to remove any person of Japanese origin from his or her home, and gave the Custodian of Enemy Property jurisdiction over the evacuees' property. More than 2,000 men had already been sent to work in road camps in interior British Columbia. Any who resisted were sent to a concentration camp at Angler, Ontario. There they wore clothing with red circles painted on their backs to make them easy targets, should they try to escape. Four hundred and fifty-two were still in custody at Angler when the war ended. Another 4,000 Japanese Canadians were sent to work on sugar beet farms in Alberta, Manitoba and Ontario. The rest were to be sent to the interior of British Columbia.

As a first step, Japanese Canadians were collected in the Pacific National Exhibition grounds in Vancouver where they were housed in converted livestock pens. In late spring they were sent to mining towns and newly built shack towns in the interior of the province. There the men working in the road camps were allowed to rejoin their families. Evacuation to the interior continued all that summer and into the fall. Finally, all Japanese Canadians, well-to-do, middle-class and poor, had been evacuated from their homes on the west coast. (The only exception made was in the case of Japanese Canadians who had married Whites.) Their land, their homes, and their personal property were taken from them.

By the time the evacuation was completed, Japan's star was waning. The rapid Japanese advance in the South Pacific was at last checked at the Battle of Midway on June 6, 1942. It was now clear that Japan could not win the war. The possibility of a Japanese invasion of the west coast of North America, always remote, was no longer a strategic consideration. The grounds for the evacuation had ceased to exist. So now the question was—what to do with the Japanese Canadians? Should they be allowed to return to the west coast? Should they be dispersed all over Canada? Or should they be sent to Japan when the war ended?

Members of Parliament from British Columbia were in no doubt. The Japanese Canadians should not be allowed to return to the west coast. At the very least they should be dispersed; better still, send them to Japan. Only the voice of Angus MacInnis was raised in defence of the principles for which Canada had ostensibly entered the war. On June 30, 1943, amid cries in the House for "repatriation"of the Japanese Canadians, MacInnis said:

> Because this is a question which must be decided on principles, principles I believe such as are laid down in the Atlantic charter, the first thing I am going to do is to make my own position clear and definite beyond the possibility of a doubt either in this house, in my own province or anywhere in Canada.
>
> Canada is at war with Japan. Canada is also at war with Germany and Italy. I see no reason why we should deal with the population of Japanese origin among us any differently from the way in which we deal with those of German and Italian extraction. If we deal with them differently— and we have done so—we do it on account of racial prejudice. So far as I have been able to ascertain; so far as anything that has been said in this house is concerned, this population of Japanese origin in the Dominion of Canada has been just as loyal as any other section of the people; and note this, no other section of the people has been treated in the way that these people have been treated. They have indicated their loyalty...by their willingness to enlist. Very few of them, however, were allowed to get into the armed forces...and the reason for that is not one that Canada can be very proud of. They were not allowed to enlist because it was feared that their services to the country would strengthen their claims for the full rights of citizenship after this war was over.

MacInnis was born in Prince Edward Island, and came to British Columbia when he was in his mid-20s. Before entering politics, he was employed as a street railwayman in Vancouver. He was first elected to the House as MP for Vancouver East in 1930. He served in the House until his retirement in 1957. In 1940 he was the only CCF MP elected from British Columbia. MacInnis displayed political courage throughout his political career, but never more so than during the years when he was the lone defender of the Japanese Canadians in the House of Commons. He concluded his speech:

> ...I want to put myself definitely on record as being opposed
> to what is called repatriation of persons of Japanese origin
> in Canada...it would not be repatriation in the proper sense;
> it would be deportation or exile for these people....

But the government could not be dissuaded. Events were
in train. The Japanese Canadians had been evacuated from
their homes and their property had been confiscated. By
July, 1944, some 4,000 of them had relocated east of the
Rockies. But the great majority were still in the camps in
the interior of British Columbia, forbidden to return to the
west coast. King decided to force them to choose between
relocating east of the Rockies and "repatriation" to Japan.
They were not to be allowed to return to the west coast.
A notice posted in the camps read:

> Free passage will be guaranteed by the Canadian govern-
> ment to all repatriates being sent to Japan, and all their
> dependants who accompany them, and including free
> transportation of such of their personal property as they
> may take with them.

Another read:

> Japanese Canadians who want to remain in Canada should
> now re-establish themselves east of the Rockies as best
> evidence of their intentions to co-operate with the govern-
> ment policy of dispersal. Failure to accept employment east
> of the Rockies may be regarded at a later date as lack of co-
> operation with the Canadian Government in carrying out
> the policy of dispersal.

A wish to return to the west coast, their home for three
generations, was to be held over their heads as "lack of
cooperation" in carrying out government policy.

What choice did the Japanese Canadians have? The
orders-in-council which forbade them to return to their
homes on the west coast were still in force. At the same
time, they knew they would not be well received in the
other provinces. Angry and bitter, many of the Japanese
Canadians agreed to be "repatriated" to Japan. These, together with their children, exceeded 10,000. This was not

repatriation. Japan was not their homeland; it was a country the majority of them had never seen. Their consent was obtained by foreclosing any other possibility. Thousands of persons—two-thirds, in fact, of those who signed applications for "repatriation"—later applied to cancel them.

Mackenzie King appeared and reappeared in the saga of the Japanese Canadians. In 1907, he had investigated the attacks on "Little Tokyo" in Vancouver. In 1928, as prime minister, he had restricted Japanese immigration. In the 1940s, as prime minister, he presided over the measures by which the Japanese Canadians were deprived of their liberty and their property. King had entered politics as a self-proclaimed reformer dedicated to humanitarian principles. Yet for King, few issues seemed to rise above the level of political management; indeed, his skill in this has given him a notable reputation among historians. No matter that Churchill and Roosevelt had proclaimed in the Atlantic Charter the ideals for which a world war was being fought. These ideals could wait for another day. Whenever he was called upon to support his principles with respect to the Japanese Canadians, he gave way before the strident calls for measures against them—restriction, evacuation, confiscation and deportation.

The Canadian policy of "repatriation" or dispersal of the Japanese Canadians, undertaken on grounds of national security, was morally wrong. Throughout the war, not a single Japanese Canadian was ever charged, let alone convicted, of espionage. King's policy of "repatriation" or dispersal was founded on racial prejudice and political convenience. Even those Japanese Canadians who had complied with the government demand to relocate east of the Rockies, as 4,000 of them had by 1944, were not to be given the rights of citizenship. The provinces east of the Rockies had little or no Oriental population and had not enacted measures to disqualify them as electors. So there was nothing to stop the Japanese Canadians claiming the right to vote in federal elections. What did King's government do? In 1944, it had the House of Commons pass a bill to prevent the Japanese Canadians who had relocated east of the Rockies from voting in federal elections.

Perhaps no aspect of the whole affair was as shabby as King's refusal to allow the Nisei to enlist in the Canadian armed forces. The United States had established an all-Japanese unit, the 442nd Regimental Combat Team, which served with distinction in Europe. King refused to hear of such a thing for Canada until finally, in the spring of 1945, and by specific British request, he allowed 150 Nisei to enlist in the Canadian Intelligence Corps to serve as interpreters for Allied units in southeast Asia.

In the general election of June 2, 1945, King was again returned to office. On August 14, 1945, the Japanese government surrendered unconditionally, and on September 2 the formal document of surrender was signed. What lay in store for the Japanese Canadians, now that the war was over? In an editorial on August 1, 1945, *The Vancouver Sun* had asked that question. "What British Columbians want to know is whether the Japs can be sent out of the country and kept out."

The new Parliament convened in September. King, adding the finishing touches to the Speech from the Throne, wrote in his diary that "the speech contains a profession of my belief in this world being ruled by moral law...." King's world of moral law was, of course, his own strange world. The evacuation in 1942 of the Japanese Canadians had been carried out under authority of the War Measures Act. But the extraordinary powers conferred on the federal government by the Act may only be invoked in case of "war or insurrection, real or apprehended." The war was over, so the federal government had Parliament enact, on October 5, 1945, the National Emergency Transitional Powers Act, which continued the powers assumed by the federal government under the War Measures Act. Acting under the new legislation, the cabinet, on December 15, passed orders-in-council providing for deportation of all Japanese Canadians who had requested "repatriation" in 1944 and for the loss of their Canadian citizenship.

King's policy would make these Japanese Canadians a

people without a country. His insensitivity to the enormity of his government's action was complete. Announcing to Parliament the government's policy of deporting loyal citizens who had committed no crime, King's gift for the banal did not fail him. "May I say that we have sought to deal with this problem and in doing so we have followed that ancient precept of doing justly but also loving mercy, and the Orders-in-Council...will give expression to that approach."

The first of the orders-in-council recited that "Whereas during the course of the war with Japan certain Japanese nationals manifested their sympathy with or support of Japan by making requests for repatriation to Japan and otherwise...." King had decided to treat Japanese Canadian requests for "repatriation" made in 1944, requests that the federal government had solicited from them, as evidence of disloyalty. The order continued,

> And Whereas it is deemed desirable...to deport the classes of persons referred to above; and Whereas it is considered necessary by reason of the war, for the security, defence, peace, order and welfare of Canada, that provision be made accordingly.

Thus, "by reason of the war" that had ended in August, more than 10,000 people, as to whom there was no evidence of disloyalty, were to be banished for "[manifesting] their sympathy with Japan," something for which there was no evidence either.

The orders-in-council provided for the deportation to Japan of any person of 16 years or more who had requested repatriation, including Japanese nationals, naturalized citizens, and persons of Japanese descent born in Canada, together with their wives and any children under the age of 16. Naturalized or Canadian-born citizens who were deported would lose their Canadian citizenship. Altogether, 10,347 Japanese Canadians were to be "repatriated." Three-quarters were Canadian citizens; half of these were Canadian-born.

But the war had ended in August, and thousands of the

Japanese Canadians applied to cancel their requests for "repatriation." Moreover, some Canadians were now beginning to feel a sense of shame over what was happening, and they began to come to the aid of the Japanese Canadians. The protests they made led to concessions by the government. An announcement was made that naturalized and Canadian-born Japanese (but not Japanese nationals) who had applied for cancellation of their requests for "repatriation" before September 2, 1945, the date of the official signing of Japan's surrender, would be considered. The government justified this limitation by asserting that persons who had applied only after Japan's surrender must have been hoping that Japan would win the war, else why didn't they apply earlier?

The campaign against deportation continued. Applications for *habeas corpus* were brought to test the legality of the orders-in-council. King agreed to refer the question of the legality of the orders-in-council to the Supreme Court of Canada. On February 20, 1946, the court handed down its decision. Chief Justice Thibaudeau Rinfret held that the cabinet "was the sole judge of the necessity or advisability of these measures," and a majority of the Supreme Court agreed with him.

The orders-in-council spoke of deportation. Every nation has the right to exclude aliens. So the Japanese immigrants to Canada who had never taken out Canadian citizenship could be deported to Japan, where they still held citizenship. Given that those who were to be deported had signed requests for "repatriation," the matter was straightforward, at least in a strictly legal sense. But the concept of deportation had no application to Canadian citizens. A nation cannot deport its own citizens. If it forcibly expels them, it is banishing them—sending them into exile. The government had based its argument in support of the orders-in-council on its right to send Japanese nationals back to Japan, to repatriate them. But could the government deport naturalized or Canadian-born citizens? Under international law it could not. Thus the orders-in-council in effect stripped Japanese Canadians of their citizenship. But that did not make them citizens of Japan. They had no right to enter any other nation. They would become state-less persons, for Canada could not force these unwilling persons upon Japan. There was no treaty or international convention between Canada and Japan that provided for this contingency. King's government had, however, ar-ranged with General Douglas MacArthur, commander of the Allied occupation forces in Japan, for Japanese Cana-dians to take up residence there. But the question of law still remained: Could the government of Canada banish its own citizens?

The Supreme Court held that the War Measures Act did confer such power on the federal government. The court did, however, balk at the orders banishing wives and chil-dren. These, they said, could not be justified, it being in no way apparent that such deportation was necessary "for the security, defence, peace, order and welfare of Canada." Two of the judges would also not go along with the de-portation of native-born Canadian citizens. One of the dissenting judges, Mr. Justice Ivan Rand, confronted the real issue. Had the government taken these steps against the Japanese Canadians in the interests of national security or because of racial prejudice?

> Now I must deal with this case as if, instead of a Canadian national of Japanese origin, I were dealing with that of a natural born Canadian national of English extraction who sympathized with Mosley or a French Canadian national who thought de Valera's course justified. I am asked to hold that, without a convention with those countries, the Government may, under the War Measures Act, and with-out affecting the national status or citizenship rights of these persons, issue an order for their deportation, on those foreign shores. I am unable to agree with that contention.

An appeal was taken to the Privy Council, which handed down its opinion on December 2, 1946. It went even further than the majority in the Supreme Court of Canada and held that the orders-in-council were valid in all respects and that even the forcible deportation of wives and children was valid. These judgements of the Supreme Court of

Canada and of the Privy Council reveal how much the judges were inclined to defer to the cabinet. The issue was regarded as one for political judgement, in no way subject to the jurisdiction of the courts. The War Measures Act gave the cabinet power to act and, so far as the Privy Council was concerned, that was the end of the matter. So the Japanese Canadians were banished by their own government. (The last Canadian before them to be banished had been Louis Riel in 1875.)

The judges had confined their judicial examination of the orders-in-council to the bare bones of the statute. Had the War Measures Act conferred on the cabinet the power to pass the orders? No one suggested that this extraordinary power should be given a strict construction. The war had ended and Japan was *in extremis*, but none of the judges thought it appropriate to scrutinize closely the necessity for the cabinet's retention of these powers now that we were no longer at war. The orders-in-council were permitted to stand, and the judges upheld the government's right to expel Japanese nationals who had not in any way transgressed the immigration laws or the Criminal Code and effectively to deprive thousands of Canadians who had committed no crime, and were guilty of no disloyalty, of the most basic right of citizenship.

These orders-in-council were racist. That is a word perhaps too easily used nowadays. We can understand the true meaning of racism, however, and the danger it represents, by reference to the Japanese Canadians. They were singled out because they were a race and culture different from the majority. Yet only Mr. Justice Rand confronted this issue.

But not all Canadians agreed with their government and the courts. New ideas of human rights and human freedom were gaining currency in the world. No longer were there just a few protesting against the federal government's policy; now there were many. On January 24, 1947, King gave in. The government, he announced, would not carry out its deportation program after all. But, by this date, almost 4,000 persons, half of whom had been born in Canada, had left for Japan. No doubt many of them would have remained in Canada, rather than share postwar Japan's bleak prospects, had not the years of persecution embittered them to the point where they had no reason to stay in Canada and no faith in Canada. We must think of them as exiles.

There was no attempt made in the United States to send the Japanese Americans to Japan. There had been, after Pearl Harbor, an outbreak of anti-Japanese hysteria in California, followed by the evacuation and internment of 120,000 Japanese Americans from the west coast. These measures had been upheld by the Supreme Court of the United States on the ground of the paramountcy of national security. But on December 17, 1944, the United States government rescinded the orders excluding the Japanese Americans from the west coast and announced that all detention centres would be closed down within one year. Japanese Americans were permitted at once to return to California and the west coast. Certainly, no attempt was made to banish them to Japan.

In April, 1947, the Canadian cabinet formally revoked the orders-in-council which had sent the Japanese Canadians to Japan. But the orders-in-council passed in 1942 stood. Japanese Canadians still could not return to the west coast. In 1948, three years after the war had ended, they could not travel freely in British Columbia or fish commercially anywhere in Canada. In that year one of them was sentenced to a year's hard labour for returning to British Columbia without permission. So the Japanese Canadians living in the camps could not return to the west coast nor, if they went east of the Rockies, could they return to the province. They were entangled in a network of bureaucracy hardly to be imagined.

On June 15, 1948, Parliament granted to Japanese Canadians who were citizens the right to vote in federal elections. But though these citizens at last could vote in federal elections, they still could not return to the west coast. The orders-in-council that forbade them to do so were finally rescinded in 1949, four years after the end of the war. By that time, many of them had settled east of the Rockies, especially in Ontario; in fact the largest population of Japanese Canadians in Canada now is in Toronto. In that same year, 1949, they were given the right to vote in provincial elections in British Columbia as well. In 1949, the United Fishermen and Allied Workers Union agreed to let Japanese Canadians return to the fishing industry in the province.

Mackenzie King could write in his Diary that it was "fortunate the use of the [atomic] bomb should have been upon the Japanese rather than upon the white races of Europe." But public attitudes were changing. With Japan defeated and prostrate, it was impossible to regard that nation as a threat to Canada. The tendency of anti-Oriental feeling to abate, which had been discernible during the early 1930s, once again became evident. The war had been fought for the ideals of liberal democracy, and Canadians felt that these ideals had a place in postwar society. The world stood appalled by the holocaust to which racial hatred in Europe had led. Canada had become a member of the United Nations Organization, and a subscriber to the Universal Declaration of Human Rights. Racism was no longer in vogue.

In the postwar years the principal concern of the Japanese Canadians was to establish themselves and their children in Canadian society. They wished only to be inconspicuous, and in Toronto deliberately dispersed themselves about the city. Many of the Nisei moved into professional and white-collar occupations, and their acceptance and assimilation, which had once been thought to be impossible, occurred virtually unnoticed. Intermarriage became commonplace. The years of abasement were over.

Had the evacuation been a blessing in disguise? Some have suggested that the social and economic integration of the Japanese Canadians would not have occurred if they had not been evacuated and dispersed during and after the war, that it was the evacuation itself that secured for the Japanese Canadians equality of opportunity. Evacuation and dispersal were justified *ex post facto* as the useful tools of social engineering. Certainly before the evacuation, Japanese Canadians were confined to urban and rural ghettos in British Columbia, and there is no question that since the war, dispersed about the country, they have thrived as never before.

Was this progress attributable to the evacuation? Some Canadians of Japanese descent take this view. It is a view which, in the United States, Senator Hayakawa has stressed. But it was progress already observed even before the outbreak of war with Japan and the evacuation. Given the racial barriers confronting them, it is not surprising that the integration of the Japanese Canadians did not take place until the 1950s and 1960s. But once the series of liberalizing measures had been passed, integration proceeded swiftly. No doubt it was accelerated by evacuation and dispersal. But it was bound to occur in any event. Consider the Chinese Canadians of British Columbia. Like the Japanese Canadians, they were restrained by barriers of law and prejudice before the Second World War. They were not evacuated and dispersed. But they were given the right to vote in British Columbia in 1947. The barriers that had confronted them were lifted. The Chinese Canadians, like the Japanese Canadians, were the beneficiaries of an increasingly liberal spirit in Canadian society.

The "it was all for the best" argument is founded on the notion that the state has the right to scatter the members of any minority whenever it is deemed to be for their own good. If the evacuation of the Japanese Canadians from their homes can be justified as social engineering, which of us will be the next group to be scattered, our communities destroyed, our property confiscated—all in our own best interest?

Such wrongs are beyond redress. The confiscation of property, however, is amenable to redress. Yet there has not been adequate redress for the loss of the Japanese Canadians' property. Their fishing boats, impounded at the very beginning of the war, were sold without any compensation to their former owners. As for the rest of their property, after evacuation it was vested in the Custodian of Enemy Property, who had wide discretionary powers to dispose of it. Without the owners' permission—indeed, over their protests—the Custodian sold their property, often at ridiculously low prices. For instance, Japanese Canadians owned some 700 farms covering about 13,000 acres in the Fraser valley. They were appraised, together, at $836,256 (approximately $64.00 an acre for the finest agricultural land in British Columbia)—that is what the owners received for them—and held by the government for soldiers then serving overseas. The irony is that some of these farms belonged to Japanese Canadians who had served in Canadian forces during the First World War. Feelings of the Japanese Canadians were summed up in a letter that one of them, Muriel Kitagawa, wrote to the Custodian of Enemy Property after her home had been sold.

Who would have thought that one day I would be unable to stand up for my country's government, out of sheer shame and disillusion, against the slurs of the scornful. The bitterness, the anguish, is complete. You, who deal in lifeles figures, files and statistics, could never measure the depth of hurt and outrage dealt out to those of us who love this land. It is because we are Canadians that we protest this violation of our birthright.

Looking back, it is easy to condemn those who called for evacuation, internment, and deportation of the Japanese Canadians. But what would we do today if some other minority were the object of racial hatred? How many of us would have the courage to take an unpopular stand against an inflamed majority? It is not enough to say that it won't happen again. In a crowded world, Canada will continue to be a land to which peoples from all over the world, of every race, wish to come. And they are coming.

Canada opened its doors to Asian immigrants in the 1960s. Perhaps the counterparts today of the Chinese and Japanese immigrants of the nineteenth century are the immigrants from India and Pakistan. Since the early years of this century, Canada had virtually excluded immigration from the Indian subcontinent. As late as 1941 there were no more than 1,500 East Indians in Canada. Since the 1960s, however, immigration from India, Pakistan and Sri Lanka has risen dramatically. This has had a visible impact on many communities in British Columbia and in other provinces, too, for these immigrants do not arrive only on the west coast, by sea, as in the old days. Today they arrive by air, and their destinations may include Winnipeg, Toronto or Montreal. Thus people from the Indian subcontinent may now by found in increasing numbers in many Canadian centres. East Indian immigrants appear to some Canadians as alien, clinging to their own language, dress and customs. There has been a recrudescence of racial feeling, directed against these most recent Asian immigrants. There have been beatings, vandalism, and fire bombings in communities with significant East Indian populations. But these have been isolated outbreaks, generally deplored by all.

The racial virus has been so far kept in check in British Columbia and the other provinces. There has been no attempt to erect a network of discriminatory laws and regulations. There is today a liberal establishment ready to speak out in support of the rights of Asians in Vancouver or West Indians in Toronto or Moroccans in Montreal. There are human rights commissions at the federal level and in every province. And there are the provisions of the Charter of Rights. These things give minorities the confidence to speak out, to protest the violation of their freedom, and to assert their claim to rights we have all been taught they should enjoy.

But might one of the provinces nevertheless have the power to pass racist legislation in the future? Might the federal government, in the exercise of its emergency power, invoke the War Measures Act against a racial minority again? How secure actually are racial minorities in Canada?

The Charter guarantees to every individual the right to equality under the law and the right to the equal protection of the law "without discrimination based on race, national or ethnic origin, (or) colour." But the Charter also says that the rights set out in it are subject to "such reasonable limits prescribed by law as can be demonstrably justified in a free and democratic society." When may such reasonable limits be imposed on the right of a racial minority to the equal protection of the law? I suppose the answer is that it may be done when a majority in Parliament or any of the legislatures imposes such a limitation and the courts find such action to be demonstrably justifiable. The War Measures Act could still be invoked. So will the Charter change anything? I think it will. There is an explicit recognition of the right of racial minorities to equality under the law. The Charter also requires the courts to determine for themselves whether or not a particular statute is demonstrably justifiable, and not simply to accede to the judgement of the politicians as they did in 1946.

The fact remains, however, that the Constitution, the Charter, and the law will not provide complete protection for racial minorities. It would be difficult to draft a statute that did. Equality for racial minorities depends, in the end, on the attitudes of the citizenry. But we have progressed. The trial and torment of the Japanese Canadians have taught us something about the obligations of citizenship in Canada. In British Columbia legislators used to strive to devise statutes that would limit the rights of racial minorities. In 1981, the legislature of the province passed the Civil Rights Protection Act to combat racism by prohibiting racist propaganda. Similar legislation was passed in Saskatchewan in 1979. This type of legislation presents a problem. Discrimination in employment, housing, and so forth on racial grounds can properly be made subject to the sanctions of the law. These are overt acts of discrimination. But legislation banning racist propaganda, such as the federal legislation of 1969 banning hate propaganda, entails the enactment of curbs on freedom of speech, something not to be undertaken except for the most compelling reasons and, in the case of racial intolerance, with an awareness that legislation may not be the answer to every evil in the state. While the wisdom—and efficacy—of such legislation is open to question, the change in public and legislative attitudes is important. Such legislation affirms society's commitment to racial equality.

The third generation of Japanese Canadians, the Sansei, have grown up without the linguistic and cultural connections that the Issei handed on to the Nisei. But this does not mean the Japanese Canadians are vanishing. Like the Acadians, the story of their expulsion has provided them with a legend, has given them a graphic tale of the hardships of their parents and their people, of those who came before them to Canada. Today, the Sansei are trying to strengthen their links with the past and to redress past wrongs. But the sense of vulnerability still persists. Should the Japanese Canadians, even today, be silent about the past, lest reminding others of it provoke another outbreak of racism? In *A Dream of Riches*, a book published by The Japanese Canadian Centennial Project in 1978, to commemorate the history of their one hundred years in this country, the Japanese Canadians have given their answer:

> Let us break this self-damaging silence and own our history. If we do not, estrangement from our past will be absorbed and driven deeper, surfacing as a fragmentation in ourselves and coming generations. But in retracing the journey of our people through time, in going back to our roots, we find ourselves made whole, replenished in spirit. We return from that journey deeply proud of our people, of their contribution to this country.

The need to remember is expressed even more graphically by Emily, one of the characters in *Obasan*, a novel about the Japanese Canadians during the Second World War, by Joy Kogawa, published in 1981. Replying to her niece, Naomi, who wishes to remain silent, Emily says,

> You are your history. If you cut off any of it, you're an amputee. Don't deny the past....Denial is gangrene.

The racism once made legitimate by our political institutions is no longer legitimate. But as long as it finds a place in our collective psyche, it will constitute a threat, sometimes near, at other times far off, but there. Nothing is to be gained by pretending it doesn't exist, or by temporizing with evil. Each of us has an obligation to uphold the regime of tolerance. In *A Dream of Riches* the Japanese Canadians have expressed what should be the aspiration of us all:

> Having gained our freedom...we must not lose sight of our own experience of hatred and fear. Too often we have heard "damn Jew," "lazy Indian," from those who were once called "dirty Japs." The struggle of the generations and the meaning of the war years is completely betrayed if we are to go over to the side of the racist. Let us honour our history...by supporting the new immigrants and other minorities who now travel the road our people once travelled.

FIVE

The Communist Party and The Limits of Dissent

THE RISE OF Marxism during the past century and its adoption by the Soviet Union as a state ideology have confronted Western nations with an external challenge. At the same time, Communism has confronted the Western nations with an internal challenge that is, in some ways, more testing than the overt threat represented by Soviet military strength and influence in the world. In Canada, this internal challenge does not lie in the possibility that Communists may acquire actual power and influence; the challenge is to our attitudes, to our institutions, and to our ideas about the limits of dissent.

Although the threat which domestic Communism presents has nearly always been exaggerated, the presence of Communists in our midst and the beliefs they espouse have pressed the regime of tolerance to its farthest limits. How should a democracy deal with Communists? Ought we to concede freedom of speech to those who would deny that freedom to the rest of us, if they could? The Charter of Rights and Freedoms entrenches freedom of expression. Canadians will thus be forced to face this question anew.

The Communists reject our political and economic system. Relying upon the imperatives of history as laid down by Marx and Lenin, they foresee the violent end of capitalism (including its social democratic variants) and liberal democracy and the assumption of power by the workers. If the Communists simply foretold the fall of capitalism and the breakdown of democracy as we know it, that would not be abuse of freedom of speech. Prophecy does not constitute sedition. But when prophecy is mixed up with arguments that are intended to accelerate the inevitable course of history, questions of civil liberty may arise. The ways in which Canadian institutions—our parliaments and police, our courts and lawyers, our industrial tribunals and trade unions—have dealt with the Communist party show how far we have been prepared to accept, and to act on, our professed belief in a free marketplace of ideas. In tracing the relations between our institutions and the Communist party, we can learn something about the vital difference between autocracy and freedom, and between sedition and dissent.

What are the true limits of dissent in a democracy? The Charter of Rights will entrench freedom of expression and freedom of association. But, according to the Charter, the rights and freedoms that it entrenches are subject to "such reasonable limits prescribed by law as can be demonstrably justified in a free and democratic society." This is not precise language, and we should not expect it to be. Where, then, have the limits of dissent been set in the past? Where should they be set today? The Charter does not answer these questions. The Charter does stipulate that any limits that are set must be reasonable limits; and they must be limits that can be demonstrably justified. But the question still remains perplexing. Should Communists have the same right to vote, to run for office as other citizens? What about employment in the public service? Admittance to the professions? What about Communist leadership in the trade unions? Should Communists be deemed always to be agents of Soviet imperialism, even when they claim to be acting independently? Are they to be deemed to be bound by the dogmas of Marx and Lenin, even when they insist that they are not?

Some things are clear enough. The Criminal Code says that it is treason to use force or violence for the purpose of overthrowing the government of Canada or of a province. If a party of armed men, seeking to establish a new regime, invaded the Parliament buildings, we should have no difficulty in calling that treason. But then there is sedition. Sedition is not the actual use of force or violence to effect a change in government, but the advocacy of the use of force or violence to effect a change in government. When does vehement denunciation of the government become indistinguishable from urging its violent overthrow? How closely must free speech by the citizenry be scrutinized to see if any are preaching sedition? Once the authorities become engaged in studying what citizens are saying and writing, with a view to discovering seditious utterances, they tend to regard many legitimate forms of dissent as incipient sedition. Files are opened, dossiers are built up, and soon an apparatus is erected to provide state scrutiny of all of the causes which make those who govern uneasy. Then mere allegations may become sufficient to establish that someone is trying to subvert the nation; the distinction between sedition and dissent becomes a matter of labels, not of evidence.

These are questions that we struggled with in Canada long before the Communists came along. The magistrates of Halifax tried to silence Joseph Howe in 1835, when he accused them of negligence and corruption. But he successfully defended himself against the charge of sedition they brought against him. William Lyon Mackenzie, denounced by Upper Canada's Lieutenant-Governor Sir Francis Bond Head as the "arch-agitator," relentlessly attacked the Family Compact that ruled the colony. On June 22, 1837, Mackenzie wrote in his newspaper, *The Constitution:*

> I have exposed their oppressions, their peculations, their tricks of state, their conspiracies against freedom, their hostility to truth, their bribery, favouritism, rottenness and corruption. Canadians! I pray you to lend me your aid in continuing this bold, dangerous, but delightful course.

Mackenzie had been repeatedly expelled from the Assembly. But he could not be silenced. Mackenzie spoke for the freeholders of Upper Canada, then an essentially rural province, and his crusade against the merchants, lawyers, and bankers that made up the Family Compact had the support of thousands of English-speaking farmers and of the nascent working class. Their claims could not be rejected as alien: like Papineau and his followers in Lower Canada, the worst they could be accused of was republicanism. Of course, when Mackenzie crossed the boundary between dissent and sedition and took up arms against the government of Upper Canada, the government declared him a traitor and, his rebellion defeated, he fled into exile in the United States. But the boundary between dissent and sedition was clearly marked.

Dissent in the early years of this century was quite a different matter. During the Laurier years large numbers of European immigrants settled in western Canada. Many of them did not speak English and did not at once assimilate. They came not only to homestead but also to work in the new industries—in the mining towns, logging camps, sawmills, and factories. There they soon tried to organize trade unions. Campaigns against dissenters by those who held political and economic power could now be strengthened by appeals to patriotism and the need to preserve English-speaking hegemony in western Canada. The International Workers of the World ("the Wobblies"), the One Big Union, and especially the Communist party were particularly vulnerable to such attacks.

It is difficult to take the Communist party seriously today, but that has not always been the case. From the 1920s until the end of the 1950s, many people believed that the Communist party in Canada was composed of diabolically clever men and women who were able to delude the workers, outwit their employers, frustrate the police, and intimidate the voters in their grand plan to establish a Communist dictatorship. The truth, of course, is very different. From its founding in 1921, the Communist party of Canada has had little electoral support, its influence in Canadian life (except in the trade-union movement) has been marginal, and the public has, for the most part, regarded its polemics as a bore. Yet the party has been the subject of constant police scrutiny and infiltration, it has from time to time been outlawed by the federal government, and its leaders have been faced with imprisonment, internment and deportation.

In June, 1921, 22 delegates meeting in a barn outside Guelph established the Communist party of Canada. Among the 22 delegates, there was an RCMP undercover man and a representative of the Communist International (also known as the Comintern, formed in 1919 by Moscow to promote revolution in the capitalist countries). The presence within the party of agents of these two institutions illustrates why the party has failed in Canada. From the beginning, the RCMP has infiltrated it, and federal and provincial governments have harassed it. Worse for it than infiltration and harassment, however, has been its association with the Communist International. The Communist party has not been able to thrive in Canada as the instrument of a foreign power. From the beginning, others—ambitious politicians and bureaucrats at home and the Soviet Union abroad—have used the party for their own purposes.

There were, of course, Communists in Canada before 1921. The early 1900s saw a proliferation of socialist and radical organizations, particularly in western Canada. Quite a number of these organizations were formed by immigrants from Central and Eastern Europe. During the First World War, many of these immigrants who had not yet become naturalized had to register as enemy aliens, and several thousand of them were interned. In 1917, after the overthrow of the Czar, Lenin and the Communists seized power in Russia. In 1919, Canada sent troops to join other Western powers in an invasion of Russia in an unsuccessful attempt, begun in 1918, to overthrow the newly established Communist regime.

Early in the same year, a strike by workers in the building and metal trades in Winnipeg led to a general strike in that city. Essential services were stopped. The newspapers were closed down. There were no deliveries of milk and bread. The city police voted to go on strike, but stayed on duty at the request of the Central Strike Committee established by the striking unions. Other workers throughout western Canada went out on sympathy strikes. Thirty-five thousand workers were on strike in Winnipeg, 60,000 were out altogether across western Canada, from Winnipeg to Vancouver. The federal authorities were alarmed. They took the view that the Winnipeg strike was the first step in a revolutionary plot to install a Communist government in Canada. John W. Dafoe, editor of *The Manitoba Free Press*, denounced the Central Strike Committee as the "Red Five." As for their followers, Dafoe said that the time had come "to clean the aliens out of this community and ship them back to their happy homes in Europe which vomited them forth a decade ago."

The "Red Five" were not Communists. A Royal Commission reported in July 1919 that there was no evidence to support the notion that Communists had led the strike or that its purpose was to overthrow Canadian institutions and establish a Soviet regime in their place. Professor D. C. Masters in *The Winnipeg General Strike* reached the same conclusion. The real cause of the strike was, according to the commissioner, H. A. Robson, K.C., the desire of the workers to achieve adequate rates of wages to combat post-war inflation. Thus issues of union recognition and collective bargaining rights, not any plan for a Communist takeover, constituted the heart of the matter. But a pattern had been established. Demands for collective bargaining rights and attempts to organize trade unions could be denounced as being Communist-inspired, and any movement for a wider sharing of political and economic power could be stigmatized as an attempt to subject Canada to an alien system whose adoption would entail the loss of all our freedoms.

At the time of the Winnipeg strike, Prime Minister Robert Borden's minister of justice, Arthur Meighen, who was soon to be Borden's successor, had Parliament amend the Criminal Code by the enactment of Section 98 (s. 98) which outlawed "unlawful associations."

> Any association...whose professed purpose...is to bring about any governmental, industrial or economic change within Canada by use of force, violence or physical injury to person or property, or by threats of such injury, or which

teaches, advocates, advises or defends the use of force, violence, terrorism, or physical injury to person or property...in order to accomplish such change, or for any other purpose, or which shall by any means prosecute or pursue such purpose...or shall so teach, advocate, advise or defend, shall be an unlawful association.

No reasonable person disputes the proposition that a society cannot tolerate violence directed against its institutions. For this reason there are provisions in the Criminal Code covering treason and sedition. But the enactment of Section 98, the language of which is wide enough to encompass the extravagant rhetoric of a trade-union meeting, or the passionate condemnation of the established order at a student demonstration, or even the words of a Laurier on the Champs de Mars, went far beyond the needs of the time, or indeed of any time.

There were stringent penalties associated with s. 98. To become a member of an unlawful association, or to be an officer of one, or to wear a badge or button indicating membership, or to contribute dues were crimes punishable by up to 20 years' imprisonment. The legislation also provided that anyone who attended a meeting of an unlawful association, or spoke publicly on its behalf, or distributed literature about it, should be presumed to be a member of it in the absence of proof to the contrary. The RCMP could seize, without warrant, all property belonging to or suspected of belonging to an unlawful association. The owner of a hall who permitted any unlawful association to meet there was liable to five years' imprisonment or to a fine of $5,000.

What, it may be argued, is wrong about this kind of legislation? Shouldn't any organization which advocates the overthrow of the government by force be subject to constant surveillance, and to prosecution? The trouble is that, once such legislation is enacted, it has to be enforced. The police, army intelligence, or some other body has to be mandated to watch over the political life of the nation. There are always ambitious bureaucrats eager to undertake the task. This is what happened after Section 98 was enacted. In November, 1919, the Royal North-West Mounted Police was constituted as a national police force, to be known as the Royal Canadian Mounted Police (RCMP), and given responsibility for national security. Together with the army, provincial police forces, even municipal police forces, they spied on unions, socialist and social democratic organizations, ethnic clubs and schools. This attempt to categorize, classify, and control these expressions of social, economic, and ethnic solidarity has continued in one form or another to the present. What, then, is to be done?

There is no simple answer, for democracies must defend themselves against subversion. But they must also be true to the ideals of freedom of speech and of association which are essential aspects of the democratic order. The ferment of social change takes many forms. Some of them are alarming to leaders of government and industry, and to the RCMP. But to adopt the kind of legislation that is the hallmark of the regimes of frightened autocrats the world over is altogether a mistake. The consequences of the denial of freedom of speech cannot be overestimated. Freedom of speech is in a sense man's calling, the necessary condition of all other freedoms. Restraints designed to curtail speech that is critical of the established order, measures founded on the idea of intellectual guilt by association—these are characteristic of totalitarianism, not democracy. Dissent is often tinged with rhetoric that, wrenched from its context, may be fitted within the usual categories of illegality. But if dissent is made the subject of repressive measures, the grievances underlying it will not be understood, and remedies to alleviate them will not be considered. It is one thing to adopt a truculent manifesto, or to make a speech or pass a resolution expressing vehement opposition to existing political or economic arrangements, but quite another to incite to violence. The distinction is vital.

Section 98 remained on the statute books until 1936. Federal and provincial governments used it to harass not only the Communist party and other left-wing political organizations, but also the trade unions. In 1932, F. R. Scott wrote in *Queen's Quarterly* that "for permanent restriction of the rights of association, freedom of discussion, printing and distribution of literature, and for severity of punishment, [it] is unequalled in the history of Canada and probably of any British country for centuries past." But s. 98 was not to be the only law of its kind: the mould was not broken. It was the model for the regulations passed under the War Measures Act during the Second World War to suppress aliens and dissenters, and for the regulations passed under the War Measures Act in October, 1970.

Thus, even before the Communist party of Canada had formally organized itself, before the 22 delegates had convened in the barn near Guelph, there was legislation on the statute books that could be used to limit its political activity. Throughout the 1920s and the 1930s, the police, acting under s. 98, harassed the party, broke up meetings, dispersed audiences, raided party offices, confiscated party literature, and arrested party activists.

During these early years, the Communist party consisted largely of landed immigrants, especially Russians, Ukrainians, and Finns. It was a movement of social protest, particularly in the western provinces, for immigrant workers. As Professor Donald Avery has written in *Dangerous Foreigners*, it provided a haven for them that no other working-class organization or political party was prepared to provide. With a membership that consisted largely of aliens, the party ranks were highly vulnerable to deportation proceedings. Under s. 41 of the Immigration Act, which Parliament had enacted in April, 1919, and which, together with amendments passed in June, 1919, during the Winnipeg general strike, was a companion piece of legislation to s. 98 of the Criminal Code, the federal government had the power to deport any alien or even a Canadian citizen who had not been born in Canada, who advocated "the overthrow by force...of constituted law and authority." Hundreds of foreign-born Communists were deported (according to June Callwood, in *Portrait of Canada*, over

7,000 suspected "Communists" were deported in 1932 alone), and so were hundreds of foreign-born trade-unionists. Commissioner J. H. MacBrien of the RCMP said that when Canada had rid itself of foreigners "there would be no unemployment or unrest."

An indigenous Canadian political party might have overcome such harassment, but the Communist party of Canada followed the party line as laid down in Moscow. The party line was, of course, designed to serve the interests of the Soviet Union, which meant that its followers in Canada were under an obligation to justify Soviet policy in all circumstances. This helped to prevent the party from attracting significant numbers of followers. The party still labours under this crippling duty, but today its tortured and tortuous attempts to justify the foreign policy of the Soviet Union are little noticed, except by other political organizations on the far left, and their furious attacks on persons who still follow the official party line are far more vitriolic than criticism the Communist party of Canada attracts from any other quarter.

The life of Tim Buck exemplifies the loyalty of Canadian Communists to Moscow. Buck became secretary-general of the party in 1929, and he was its chief spokesman until 1962. He visited the Soviet Union often and, as a reward for fidelity, he received on his eightieth birthday the Order of the October Revolution. In 1967, Buck wrote in *Canada and the Russian Revolution*:

> The new Soviet state brought into being by the Great October Revolution has withstood, invincibly, all the attacks from without and has overcome, brilliantly, all the varied difficulties encountered within, in the course of building a completely new and historically higher social order....Above all, their magnificent role in mankind's striving to prevent world nuclear war places them in the forefront of the democratic forces which embody our hope for peace and democratic progress.

To us Buck's devotion may seem misguided. But Buck and his comrades felt that they were soldiers in an international army that would triumph in the end. It seemed to them that a new world was being built in the Soviet Union. There the first proletarian revolution in history had produced a regime which was constructing the socialist order. They had a deep faith—a religious faith—in Marxian doctrine, and persecution served to strengthen the faith of these true believers. There was no more inclination in the party to question the policy laid down by Moscow than there was among Roman Catholics in the twelfth century to question the dogmas of the Church. There were no proletarian revolutions after 1917—there have been none in the West to date—but the Communists were prepared to wait. They believed that their prophet would be vindicated.

The Communists paid for their loyalty to their convictions. On August 11, 1931, Buck and eight others were arrested in Toronto and charged under s. 98 with being members of an unlawful association. They were doing nothing in 1931 that they had not been doing for years. Despite constant harassment, they had run candidates in municipal, provincial, and federal elections. But in 1931, the attorney-general of Ontario preferred an indictment against Buck and his colleagues, alleging that they were "members of an unlawful association, to wit, the Communist party" and they "did act or profess to act as officers of an unlawful association, to wit, the Communist party." They were also charged with seditious conspiracy.

An RCMP officer who had infiltrated the party gave evidence against them, and party literature was introduced as evidence. One of the publications described the party's proceedings in the barn near Guelph.

> The result of the Constituent Convention is the Organization of the vanguard of the Canadian working class into the Communist party of Canada, Section of the Communist International, with a programme of Mass-action as the vital form of proletarian activity, armed insurrection, civil war as the decisive, final form of mass-action for the destruction of the Capitalist State, proletarian dictatorship in the form of Soviet power as the lever of the Communist reconstruction of society.

The Crown argued that this and other publications in the same vein brought the party squarely within the prohibitions of s. 98, that the Communist party intended to bring about governmental, industrial and, economic changes within Canada by the use of force, violence, or physical injury to persons or property, and that the party advocated such methods of securing change. Buck and the others explained that, according to Marx and Engels, the capitalist class must inevitably clash with the working class—it is the dynamic of history. They were not urging violent change, they were predicting it. This was a difficult point to make, especially when confronted with the hyperbole used in their publications. Eight of those accused, including Buck, were found guilty, and Buck and six others were each sentenced to five years' imprisonment. An appeal failed, except on the count of seditious conspiracy; the convictions under s. 98 stood. Buck was released from prison in November, 1934.

Buck never did become the leader of the left in Canada. The man who did, J. S. Woodsworth, was Buck's implacable foe. Woodsworth had gone to jail himself at the time of the Winnipeg general strike. Then he entered Parliament as a representative of the Independent Labour party. From the beginning, Buck realized that Woodsworth was the Communist party's most dangerous enemy. In 1929, Buck had declared that "the eyes of our party membership must be focused upon the menace of social reformists." Buck was right, and Woodsworth went on to become, in 1933, the leader of the Co-operative Commonwealth Federation (the CCF), a socialist party that had no allegiance except to Canada. The establishment of the CCF precluded any possibility that Communism might ever become a mass movement of the left in Canada.

There has always been a quixotic aspect to the Communist party's campaigns for elected office in Canada. When they have put up candidates, they have generally received only a scattering of votes. In January, 1933, Communist candidates did win control of the municipal council of Blairmore, Alberta, and, in true comic-opera style, they renamed the town's main street "Tim Buck Boulevard." The CCF entered its first federal campaign in the general election of 1935, and it polled 20 times the vote the Communists received. Thereafter, the Communists sought alternately to ally themselves with or to destroy the CCF. Woodsworth was unalterably opposed to an alliance with the Communists, and ruthless in the measures he took to prevent them from subverting the CCF. Nevertheless, he led the battle in Parliament to repeal s. 98 and thereby to end the harassment of the Communists. Woodsworth said at the time that repeal of s. 98 "can only benefit our worst enemies," but, for him, for political freedom to be meaningful, there had to be freedom for all political parties.

Although the Communist party failed in electoral politics, it was a vital factor in the trade-union movement during the 1920s and 1930s. In 1924, Buck stood for the presidency of the Trades and Labour Congress of Canada (TLC), then the only national labour organization in the country, and he won 20% of the vote. After that, Communist strength in the TLC declined. Then, in 1930, the Communists founded the Workers' Unity League, consisting of unions in the mining, lumbering, clothing, and textile industries. However, in 1935, the Comintern, calling for a united front of the working class around the world to resist fascism, ordered the Workers' Unity League to disband and the unions affiliated with it to join the TLC. In the TLC these unions became a minority, and thus the influence the Communists had established among the League unions was dissipated. Not for the last time did the Communists, because of their political allegiance to Moscow, lose much of the influence they had painstakingly gained in the trade-union movement.

In 1935, industrial unions in the United States established the Congress of Industrial Organizations (CIO). Soon it had millions of members in the steel, automobile, rubber, smelting, and electrical industries. The TLC in Canada was not prepared to organize the workers in these industries, so Canadian workers sought assistance from the CIO. But the CIO was in no position to assist, its resources and manpower being committed to the struggle to expand union activity in mass-production industries in the United States. So the Communists in Canada, with their experience in the Workers' Unity League unions behind them, moved into the breach. As Tim Buck said, "Our Party had trained and developed a whole cadre of people who knew about unions and knew how to go about organizing them. And the Party members, even though they didn't work in the industry, would go out distributing leaflets, helping to organize the union." The party's trade-union department, headed by J. B. Salsberg, sent organizers into these industries throughout Canada. Professor Irving Abella, in *Nationalism, Communism, and Canadian Labour*, does not stint his acknowledgement of the Communists' role in the formation of the CIO unions in Canada during the late 1930s and early 1940s.

> ...there seems little doubt that the contribution of the Communists to the creation of the CIO in Canada was invaluable. They were activists in a period which cried for activity; they were energetic, zealous, and dedicated, in a period when organizing workers required these attributes. They helped build the CIO, and helped it grow until it was strong enough to do without them. They did the work that no one else was willing or able to do....
>
> The large CIO unions, Steel, Auto, Electric, Woodworkers, Mine-Mill and Textile, were organized at the beginning by Communists and were all, at one time or another in their history, dominated by the party....[The founders of these unions in Canada] were all active members or supporters of the party, as were a host of other nameless, young, dedicated organizers who spread out the length and breadth of Canada in the 1930s to bring unionism to the unorganized.

Not surprisingly, the CIO unions established in Ontario, where Canada's manufacturing industries were most heavily concentrated, were attacked as Communist. Industrialists and their principal ally in government, Premier Mitchell Hepburn of Ontario, were determined to stop industrial unionism, and they found it convenient to denounce the

CIO unions as Communist—and they were right in that many of the men and women engaged in organizing these unions were Communists. The CIO unions were also denounced as Communist in Quebec where Maurice Duplessis, a nationalist demagogue and fierce enemy of Communists, trade unions, and all left-wing movements, was elected premier in 1936.

When Mackenzie King was returned to office in 1935, he fulfilled an election promise and in 1936 repealed s. 98. The Communists quickly took advantage of this unaccustomed freedom to distribute leaflets in the Legislative Assembly in Quebec City, and just as quickly (1937) Duplessis passed "An Act to Protect the Province Against Communist Propaganda." This statute, which became known as the Padlock Act, made it illegal for any person who owned or occupied a house to use it or to allow any other person to use it to propagate Communism. It gave the attorney-general of the province the power to padlock any house and evict the occupants if he was satisfied that anyone was making use of it to propagate Communism. It also made illegal the publication or distribution of any newspaper, periodical, or pamphlet "propagating or tending to propagate Communism or Bolshevism."

The Padlock Act, Duplessis's version of s. 98, was designed to curtail freedom of speech and freedom of association. The Act had widespread support among the Roman Catholic clergy and the Quebec populace. There were few French Canadians in the Communist party, which was atheistic and insensitive to Quebec nationalism. The Padlock Act did not define Communism or Bolshevism, but Duplessis supplied his own definitions. He described the CCF as "a movement of Communist inspiration," and the CIO as "Communistic." Duplessis was unmoved by protests, and he used the Act again and again to suppress political dissent and to curb the trade-union movement. Twenty years were to pass before the question of the Act's constitutionality reached the Supreme Court of Canada.

It was in the trade-union movement, itself, however, that the Communist party was most embattled. While politicians and industrialists ranted about Communists, their dire warnings were largely based on fantasy. It was not the Hepburns and the Duplessises nor the RCMP who defeated Communism in Canada, it was the CCFers and their anti-Communist allies in the trade unions. The Communists' rivalry with the CCF in the electoral field was repeated in the unions. The CCFers confronted the Communists where they were most powerful and, in many cases, they succeeded in ousting them from the very unions they had organized in the first place.

In 1940, the CIO in Canada merged with the All-Canadian Congress of Labour to form the Canadian Congress of Labour (CCL). The Communists had dominated the CIO, but they were a minority in the new organization. At the founding convention of the CCL, delegates passed a resolution condemning Communism, along with Nazism and Fascism. Thereafter, CCF trade unionists were in the ascendant in the CCL, although the struggle between them and the Communists for control of the unions still led by the Communists continued for more than a decade. The Communists bitterly resisted losing power. They were determined to hold the ground they possessed and, where they could, to add to it. In 1943, a CCL commission reported on the methods the Communists had used to gain control of the Boilermakers' Union in Vancouver.

> By a process of strategy, relative terror, and with a definite organized campaign, these adventurers sought to discredit the builders of the union by slander and ridicule, and union meetings became a nightmare where order disappeared and disorder took its place. Political generals placed themselves strategically in the meetings of the unions, and on an organized basis were able to disorganize them to such an extent that the sincere trade unionists became disgusted and invariably left, thereby leaving the business of the union in the control of these political strategists.... Owing to this unhealthy, chaotic state of affairs, many members became thoroughly disgusted, and desisted from attending the meetings of the local union. This was responsible for the development of apathy among a large section of the

membership, and as time went on the attendance at meetings of the union decreased to such an extent that those whose main purpose was to secure political control were enabled to take virtual possession of it....

The most interested group represents what is commonly known as the Communist Party. It is well organized and has been successful in burrowing its way into the councils of the union and a number of positions of authority.... Many individuals from all parts of the country and from various industries who were regarded as outstanding Communists...have apparently concentrated their numbers and strategy inside practically all shipyard workers' unions in Vancouver, and in the Boilermakers' Union more than any other organization. Certain individuals who were regarded as members of their political organization left salaried positions with other unions to obtain employment in the shipyard, evidently for the purpose of securing membership in the Boilermakers' Union and concentrating their political forces in it.

Their first step seems to have been to obtain minor positions in the union and to use such positions to secure employment for more members of this Party in the shipyards. Their next step was to place their members in the more influential positions in the union, with the object of securing control of its treasury....

The evidence indicates that the next step in their program was designed to assure election of large delegations to conventions of the Canadian Congress of Labour, with the ultimate object of acquiring control of the Congress itself.

There is, of course, nothing uniquely Communist about such methods. They are meat and drink to persons of many parties and organizations who are determined to prevail on behalf of some great cause. Whatever their methods, the Communists' efforts were to a large extent nullified by their devotion to Moscow. Nothing better illustrates their thralldom to the official Soviet party line than their attitude towards the Second World War. Throughout the late 1930s, the Communist party of Canada had pursued an anti-fascist line, urging the Western democracies to join with the Soviet Union to stop Hitler. But when in August, 1939 Hitler signed a pact with Stalin, the Canadian Communists had to turn their arguments inside out. When war broke out in September, 1939, Tim Buck, bound by the party line, defended the Nazi-Soviet Pact. The party's slogan was, "Withdraw Canada from the Imperialist War." But when Hitler invaded the Soviet Union in June, 1941, the party line changed again. Now an imperialist war became a people's war; indeed after June 22, 1941, Buck and his fellow Communists castigated the CCL leadership for not cooperating fully in the Allied effort against Hitler. Given such wild fluctuations in policy, the standing of the Communist party among rank-and-file trade unionists was bound to suffer.

On November 16, 1939, the federal government passed an order-in-council to ban the Communist party. As a result, 110 Communists were interned, and Tim Buck fled to the United States. When Hitler invaded the Soviet Union in June, 1941, the Soviet Union became our ally. Buck gave himself up and a month, later, he and the interned Communists were released. The government did not, however, lift its ban on the party, so in 1943 the Communist party established "a new party of Communists," the Labour Progressive Party (LPP). The new party renounced the use of violence as a means of achieving a change of government in Canada.

The LPP, led by Buck, did better at the polls than it had as the Communist party. On August 9, 1943, an LPP candidate, Fred Rose, defeated David Lewis, the national secretary of the CCF, in a federal by-election in Montreal. For the first time, the party had elected one of its members to Parliament. But within two years, Rose, the instrument of the Communist party's most important electoral breakthrough, was to become the symbol of its greatest setback.

For a time, the LPP collaborated with the Liberals. When MacKenzie King called a by-election in Grey North for February 5, 1945, to obtain a seat in the House for his newly appointed minister of defence, General A. G. L. McNaughton, the Communists denounced the CCF because they ran a candidate against him. In the general election in June of that year, the LPP urged the re-election of the Liberals. There were even friendly meetings between prominent Liberals (including a member of King's cabinet) and LPPers—when under that same Liberal government the Communist party was still banned.

In the general election of August, 1945, the LPP contested 67 ridings. Fred Rose was re-elected, but he was still the only Communist to win a seat. Within a month of the election, on September 5, 1945, Igor Gouzenko, a cipher clerk at the Soviet Embassy in Ottawa, defected and sought asylum in Canada. Gouzenko brought with him evidence of a Soviet spy-ring in Canada. He also had evidence to show that Fred Rose and Sam Carr, a senior official of the LPP, had been working for the Soviet military attaché in Ottawa.

Mackenzie King learned of Gouzenko's defection on the morning of September 6. On September 11, King and members of his cabinet met a delegation of trade-union leaders, including C. S. Jackson, a Communist and founder of the United Electrical Workers in Canada. That evening, King wrote in his diary:

> This, however, I want to record. I am told that all who were present were communists. Jackson, who did much of the speaking, was interned for three years during the war. Also one or two others were interned. One had just been dismissed from a position in a Labour Union. All had very dour and bitter countenances. I thought Jackson very skillful. On the other hand, I did feel, by trying to be as sympathetic as possible, that they were a hard and dangerous lot. Their presence in Ottawa and the kind of demonstrations they had been making, along with the presence today of another group of the seaman's union, demanding the retention of war bonus in time of peace, with what I learn of other movements, makes clear that Canada is more or less honeycombed with communist leaders who have a close association with the movement in the U.S. and that all are very closely associated with the movement in Russia.

On October 6, 1945, the government passed a secret order-in-council under the National Emergency Transitional Powers Act (referred to in Chapter 4) which empowered the RCMP to detain persons suspected of communicating information to a foreign power and to interrogate them under conditions to be determined by the minister of justice. Mr. Justice Robert Taschereau and Mr. Justice Roy Kellock of the Supreme Court of Canada were appointed royal commissioners to take evidence from Gouzenko and to interrogate suspects. The Royal Commission on Espionage held hearings *in camera*, and persons brought before it for questioning had no right to bail or to counsel.

King was concerned by the fact that the suspects were detained incommunicado, and that the Royal Commission carried out its interrogations *in camera*. He was eager to revoke the secret order-in-council, as much from concern for his own reputation as in the interests of justice. On April 1, 1946, it was revoked and, on April 7, King noted in his diary,

> I continue to feel more and more put out at the course adopted by the espionage Commission in detaining the persons whom they had before them. It has done irreparable harm to the party and my own name will not escape responsibility. Only the documentary knowledge I had in advance and its bearing on the safety of the State could have excused the course taken. Even there I think the ends of justice would have been better served by risking more in the way of possible loss of conviction.

The Royal Commission on Espionage submitted its final report on July 15, 1946. As the result of its work, 18 persons were brought to trial, eight of whom were found guilty and served prison sentences and one of whom was fined; the rest were acquitted either in the first instance or on appeal. Rose had already been convicted (under the Official Secrets Act) on June 20, 1946, and he received a six-year sentence. Sam Carr disappeared after Gouzenko's disclosures. He was later arrested in New York, returned to Canada, tried, and sentenced to six years' imprisonment on April 8, 1949.

With the Gouzenko affair came the Cold War. The LPP (which began once again in 1960 to call itself the Communist party of Canada) went into a decline from which it has never recovered. Krushchev's revelations of Stalin's crimes, the Sino-Soviet split, the Soviet Union's own imperialist policies, and the repression of dissent in the Soviet Union and in eastern Europe have all led to a splitting off of opinion on the far left and have created a multitude of Marxist parties in Canada, which today compete with one another for a handful of votes.

The Cold War led to troubles not only for the Communists. The Gouzenko affair was the pretext for an onslaught against anyone in the public service, the universities, and the trade unions who had left-wing opinions. Fred Rose and others in high places had been found guilty of espionage—but did that mean that every Communist and former Communist was disloyal? Few paused to consider the question. John Grierson, chairman of the National Film Board, was forced to resign his office. Herbert Norman, Canada's ambassador to Egypt, was driven to suicide by United States Senator Joseph McCarthy's allegations. Let there be no mistake: some of these men were or had been Communists. But were they, therefore, fair game? Should they have been hounded from any post of responsibility, along with many who had never been connected with the Communist party, without knowing what accusations had been made against them, or by whom?

The trade-union movement had to confront these questions, and in many ways trade-union halls were the fiercest battleground of the Cold War. There the Communists, although vulnerable, were organized, still influential, and they held many important offices. But the Communist inroads could not be held. In 1949, the Trades and Labour Congress of Canada expelled the Communist-led Canadian Seamen's Union, and it passed a motion calling on all affiliated organizations to remove Communists from union office. The CCL mounted a similar anti-Communist drive, a far more serious affair than the TLC's because the Communists still exercised real influence in many of the unions affiliated to the CCL.

The leadership of the CCL challenged the Communists within the trade unions they controlled. The International Woodworkers of America and the United Auto Workers turned out their Communist leaders before the 1940s were over. Some unions, such as the Mine, Mill and Smelter Workers and the United Electrical Workers, could not be "liberated from within," as Professor Gad Horowitz delicately described the operation in *Canadian Labour in Politics*. The CCL tried to loosen the Communists' hold on these workers by expelling their unions. After the outbreak of the Korean War in July, 1950, the CCL adopted a constitutional amendment giving the executive council of the CCL authority to expel any union which was "following the principles and policies of the Communist Party." Sometimes expulsion didn't work, and workers continued to support their Communist leaders. Members stayed with the Mine, Mill and Smelter Workers' Union and refused to join the United Steel Workers of America, the CCL affiliate they were supposed to join. Nor would members of the United Electrical Workers' Union join the International Union of Electricians, another CCL affiliate, after their union had been expelled. Nevertheless, by 1951, there were no longer any large Communist-dominated or even Communist-influenced unions in the CCL. They all had been taken over or expelled.

The leadership of the CCL believed that it was in the best interests of the trade-union movement to exclude Communists from positions of power. So long as the Communists dominated a bloc of unions within the CCL, there would be divisions within the CCL not only with respect to foreign policy but also in matters related to domestic trade-union policy. Disputes over what Canada's response ought to be to Soviet activities abroad were one thing, but contradictory policies with regard to strikes, lockouts, legislation, and support for the CCF could only be an embarrassment to the CCL and injure the long-term interests of the workers. But the drive to eliminate Communist influence in the trade unions was greatly enhanced by the pathological anti-Communism that prevailed during the late 1940s and early 1950s. This infected public life and many of the professions, and manifested itself stridently in the trade-union movement. Of course, in the trade unions the Communists were not a chimera; there they held real power.

Lenin's published admonitions *On Trade Unions* left Canadian Communists no alternative except to regard trade unions as instruments for advancing the proletarian revolution under the close supervision of the party. That was the theory. It is a theory that is enforced in the Soviet Union. But in Canada, where the Communist party has no political power, the theory could not be implemented in its full rigour. The Communists held office in the unions they led because they had represented their members faithfully and well. The actions taken to oust them reflected this fact. Meetings were held, charges laid, and resolutions passed under the aegis of the CCL. Yet seldom were these proceedings based on the fact that the members of the unions concerned had chosen Communists to lead them. Charges against the Communists were based on pretexts, although everyone concerned, including the union members themselves, knew that what was involved was a mortal struggle between the CCL and the Communists. Whatever may be said of the methods the Communists had used to gain and retain control of these unions, they were no worse than the methods used to oust them. Professor Abella has criticized the expulsion of the Communist-dominated unions from the CCL:

> Unquestionably, very few members of the expelled unions were Communists. Their sole crime was simply their insistence on electing leaders to whom the Congress objected. Men such as Jackson, Harris, Murphy, and Pritchett were men whose contribution to the industrial labour movement in Canada cannot be denied or easily matched. That their membership was devoted to them despite their political ideas seems to indicate that the rank and file were satisfied with their leadership. If the opposition to these men in

their own unions could not defeat them democratically, then that was hardly sufficient reason for the Congress to help them with undemocratic procedures.

The CCL did not observe due process in its drive to expel the Communist-led unions, nor was due process observed by its member unions in the proceedings whereby they removed officers and expelled members thought to be Communists or fellow travellers. Granted that conflicts within the trade-union movement are not conducted according to Marquess of Queensbury rules, nevertheless, the robust traditions of trade-union democracy were diminished.

The Communists believe their cause is the workers' cause and that there is a complete identity of interest between the workers and the party. To be sure, the Communist objective is the erection of a system in which the trade-union movement is the creature of the party, and wholly subordinate to the party. The consternation of Soviet leaders over the rise of an independent trade-union movement in Poland may be cited as evidence of the rigidity with which Communist doctrine is sought to be enforced. (It may be cited, too, as evidence of the unwillingness of the Soviet rulers to allow any loosening of the bonds which hold their empire together.) But as for Communists in the trade-union movement in Canada, preoccupied with day-to-day trade-union business, in a free society, why should they be presumed not to be working in the best interests of their members? Their members are the best judges of whether or not the interests of the union are being subverted to the interests of the party. During the height of the Cold War in the 1950s, however, it was not conceded that Communists could be expected to use their offices in the trade-union movement loyally on behalf of their members. International unions, whose headquarters were in the United States, often dismissed local officers in Canada believed to be Communists, and sometimes even placed local unions under trusteeship because they had elected Communist leaders. In this way, many Communists were removed from union office. Together with many ordinary members, they were often also expelled from the union itself. So also were many CCF trade-union officials and members and even, in the drive to purge dissidents, some who belonged to the Liberal or Conservative parties or had no political affiliation at all. In some cases those expelled were denied the right to work at their trade.

Anti-Communism waned in the late 1950s. In 1956, the TLC and CCL came together to form the Canadian Labour Congress (CLC). By the end of the 1960s, the CLC and most of its affiliates had ceased to exclude Communists from office and had made peace with the Communist-led unions that had held out against the CCL. But not before the trade-union movement, in the spirit of Section 98, had acted to curtail freedom of speech and freedom of association.

The anti-Communist zeal evident in the trade-union movement during the 1950s was not overtly matched in Parliament. The federal government was not prepared to ban the LPP, as it had banned the Communist party in 1940. Of course, the Liberal government of the day understood exactly where the Communists' real influence lay and, after a series of strikes on the Great Lakes by the Communist-led Canadian Seamen's Union (CSU), the government decided to destroy the union. In 1950, a year after the CSU had been expelled from the TLC, the Canada Labour Relations Board decertified the CSU on the ground that it was Communist-dominated and, therefore, not a union under federal law. In perhaps the most cynical act of the St. Laurent government, Hal Banks, a gangster from the United States, was invited to reorganize the seamen on the Great Lakes. Banks was to be a continuing embarrassment to the St. Laurent government.

The provinces also took measures to combat Communism in the trade unions. The Labour Relations Board in Duplessis's Quebec decertified the Communist-dominated unions that the CCL had expelled. But when the Nova Scotia Labour Relations Board also tried to decertify a trade union because it was led by Communists, the ensuing litigation went all the way to the Supreme Court of Canada.

The case concerned the Maritime Workers Federation of Nova Scotia, the secretary-treasurer of which, J. K. Bell, was a member of the LPP. The provincial Labour Relations Board refused to certify the union as the bargaining agent for the employees of a firm called Smith and Rhulands Ltd., despite the fact that the union had signed up a majority of the firm's employees and had fulfilled all of the other requirements for certification. The Board considered that Bell, a Communist, was the dominating influence in the union and that, as a Communist, he was committed to the overthrow of democratic institutions and to the establishment in Canada of a dictatorship subservient to the Soviet Union. The Board therefore denied that this local union could be certified as the bargaining agent for the employees:

> The Communist party differs essentially from genuine Canadian political parties in that it uses positions of Trade Union leadership and influence as a means of furthering policies and aims dictated by a foreign Government. Statements and actions of Communists show that their policy is designed to weaken the economic and political structure of Canada as a means of ultimately destroying the established form of Government.
>
> Consequently to certify as bargaining agent a Union while its dominant leadership and direction is provided by a member of the Communist party would be incompatible with promotion of good-faith collective bargaining and would confer legal powers to affect vital interests of employees and employer upon persons who would inevitably use those powers primarily to advance Communist aims and policies rather than for the benefit of the employees.

The union took the Labour Relations Board to court and the Supreme Court of Nova Scotia held against the Board. Smith and Rhulands Ltd. then appealed to the Supreme Court of Canada, which, in a four to three decision, upheld the union's right to be certified.

Mr. Justice Ivan Rand, who had dissented from his colleagues in the Japanese-Canadians case in 1946 (see Chapter 4), spoke for the majority in this case. He asked whether or not the fact that the secretary-treasurer of the union was committed to Communist doctrine constituted grounds for the Board to deny the union members whom he represented the right to bargain collectively:

> No one can doubt the consequences of a successful propagation of such doctrines and the problem presented between toleration of those who hold them and restrictions that are repugnant to our political traditions is of a difficult nature. But there are certain facts which must be faced.
>
> There is no law in this country against holding such views nor of being a member of a group or party supporting them. This man is eligible for election or appointment to the highest political offices in the Province: on what ground can it be said that the Legislature of which he might be a member has empowered the Board, in effect, to exclude him from a Labour Union? Or to exclude a Labour Union from the benefits of the statute because it avails itself, in legitimate activities, of his abilities? If it should be shown that the Union is not intended to be an instrument of advantage and security to its members but one to destroy the very power from which it seeks privileges, a different situation is presented....The [Labour Relations Act] deals with the rights and interests of citizens of the Province generally, and, notwithstanding their private views on any subject, assumes them to be entitled to the freedoms of citizenship until it is shown that under the law they have forfeited them.

Such, in Rand's opinion, had not been shown. All that had been established was that a man who was a Communist had been elected to office by the members of his union. Rand continued,

> To treat that...as a ground for refusing certification is to evince a want of faith in the intelligence and loyalty of the membership of both the Local and the federation. The dangers from the propagation of the Communist dogmas lie essentially in the receptivity of the environment. The Canadian social order rests on the enlightened opinion and the reasonable satisfaction of the wants and desires of the people as a whole: but how can that state of things be

advanced by the action of a local tribunal otherwise than on the footing of trust and confidence in those with whose interests the tribunal deals? Employees of every rank and description throughout the Dominion furnish the substance of the national life and the security of the state itself resides in their solidarity as loyal subjects. To them, as to all citizens, we must look for the protection and defence of that security within the governmental structure, and in these days on them rests an immediate responsibility for keeping under scrutiny the motives and actions of their leaders. Those are the considerations that have shaped the legislative policy of this country to the present time and they underlie the statute before us.

Rand rejected the notion of guilt by association. There must, he said, be evidence.

I am unable to agree, then, that the Board has been empowered to act upon the view that official association with an individual holding political views considered to be dangerous by the Board proscribes a labour organization. Regardless of the strength and character of the influence of such a person, there must be some evidence that, with the acquiescence of the members, it has been directed to ends destructive of the legitimate purposes of the Union, before that association can justify the exclusion of employees from the rights and privileges of a statute designed primarily for their benefit.

This judgement, remarkable in the early 1950s, was delivered by a remarkable man. Ivan Rand was born in Moncton in 1884. After a BA at Mount Allison University, he studied law at Harvard. A man of firm convictions and deep scholarship, he was appointed to the Supreme Court of Canada in 1943. The judgements he wrote during his 16 years on the Supreme Court constitute the most profound contribution that any Canadian has made to the definition of a free society. He was, as Professor Edward McWhinney has said, "...The philosopher of Canadian constitutional law—the judge who thinks through the mass of disparate detail in the case law to the great, universal organizing principles in terms of which alone the scattered details have significance...."

The case of Smith and Rhulands Ltd. is a reminder that trade unionists who were members of the Communist party have, at the same time, been responsible for improving wages and working conditions in many industries. Very often as union officers they have received full support from trade unionists while at the same time they have received only a derisory number of votes from those same trade unionists in their campaigns for public office. Trade unionists have shown themselves to be quite capable of distinguishing between trade-union activity and other forms of political activity.

Of course, the Soviet Union has used spies and secret agents in the West, and there have been traitors in the Communist party of Canada, as the Gouzenko affair demonstrated. During the 1950s, there was ample reason for concern about Soviet espionage, but the torrent of public and, worse still, of clandestine allegations ruined many reputations, destroyed many careers, and left many workers without the right to work at their trade, often on the strength of nothing more than allegations of disloyalty to their country, their profession, or their union.

Not only working men were denied the right to follow their trade. Many others were denied admittance to the professions because of some association with Communism. Perhaps the best known case is that of Gordon Martin, a law graduate of the University of British Columbia, who applied for admission to the Bar of British Columbia. The province's Legal Professions Act requires any person called to the Bar to take an oath to oppose "all traitorous conspiracies." The Benchers of the Law Society of British Columbia, the governing body of the legal profession, refused to allow Martin to be called to the Bar because he was a member of the LPP and he had campaigned for public office as an LPP candidate. The Benchers asserted that Communist doctrine and practice represent a traitorous conspiracy. Martin insisted that he belonged to a legal political party. The Benchers maintained that,

> The fact that the Government because of reasons of policy has not proceeded against Communists is not to give the

so-called Labour Progressive Party any stamp of approval of legality. In the view of the Benchers the Labour Progressive Party is an association of those adhering to subversive Communist doctrines. It is not in the ordinary sense a political party at all, inasmuch as a Canadian political party must of its very nature owe allegiance to the Canadian democratic system. A party which adheres to revolutionary Marxism cannot owe allegiance to Canada and, therefore, is not a political party, in the sense that political parties are known in democratic countries.

The decision against Martin did not depend on his having said or done anything inimical to the welfare of Canada. To the Benchers, notwithstanding that Martin had stated that he was opposed to the use of violence, his association with the Communist party meant that he was not a person of good repute and not fit to be called to the Bar.

Martin took his case to the British Columbia Court of Appeal, which held it could not interfere with the Benchers' right to decide who may be called to the Bar. But the judges who sat in the case felt obliged to excoriate Communism. Mr. Justice C. H. O'Halloran warmly commended the attempts of trade unions and universities "to rid themselves of men and women professing Communist beliefs." He said, "It has come to be universally accepted in the Western nations that it is dangerous to our way of life to allow a known Communist or Communist sympathizer to remain in a position of trust or influence." Mr. Justice Norman Robertson concluded that the government of Canada would not knowingly employ a Communist. A Communist could not be a loyal Canadian citizen. Mr. Justice Sidney Smith held that joining the LPP was, of itself, an overt act. No Communist could be loyal to Canada; therefore, anyone who was a member of the party was unfit to be a lawyer. There need be no other evidence that the candidate had said or done anything to subvert Canadian institutions. The Martin case was not, regrettably, appealed to the Supreme Court of Canada.

Few persons would have argued with the judges in the

Martin case during the early 1950s. Yet Mr. Justice Rand, in the Smith and Rhulands Ltd. case, had rejected the idea that a person's membership in the LPP allowed the court to draw any conclusion it wished, founded on whatever sources it could call to mind, about that person's political beliefs and intentions. There must, he said, be evidence. It must be shown that a person seeks to subvert our institutions.

The early 1950s saw many attempts to curb political expression not only by Communists, but also by anyone else who questioned the foreign policy of the West. Anyone who did speak out was liable to be denounced as a Communist, a manifestation of the tendency, which may still be observed today, to reduce any complex issue to simplistic terms. Labels pasted on those on either side may stick, and no one will then notice what the combatants' beliefs really are. This may virtually disarm persons who have a right to be heard.

Patience and courage are required to reject insistent demands for repressive action against political dissenters. Sometimes our political leaders do not exhibit such courage, nor is it always to be found in judges. Whereas politicians may find plausible excuses for giving way, there can be none for judges. Yet, in the grip of a fervent patriotism, they sometimes slipped completely clear of the reins of judicial office.

But Mr. Justice Rand never lost his objectivity. This tall, austere man from the Maritimes was to write one more judgement dealing with both freedom of speech and the Communist party. In 1957, Duplessis's Padlock Act came before the Supreme Court of Canada in a test case, *Switzman vs. Elbling*. A tenant in Montreal sought a declaration that the attorney-general of Quebec had no right to padlock her house. The Quebec courts ruled against her. But the Supreme Court of Canada held that the Padlock Act was unconstitutional because it was "criminal law," and the provinces cannot enact legislation in relation to "criminal law." To that extent, the BNA Act imposed very real constraints on provincial power to limit free speech. Rand's judgement in this case is the clearest affirmation of freedom of speech that has ever been handed down from Canada's highest court. Counsel for the government of Quebec had argued that the Padlock Act was legislation related to civil rights within the province. To this assertion, Rand replied,

> The aim of the statute is, by means of penalties, to prevent what is considered a poisoning of men's minds, to shield the individual from exposure to dangerous ideas, to protect him, in short, from his own thinking propensities. There is nothing of civil rights in this; it is to curtail or proscribe those freedoms which the majority so far consider to be the condition of social cohesion and its ultimate stabilizing force.

"The object of the legislation," Rand pointed out, "is admittedly to prevent the propagation of communism and bolshevism, but it could just as properly have been the suppression of any other political, economic or social doctrine or theory...."

It was argued that the ban was a local matter and, therefore, that it came within provincial jurisdiction. There was said to be a special need to protect the intellectual and social life of Quebec against subversive doctrine, a need that did not exist in the English-speaking provinces. Quebec was too backward, its population too intellectually ill-equipped to deal with the theories of Marx and Lenin. This contention was wholly patronizing. The astonishing thing is that it could be advanced, in 1957, by the attorney-general of Quebec. Rand dealt with it:

> ...Canadian government is in substance the will of the majority expressed directly or indirectly through popular assemblies. This means ultimately government by the free public opinion of an open society, the effectiveness of which, as events have not infrequently demonstrated, is undoubted.
>
> But public opinion, in order to meet such a responsibility, demands the condition of a virtually unobstructed access to and diffusion of ideas. Parliamentary government postulates a capacity in men, acting freely and under self-

restraints, to govern themselves; and that advance is best served in the degree achieved of individual liberation from subjective as well as objective shackles. Under that government, the freedom of discussion in Canada, as a subject-matter of legislation, has a unity of interest and significance extending equally to every part of the Dominion. With such dimensions it is *ipso facto* excluded from head 16 as a local matter.

This constitutional fact is the political expression of the primary condition of social life, thought and its communication by language. Liberty in this is little less vital to man's mind and spirit than breathing is to his physical existence.

Le Devoir, commenting on the judgement in the Padlock Act case, asked "whether the defence of freedom must go so far as to defend and to respect an alleged right to propagate error." That, of course, is precisely the point. Without the right to propagate error, there cannot be true freedom of speech, no real exchange of ideas. It is not the function of the government to keep the citizen from falling into error; it is the function of the citizen to keep the government from falling into error. Those chosen to watch over national security, whether they be members of the RCMP or of a civilian agency, should bear this constantly in mind.

All that is left of the Communist party in Canada today is a hide-bound, Stalinist rump. Yet, the party's turbulent history has revealed the true limits of dissent in this country. The Communists, and their latter-day Marxist progeny, have pressed dissent to its farthest limits. But the history of the party has surely demonstrated that the Communists should be protected in their enjoyment of the same freedom of speech and of association as the majority of Canadians, who may abhor their ideas. Any restraint on their freedom is a restraint on the freedom of us all. To scan the public statements of radicals, to build up dossiers on them, to pass on information about what they have said or what someone thinks they may have said, to suggest that they are adherents of this group or that, to use such information to deny them employment, or advancement, or to deport them—all of these activities inhibit freedom of speech, and impose a check on freedom of association.

Such surveillance has not been limited to the Communist party. The McDonald Commission reported that in 1977 the RCMP had files on more than 800,000 Canadians. This is appalling. Mr. Justice McDonald and his colleagues have proposed that there be strict limitations on domestic spying. But the time will inevitably come when those responsible for national security will seek to extend their mandate. Such requests should, as the disclosures of the McDonald Commission show, be received with skepticism. In any free society there is a proliferation of groups, espousing any number of causes which challenge the assumptions by which we live. Their rhetoric is often fierce, though this usually indicates a sense of frustration as much as revolutionary intention. Yet it is enough to bring them within the purview of the government's well-meaning guardians of intellectual virtue. Robin Bourne, formerly assistant deputy minister in the solicitor-general's department, in charge of the security planning and analysis branch, asked about the RCMP's surveillance of radicals in the 1970s, said:

> We were a little naive in those days....These people wanted social change and that was a new thing, and when we investigated them they turned out to be Canadians just like us.

When measures are proposed to curb the rights of Communists or others who are said to seek the forcible overthrow of our government, the measures will be defended on the ground that they are "reasonable limits" that can be "demonstrably justified" under the Charter of Rights. It will be said that our institutions themselves must be preserved or all of the rights and freedoms in the Charter may be set at naught. But there are already federal laws against treason and sedition. Are other restraints needed? Another Section 98? Another Padlock Act? Surely not! If we have confidence in our institutions, then we must permit dissenters to argue that they should be set aside, or to insist upon the inevitability of their destruction, or even to assert that anyone who reflects upon the injustices they perpetuate will help to destroy them. But unless there is a clear and urgent call to others to overthrow these institutions by force (and the laws against treason and sedition are adequate to cope with this possibility), a free and democratic nation should not attempt to restrain dissent.

It comes down to a question of evidence or of labels. If we say that simply joining the Communist party is evidence of disloyalty to Canada, to the government, to a trade union, to a profession or to a university, then we shall be told that for any citizen to join any group labelled extremist (whether of the left or right) disqualifies him or her from the ordinary rights of citizenship. Furthermore, those whose names appear on such a group's list of members, or those who have joined them in a demonstration, or attended a meeting, or handed out leaflets, may be subject to the same label, to the same disqualifications, without any evidence of disloyalty and without due process. Men and women should be punished for what they do, not for what they think.

How can we criticize Soviet authorities for their refusal to allow dissent if we cannot abide dissent ourselves? It is not surprising that the leaders of the Communist party in the Soviet Union are unwilling to dismantle the structure of power in their own country and that they are loath to see it altered in Czechoslovakia, Poland, and the other states of Eastern Europe. Neither will they permit anyone to argue that it should be altered. If Canada, with a legacy of free institutions and free speech, cannot tolerate dissent, why should we expect the Soviet Union to tolerate it? There, a bureaucratic tyranny, the absence of due process for dissenters—indeed, the refusal to countenance dissent in any form—is deeply abhorrent to independent minds. To understand why the rights of Communists must be acknowledged here in Canada is to understand why we seek the rejection of Communism abroad. In the Soviet Union, because there is no right to propagate error, there can be no freedom of speech and no freedom of association for persons who oppose what the Soviet rulers' choose to call socialism.

In the contest between the western democracies and the Communist nations, we must be careful not to cede the very things that will make the outcome of this contest significant to all people. It is not a struggle between capitalism and Communism, the eighteenth and nineteenth-century offspring of the Industrial Revolution. Rather, the question is whether or not the regime of tolerance will prevail among men and women and among the nations. This regime represents the proudest achievement of the West, our claim to the verdict of history: it is an insistence upon the right of the individual to think as he will, to believe what he chooses, and to speak his own truth.

SIX

Jehovah's Witnesses: Church, State and Religious Dissent

WE ALL KNOW about Quebec's Quiet Revolution: after the death of Premier Maurice Duplessis in 1959, the Liberal government of Jean Lesage, elected in 1960, in six years transformed the social and institutional fabric of the province. Before the Quiet Revolution, the Roman Catholic Church had been the dominant institution in the life of the province. After the Quiet Revolution the government of Quebec had become its dominant institution. One had been the custodian of conservative values; the other was clearly an agent of change.

For two hundred years, from 1759 to 1959, the Catholic Church had stood guardian to the French-speaking population of Quebec. The Church spoke not only for the next world, it was intensely concerned with this one. It educated the youth of Quebec, and it inculcated in them the values of the family, the faith, and *la nation*. The Church preserved and nourished French culture in Canada. At the same time, it also endorsed the legitimacy of British rule and of the established economic order.

The Church in Quebec was a monolithic presence, and its influence extended into every aspect of Quebec life, including politics. Notwithstanding Laurier's triumph in 1896, the Church did not retire from the political battlefield. Politicians still sought to ally themselves with the Church, and Maurice Duplessis proved himself a master in the self-cast role of champion of the people's language, customs, and faith.

Of course the Church's influence among the people of

Quebec did not suddenly collapse with Duplessis's death. For a long time, its influence was being eroded by Quebec's transformation from an agricultural to an industrial economy, by the movement of population from rural areas to the cities, and by the expansion of the mass media. There were stirrings of protest against the reactionary tendencies of Quebec institutions but there had been no concerted challenge to the alliance between Duplessis and the Church until 1949. In that year, a violent strike at Asbestos brought intellectuals, journalists, and even some clergy to the side of the embattled workers. The strike, according to Marcel Rioux in *Quebec in Question*, "[made] possible the springtime of Quebec." During the decade that followed, intellectuals such as Pierre Trudeau, trade unionists such as Jean Marchand, and journalists such as Gérard Pelletier urged the adoption of liberal and democratic ideas. They denounced clerical domination of provincial life. At the same time, a small Protestant sect, the Witnesses of Jehovah, challenged the very doctrines of the Church. No one suggests that the struggle of the Witnesses was one of the hinges on which events turned in Quebec, but the clash between the Catholic Church and the Witnesses, the confrontation between Duplessis and Jehovah, heralded the arrival of secularism in Quebec. That clash laid bare competing ideas of freedom of speech and freedom of religion.

The Jehovah's Witnesses were unlikely protagonists of secularism, but they were determined to establish their right to seek converts from Catholicism in a province where none had successfully contested the Church's control of its flock. They went to the courts to establish the right to disseminate their religious literature in the streets of Quebec, and the principles they affirmed in this struggle redounded to the advantage of religious dissenters everywhere in Canada. And political dissenters, too, for to challenge the Church in Quebec during the Duplessis regime was a political act, since any limitation of the Church's authority might lessen Duplessis's authority.

Duplessis was a Quebec nationalist whose nationalism was founded on obscurantism and repression. Pierre Trudeau, always in those days the foe of nationalism, wrote in 1956 in *The Asbestos Strike*:

> ...our nationalism, to oppose a surrounding world that was English-speaking, Protestant, democratic, materialistic, commercial and later industrial, created a system of defence which put a premium on all the contrary forces: the French language, Catholicism, authoritarianism, idealism, rural life, and later the return to the land.

The people of Quebec, according to Trudeau, had no firm faith in democracy: rather they clung to traditional values, expelling persons who dissented from or doubted them. Of all Quebec's institutions, the most powerful in its resistance to change was the Roman Catholic Church.

During the Duplessis era, between 1936 and 1959, Church and State joined in persecuting Jehovah's Witnesses, who carried their struggle for freedom of speech and freedom of religion to the Supreme Court of Canada again and again. The Charter of Rights and Freedoms enshrines freedom of speech and of religion as inalienable rights of its citizens in every province. The fervour of this small Protestant sect had more than a little to do with establishing the intellectual foundations for the Charter.

The Jehovah's Witnesses have always been zealous to spread God's word. They believe they must share their faith with others, and that other faiths must be exposed as flawed or corrupt. Theirs is not an easy task, and the world has often been indifferent and sometimes hostile to them.

The Witnesses carry out God's work in the streets, and we are used to seeing them on the sidewalks of every city in Canada. Why will they not stay inside their meeting halls and practise their religion privately? Why must they make a public nuisance of themselves in the streets? They answer that their religion calls them to bear witness to their faith. One of the most important aspects of their faith is a duty to preach to others and convert them, a duty which takes the Witnesses to the streets, and from door to door with their journals, *Awake* and *The Watchtower*.

The Witnesses believe that the Roman Catholic Church has had a malign influence on the development of Christianity and on Christian doctrine. They believe that the rise of bishops and the clergy, the establishment of monastic orders, and the cult of saints and martyrs represent a falling away from true Christianity. The rise of Protestantism did not by itself correct these evils, so God chose a small group of Christians and commanded them to restore pure worship and to preach the good news of Christ's Kingdom.

Many of the Witnesses' beliefs have set them at odds not only with other churches but also with the secular state. Their first loyalty is to God. They do not acknowledge the claims of the state to their obedience. They oppose participation in politics and the celebration of national holidays, and they will not stand to attention for national anthems. They do not consider themselves bound by earthly laws when these laws conflict with their understanding of divine law. They are ardent students of the Bible, which they interpret strictly—so strictly that, on the strength of Biblical injunction, they oppose blood transfusions, even for their children in cases where, on medical grounds, the authorities have obtained court orders to apprehend them for purposes of administering transfusions. These controversies keep the Witnesses in the public eye.

Dr. Charles Russell, an itinerant preacher in Pennsylvania, founded the movement during the 1870s, and it spread to Canada late in the nineteenth century. The Witnesses' vigorous attacks on the Catholic Church and on the Protestant denominations did not go unnoticed, but not until the First World War did the Witnesses become the objects of intense anger and persecution. The Witnesses, then known as Canadian Bible Students, opposed war, believing that a Christian should not take up arms. They therefore objected to military service, even non-combatant military service.

Professor M. J. Penton, himself a Witness, has provided an authoritative account, in *Jehovah's Witnesses in Canada, Champions of Freedom of Speech and Religion*, of the persecution (for that is what it was) of the Witnesses during the First and Second World Wars and between the wars. When, in 1917, Canada introduced conscription into military service, the Witnesses insisted they were conscientious objectors. But it was held that the Witnesses did not constitute a religious denomination; so they had to either do military service or go to prison. Many of them chose to go to prison. As well as refusing to go to war themselves, the Witnesses condemned clergymen who supported the war. The clergy were irate. Canada's Chief Censor, Colonel Ernest Chambers, was eager to impose restrictions on what the Witnesses could say and what they could publish. During and immediately after the First World War, he was their primary antagonist in Canada.

The federal government, though it did not move against the Witnesses' publications until the final year of the war (1918), did so pursuant to authority conferred by a statute passed in 1914, during the first days of the war. This was, of course, the War Measures Act. It gave the federal government wide powers to curtail the liberty of and to dispose of the property of Canadians. When the federal government began to act against the Witnesses, it did so because the Russian Revolution, which brought Lenin and the Communists to power in that country in October, 1917, had alarmed all of the Western governments, and Canada, like the others, put out a dragnet that hauled in a multitude of dissidents. The Witnesses were to find that measures adopted to curtail the activities of Communists were used with equal zeal against them. In January, 1918, an order-in-council banned *The Bible Students' Monthly*, one of the Witnesses' publications, on the ground that it was calculated to discourage enlistment. On July 18, 1918, the government banned all of the Witnesses' publications. The police made seizures of this literature: many Witnesses were charged and some were sent to prison. Colonel Chambers complained to the minister of justice that the courts were too lenient:

> Many of these individuals are peaceable people leading clean lives and with generally good reputations for honesty etc. in the community in which they live. They are decided fanatics however and persist in circulating pronouncedly pacifist, socialist and anti-war literature.

Even after the war was over, the police continued to arrest Witnesses and to seize their literature. And Colonel Chambers continued to issue warnings about the Witnesses. On December 31, 1919, he warned the deputy minister of justice that,

> The publications of the International Bible Students Association included most dangerous and pernicious, pacifist and distinct pro-enemy propaganda all the more vicious because insidious and disguised under the form of religious cant.

Chambers did not prevail, however. The federal government lifted its ban on the Witnesses' literature on January 1, 1920, and the Witnesses were free to proselytize once more. During the 1920s, they bought five radio stations across Canada. But they soon lost their licences to broadcast, without a hearing and on grounds that should have called for full debate. Though one of the Witnesses' stations, CHUC in Saskatoon, allowed the Ku Klux Klan to broadcast, it was a speech by Judge Joseph Rutherford, Russell's successor as chief spokesman for the Witnesses, at a convention in Toronto in July, 1927, and broadcast over the Witnesses' stations, that was the immediate cause of official refusal to renew their licences. Rutherford's speech seemed calculated to arouse the potentates of Church and State, not to mention the "money power."

> The masses of the people are entitled to self-government exercised by the people for the general welfare of all; but instead of enjoying such rights a small minority rules; that the money power of the world has been concentrated into the hands of a few men called high financiers, and these in turn have corrupted the men who make and execute the laws of the nations, and the faithless clergy have voluntarily

joined forces with the high financiers and professional politicians, and that the said unholy alliance constitutes the governing powers that rule the people.

Lucien Cardin, minister of the federal department of marine and fisheries, was responsible for the licensing of radio stations. In March, 1928, he refused to renew the licences of the Witnesses' stations in Vancouver, Edmonton, and Toronto. There had been, he told the House, many complaints that,

> ...the propaganda carried on under the name of Bible talks is said to be unpatriotic and abusive of all our churches. Evidence would appear to show that the tone of the preaching seems to be that all organized churches are corrupt and in alliance with unrighteous forces, that the entire system of society is wrong and that all governments are to be condemned.

This assessment of the Witnesses' broadcasts was fair enough, but was it sufficient cause for refusing to renew their licences? The question does not seem to have been raised in the House.

After losing their broadcasting licences, the Witnesses demonstrated for the first time their astonishing capacity to obtain signatures on petitions. They got up a petition for the renewal of their licences signed by 458,026 people. Their licences were not renewed. The Witnesses, however, continued to broadcast. Buying time on commercial radio stations, they carried on their attacks on both Catholics and Protestants, earning the detestation of the clergy throughout Canada. In 1932, R. B. Bennett's Conservative government established the Canadian Radio Commission, and it took over the licensing of radio stations. On January 18, 1933, the commission sent a directive to radio stations throughout Canada to advise that the speeches of "one Judge Rutherford, foreign anti-social agitator," should not be broadcast without prior submission to the commission for approval. *The Golden Age*, a publication of the Witnesses in the United States, described the chairman of the commission as "a thief, a liar, a Judas and a polecat, and therefore fit only to associate with the clergy." The Witnesses in Canada sent another petition, this one with 406,270 signatures, to Parliament. But they stayed off the air.

In that same year, 1933, the Witnesses turned their attention to Quebec. The Witnesses were the first non-Catholic denomination to seek converts among the Roman Catholic population of Quebec. Their brochures were anti-clerical and anti-Catholic. As a result, Witnesses were charged with a variety of offences, such as violating the Lord's Day Act, disturbing the peace, peddling without a licence, and even with sedition. Many were convicted; some were fined, and some were imprisoned.

The Witnesses were not daunted. They continued with their campaign, although they won few converts, for Quebec was always stony ground for them. Then, in 1936, Maurice Duplessis came to power in Quebec. He stepped up the campaign against the Witnesses, using not only existing laws but also his new Padlock Act against them, for the legislative net that statute provided was wide enough to catch a Witness as easily as a Communist.

Duplessis was defeated in 1939. But the Witnesses' respite was brief, for later that year the Second World War began and, on September 9, the federal government invoked the War Measures Act. On July 4, 1940, the federal government banned the Canadian Watch Tower Bible and Tract Society (the legal entity which owned the Witnesses' meeting halls and arranged for the printing of their literature). It became an offence to belong to the Society, and all the organization's property was placed in the hands of the Custodian of Enemy Property. The police confiscated the Witnesses' literature, seized the property of the Watch Tower Society, shut up the Witnesses' meeting halls, and prosecuted the Witnesses for being in possession of or for distributing banned literature. The Witnesses' real crime was that they opposed war, and said so. Mackenzie King said of the Witnesses,

> The literature of Jehovah's Witnesses discloses, in effect, that man-made authority or law should not be recognized

if it conflicts with the Jehovah's Witnesses' interpretation of the Bible; that they refuse to salute the flag of any nation or to hail any man; and, that they oppose war. The general effect of this literature is, amongst other things, to under-mine the ordinary responsibility of citizens, particularly in time of war.

Of course, few persons regarded the Witnesses as a serious threat to the war effort. Moreover, there was no Colonel Chambers to insist on a suitably rigorous attitude toward them. Indeed, they had defenders in Parliament, including a Conservative backbencher named John Diefenbaker. Yet it is notable how harshly the Witnesses were treated by the federal government during the Second World War. On July 23, 1942, a select committee of the House recommended lifting the ban on Witnesses and Communists, but the minister of justice, Louis St. Laurent, refused, largely because the Catholic hierarchy were opposed. According to Professor Penton, there were only 7,007 Witnesses in Canada in 1941, and some 500 of them were arrested while the group was under ban. John Diefenbaker, when he wrote his memoirs, said that the "treatment of the Jehovah's Witnesses during the war can never be justified." It was only after the Witnesses presented another petition, this one with 223,448 signatures, to Parliament, that, on June 13, 1944, the government finally lifted its ban on the Watch Tower Society.

With the end of the war, the Witnesses were again free to seek converts. In the English-speaking provinces, they met little opposition. But the Witnesses were now more determined than ever to expose the iniquities, especially in Quebec, of the Roman Catholic Church, which they considered had instigated the persecution they had suffered during the war. They believed that St. Laurent, and King's other ministers from Quebec, had been nothing more than the instruments of Roman policy.

The Witnesses returned to the streets of Quebec. There was a virulently anti-Catholic strain in their literature, and their publications contained bitter accusations against the

Catholic Church, its bishops, its priests and its schools. Cardinal Rodrigue Villeneuve and his clergy denounced the Witnesses as heretics and Communists. Homes were entered without warrants, peaceful meetings were broken up, Bibles seized, and hundreds of Witnesses charged with sedition. Irate mobs of Catholics dispersed meetings of Witnesses. The Church, which had not hesitated to try to impose its will on Laurier, was not about to allow a small but noisy Protestant sect to vilify its faith and works within its North American stronghold.

For many generations, the Roman Catholic Church in Quebec had successfully worked with the government, the schools and the courts to enforce a regime of values and attitudes that upheld the power of the Church and that encouraged the people of Quebec to vote only for politicians who defended the existing political, social, and economic order. The preservation of a religious and linguistic exclusiveness, which was essential for the protection of French-Canadian minorities in the English-speaking provinces, was enforced by Church and State in Quebec for quite a different purpose: in Quebec, this exclusiveness preserved the established order.

But even the most venerable institutions change. Today, the Catholic Church throughout the world has become a powerful champion of human rights and of the redistribution of wealth. In 1946, however, the Church in Quebec was in no mood to abide criticism or dissent. Duplessis, back in office, once more undertook to suppress the Jehovah's Witnesses, and the police made many arrests. In November, 1946, with 800 Witnesses facing trial, the Witnesses distributed a pamphlet, in both English and French, entitled, "Quebec's burning hate for God and Christ and freedom is the shame of all Canada." This pamphlet, calculated to incense any Catholic, was addressed to the people of Quebec as a reply to the Catholic mobs that had broken up Witnesses' meetings earlier that year.

Did the parish priests that have stood by and approvingly witnessed such outrages show regard or disregard for

Christian principles? And what about Quebec's law-making bodies that frame mischief by law to "get" those not favoured by the ruling elements? And her police forces that allow mobsters to riot unchecked while they arrest the Christian victims, sometimes for no more than distributing Bibles or leaflets with Bible quotations....

And what of her judges that impose heavy fines and prison sentences against them and heap abusive language upon them, and deliberately follow a malicious policy of again and again postponing cases to tie up tens of thousands of dollars in exorbitant bails and keep hundreds of cases pending?...

In a torrential downpour all the foregoing violence and injuries rain down daily upon Jehovah's Witnesses in Quebec province....

Such deeds are the outgrowth of burning hate, and cause the finger of shame to point to Canada....

Not satisfied with throwing tomatoes and potatoes and rocks, this time the Catholic hoodlums added to the bombardment cucumbers, rotten eggs and human excrement!...

All well informed persons in Canada grant that Quebec province with its 86-percent Catholic population is under church-and-state rule. In the Quebec Legislature the crucifix is placed above the Speaker's chair, and in the Quebec Parliament Buildings alongside the throne of the Lieutenant-Governor of Quebec is installed a throne for the cardinal....

All the facts unite to thunderously declare that the force behind Quebec's suicidal hate is priest domination. Thousands of Quebec Catholics are so blinded by the priests that they think they serve God's cause in mobbing Jehovah's Witnesses....

Quebec Catholics will show love for God and Christ and freedom not only by words but also by righteous deeds. They will join with the many thousands of other Quebec people, Catholic and Protestant and non-religious that have vigorously protested the wicked treatment meted out to Jehovah's witnesses in that benighted, priest-ridden province.

Quebec, Jehovah's witnesses are telling all Canada of the shame you have brought on the nation by your evil deeds.

In English, French and Ukrainian languages this leaflet is broadcasting your delinquency to the nation. You claim to serve God; you claim to be for freedom. Yet if freedom is exercised by those who disagree with you, you crush freedom by mob rule and gestapo tactics....

Quebec, you have yielded yourself as an obedient servant of religious priests, and you have brought forth bumper crops of evil fruits.

Duplessis described the pamphlet as "intolerable and seditious," and more Witnesses were arrested. In taking these measures, Duplessis was supported by the French-Canadian press, the Roman Catholic hierarchy, and the people of Quebec. The Witnesses, they agreed, had brought their troubles on themselves. Those who openly attack the faith of a righteous majority must expect to be punished for their insolence.

This way of looking at freedom of religion is, of course, at odds with the principles of democracy, an essential aspect of which is religious toleration. Reinhold Niebuhr, the Protestant theologian, has argued that the moral presuppositions that are the foundation of a society should never be withdrawn from scrutiny. Only with constant scrutiny can "the premature arrest of new vitalities in history" be prevented. A society that "exempts ultimate principles from criticism will find difficulty in dealing with the historical forces which have appropriated these truths as their special possession."

The Witnesses launched a nationwide campaign for the enactment of a Bill of Rights, and on June 9, 1947, they presented to Parliament their petition, with half a million names on it. On February 8, 1949, they presented to Parliament a second petition for a Bill of Rights, this one with 625,510 signatures on it. John Diefenbaker, their most prominent defender in Parliament during the Second World War, now made their cause his own, and he became the leading advocate of a Bill of Rights in Canadian politics. In 1960, when he was prime minister, he proudly introduced The Canadian Bill of Rights, a precursor of the Charter of Rights and Freedoms.

Many of the Witnesses that the Quebec police arrested in 1946 were charged with distributing literature without a licence, but the police laid more serious charges, also. Aimé Boucher, a farmer who had distributed "Quebec's burning hate," was indicted for sedition. The Criminal Code provides that it is sedition to publish or to circulate any document that advocates the use of force as a means of accomplishing a change in government. The key issue is seditious intent. Not every man with a seditious intent may be heard to urge, in explicit language, that the populace ought to take up arms at once to overthrow the government. The courts have always held that creating discontent or disaffection among the citizenry and promoting feelings of hatred or ill-will between different classes may be indicative of a seditious intent. But Section 138A of the Criminal Code provided (Section 60 is the successor to Section 138A in today's Code) that it is not sedition to point out errors or defects in government, or to point out aspects of the law, with a view to changing them, that are themselves producing feelings of hatred or ill-will between different classes of citizens. Boucher relied on this section of the Code as his defence. The trial judge, however, virtually directed the jury to convict Boucher. He did not tell the jury they could decide for themselves whether or not Boucher had acted in good faith under s. 138A. Not surprisingly, the jury convicted Boucher. The Quebec Court of Appeal denied his appeal.

Boucher's appeal to the Supreme Court of Canada was the first of the Witnesses' appeals to reach it, and his appeal was heard just after the abolition in 1949 of appeals to the Privy Council in Britain. The Supreme Court of Canada was now the final court of appeal for Canada. Its first decade as Canada's court of last resort was its greatest. During the 1950s no other tribunal in the English-speaking world showed as ardent a concern for fundamental freedoms, and the most powerful judgements emanating from the court were those of Mr. Justice Ivan Rand. He was profound, learned, eloquent, and he was unyielding in his devotion to civil liberties.

The decisions of the Supreme Court during the 1950s are little known, except to lawyers, and they are not well enough known even to them. The legal profession took no great interest in these important cases, the judgements were hardly discussed in law schools, and neither the media nor the public comprehended their significance. But they provide for us today uniquely Canadian insights into questions of freedom of speech and freedom of religion, and flesh out the bare bones of the guarantees of the Charter.

Boucher's appeal squarely placed the issue of the nature and scope of sedition before the Supreme Court. Rand's judgement traced the history of laws against sedition in England and in Canada, then he turned to the pamphlet itself:

> The incidents, as described, are of peaceable Canadians who seem not to be lacking in meekness, but who, for distributing, apparently without permits, Bibles and tracts on Christian doctrine; for conducting religious services in private homes or on private lands in Christian fellowship; for holding public lecture meetings to teach religious truth as they believe it of the Christian religion; who, for this exercise of what has been taken for granted to be the unchallengeable rights of Canadians, have been assaulted and beaten and their Bibles and publications torn up and destroyed, by individuals and by mobs; who have had their homes invaded and their property taken; and in hundreds have been charged with public offences and held to exorbitant bail. The police are declared to have exhibited an attitude of animosity toward them and to have treated them as criminals in provoking by their action of Christian profession and teaching the violence to which they have been subjected; and public officials and members of the Roman Catholic clergy are said not only to have witnessed these outrages but to have been privy to some of the prosecutions. The document charged that the Roman Catholic Church in Quebec was in some objectionable relation to the administration of justice and that the force behind the prosecutions was that of the priests of that Church.

Of Aimé Boucher, Rand wrote,

> The conduct of the accused appears to have been unex-
> ceptionable; so far as disclosed, he is an exemplary citizen
> who is at least sympathetic to doctrines of the Christian
> religion which are evidently different from either the Prot-
> estant or the Roman Catholic versions: but the foundation
> in all is the same, Christ and his relation to God and hu-
> manity.

Should the Court regard this pamphlet as seditious? There
could be no doubt that the Catholic population of Quebec
deeply resented the allegations it contained, and the prosecution had argued that its circulation was calculated to
create discontent among the people of Quebec and ill will
between different classes of citizens. Rand rejected this
argument. Merely tending to create discontent or disaffection or ill will among the population was not enough
to make the pamphlet seditious. There must, in addition,
be an intention to incite the people to violence.

> Freedom in thought and speech and disagreement in ideas
> and beliefs, on every conceivable subject, are of the essence
> of our life. The clash of critical discussion on political, social
> and religious subjects has too deeply become the stuff of
> daily experience to suggest that mere ill will as a product
> of controversy can strike down the latter with
> illegality....Controversial fury is aroused constantly by dif-
> ferences in abstract conceptions; heresy in some fields is
> again a mortal sin; there can be fanatical puritanism in ideas
> as well as in morals; but our compact of free society accepts
> and absorbs these differences and they are exercised at
> large within the framework of freedom and order on broader
> and deeper uniformities as bases of social stability. Similarly
> in discontent, disaffection and hostility: as subjective in-
> cidents of controversy, they and the ideas which arouse
> them are part of our living which ultimately serve us in
> stimulation, in the clarification of thought and, as we be-
> lieve, in the search for the constitution and truth of things
> generally.

The Supreme Court was unanimous in holding that
Boucher had not received a fair trial and that the trial judge

had not adequately summed up the law for the jury. Boucher's conviction could not, therefore, stand. Rand went on to ask, should Boucher stand trial again? Rand held that the Witnesses had acted in good faith and that, under s. 138A, Boucher should be acquitted.

> The writing was undoubtedly made under an aroused sense of wrong to the Witnesses; but it is beyond dispute that its end and object was the removal of what they considered iniquitous treatment. Here are conscientious professing followers of Christ who claim to have been denied the right to worship in their own homes and their own manner and to have been jailed for obeying the injunction to "teach all nations." They are said to have been called "a bunch of crazy nuts" by one of the magistrates. Whatever that means, it may from his standpoint be a correct description; I do not know; but it is not challenged that, as they allege, whatever they did was done peaceably, and, as they saw it, in the way of bringing the light and peace of the Christian religion to the souls of men and women. To say that is to say that their acts were lawful. Whether, in like circumstances, other groups of the Christian Church would show greater forbearance and earnestness in the appeal to Christian charity to have done with such abuses, may be doubtful. The Courts below have...lost sight of the fact that, expressive as it is of a deep indignation, its conclusion is an earnest petition to the public opinion of the province to extend to the Witnesses of Jehovah, as a minority, the protection of impartial laws.

The mere fact that the language may have been extravagant and that it aroused resentment did not make that language illegal, for even the intent to create hostility and ill will between different classes of citizens does not, of itself, constitute sedition. The Witnesses had had no intention of inciting violent opposition to lawful authority. A majority of the Supreme Court judges held that Boucher should be acquitted.

The Boucher case concerned freedom of speech as much as it concerned freedom of religion. Freedom of religion is not only freedom to worship, it is also freedom to practise the outward observances of religious faith—or of none. Persons who take their religion seriously may try, as the Jehovah's Witnesses do, to make converts on the streets; or they may demonstrate against policies of government they believe are contrary to Christian doctrine or biblical precept; or they may campaign at home and abroad for social justice, as believers in the social gospel do, for they do not think that prayer can be their only response to racism, starvation and oppression. All of these entail freedom of speech, freedom to disseminate literature, and freedom to campaign in the streets, in meeting halls, and on Parliament Hill. Without freedom of speech there cannot be freedom of religion.

Duplessis was still determined to remove the Witnesses from the streets of Quebec. If the laws against sedition were no longer available to him, there were still licensing by-laws. The police continued to charge Witnesses under them. One of the Witnesses, Laurier Saumur, challenged the province's power to confer on municipalities the right to pass by-laws that forbade the distribution of literature without a licence. At issue was the validity of a Quebec City by-law that prohibited distribution in the streets of any book, pamphlet, or tract without the permission of the city's chief of police. The Witnesses claimed that this by-law was an infringement on freedom of religious expression and argued that, because the province had no power to limit freedom of religion, it could not confer such a power on a municipality. The Quebec courts rejected this argument. Saumur appealed to the Supreme Court of Canada.

On October 6, 1953, the Supreme Court decided, five to four, in Saumur's favour, and seven of the nine judges wrote reasons for judgement. This surfeit of judicial writing cannot easily be summarized, but these judgements have ever since been a rich vein for lawyers seeking nuggets of judicial wisdom. As might have been expected, Rand's judgement carried many valuable nuggets. He saw that the Court had before it the same issue it had considered in the Boucher case: there can be no freedom of religion without freedom of speech. The by-law in question provided that the police had to approve what was written in a pamphlet before a licence could be issued for the pamphlet's distribution. Here was a plain case of prior restraint.

> What the practice under the by-law demonstrates is that the language comprehends the power of censorship. From its inception, printing has been recognized as an agency of tremendous possibilities, and virtually upon its introduction into western Europe it was brought under the control and licence of government. At that time, as now in despotisms, authority viewed with fear and wrath the uncensored printed word; it is and has been the *bête noire* of dogmatists in every field of thought; and the seat of its legislative control in this country becomes a matter of the highest moment.

Quebec argued that the British North America Act had given the provincial legislatures jurisdiction to pass laws related to civil rights within the province and matters of a local or private nature. Rand took the view that civil rights, in Canadian constitutional law, means private law, such as the right to enforce a contract, the right to sue in an automobile accident case, the right to sue for defamation, etc. He did not consider that civil rights included what Canadians regard as fundamental freedoms, such as freedom of speech, freedom of worship, and freedom of association. These rights, Rand said, belong to every Canadian, and no provincial legislature can take them away. Thus Rand regarded as "self-evident" the idea that legislation in relation to freedom of religion cannot be regarded as a local or private matter: "The dimensions of this interest are nationwide; it appertains to a boundless field of ideas, beliefs and faiths with the deepest roots and loyalties." This brought him back to freedom of speech, which, he said, was essential to the very idea of free institutions in a democratic society.

> Under [the] constitution, Government is by parliamentary institutions, including popular assemblies elected by the people at large in both Provinces and Dominion; Govern-

ment resting ultimately on public opinion reached by discussion and the interplay of ideas. If that discussion is placed under licence, its basic condition is destroyed: the Government, as licensor, becomes disjoined from the citizenry. The only security is steadily advancing enlightenment, for which the widest range of controversy is the *sine qua non*.

Since the 1950s, then, there have been solid legal grounds for saying that only Parliament can legislate to curtail the fundamental freedoms. In the Padlock Act case of 1957, freedom of speech was held to be beyond provincial jurisdiction. The cases of the Jehovah's Witnesses established that freedom of religion also lay beyond provincial jurisdiction. Only Parliament, in the exercise of its power to make criminal law, could pass laws in relation to the fundamental freedoms. Rand, however, did not stop there. It was not enough merely to say that the provinces could not legislate in relation to fundamental freedoms. He wished to state the issue affirmatively:

> ...freedom of speech, religion and the inviolability of the person, are original freedoms which are at once the necessary attributes and modes of self-expression of human beings and the primary conditions of their community life within a legal order.

In this, he foresaw the lineaments of the Charter of Rights, and he provided a firm philosophical basis for the idea that the fundamental freedoms lie beyond the reach of legislative authority, federal or provincial.

The series of cases in which the Jehovah's Witnesses challenged Duplessis's near-dictatorial authority reached its culmination in a suit brought against Duplessis himself. On December 4, 1946, in the month following the publication of "Quebec's burning hate," Duplessis, in his capacity as premier and attorney-general of Quebec, had the Quebec Liquor Commission cancel Frank Roncarelli's liquor licence. Why? Roncarelli, a Witness himself, had posted bail for hundreds of his fellow Witnesses. Duplessis told the press:

A certain Mr. Roncarelli had supplied bail for hundreds of Witnesses of Jehovah. The sympathy which this man has shown for the Witnesses in such an evident, repeated and audacious manner is a provocation to public order, to the administration of justice and is definitely contrary to the aims of justice. He does not act, in this case, as a person posting bail for another person, but as the mass supplier of bails, whose great number by itself is most reprehensible.

The Quebec Liquor Commission had not only cancelled Roncarelli's licence, it had disqualified Roncarelli from holding a licence to sell liquor "forever."

Roncarelli sued Duplessis for damages, claiming that his liquor licence had been cancelled illegally. Duplessis took the position that he had acted lawfully in his official capacity. The Superior Court of Quebec awarded Roncarelli $25,000 in damages, but the Quebec Court of Appeal reversed that judgement. Roncarelli took his case to the Supreme Court of Canada and, in the most famous judgement the Court has ever handed down, it restored the award of damages against Duplessis, holding, six to three, that Duplessis had acted in a private capacity, not in the exercise of any of his official powers. Duplessis had no authority as premier and no statutory mandate as attorney-general to see to the revocation of Roncarelli's liquor licence. He was, therefore, held liable to Roncarelli. The Court's judgement, although based on the Civil Code of Quebec, applies equally to the English-speaking provinces in which the common law obtains.

The Supreme Court's judgement in Roncarelli's case was handed down in 1959. The loss of Roncarelli's liquor licence had long since obliged him to close his restaurant, but the decision in the case is a powerful vindication of the rule of law and provides a definition of the appropriate limits of executive power. Rand's judgement is regarded as classic throughout the English-speaking world. Some lawyers (and even judges) have said that they find Rand's judgements difficult. True, they cannot be read swiftly, and certainly they require thought, but the truths they yield make a careful reading of them deeply worthwhile. Rand's judgements are the Canadian judiciary's greatest monument.

Duplessis had claimed that the Quebec Liquor Commission had a discretion to grant, renew, or cancel liquor licences. In prompting the commission to act, he was only urging it to do what it had the legal power to do. The commission could, at its own discretion, cancel any liquor licence. Surely, Duplessis claimed, he could not be sued for instructing the commission to do its job. Rand rejected this contention.

> In public regulation of this sort there is no such thing as absolute and untrammelled "discretion," that is, that action can be taken on any ground or for any reason that can be suggested to the mind of the administrator; no legislative Act can, without express language, be taken to contemplate an unlimited arbitrary power, exercisable for any purpose, however capricious or irrelevant, regardless of the nature or purpose of the statute. Fraud and corruption in the Commission may not be mentioned in such statutes but they are always implied as exceptions. "Discretion" necessarily implies good faith in discharging public duty; there is always a perspective within which a statute is intended to operate; and any clear departure from its lines or objects is just as objectionable as fraud or corruption. Could an applicant be refused a permit because he had been born in another Province, or because of the colour of his hair? The ordinary language of the Legislature cannot be so distorted.
>
> To deny or revoke a permit because a citizen exercises an unchallengeable right totally irrelevant to the sale of liquor in a restaurant is equally beyond the scope of the discretion conferred.

Rand described Roncarelli's disqualification "forever" as "virtually vocational outlawry."

Rand's judgement does not depend on a narrow interpretation of the statute; he looks instead to the foundation on which statutory bodies are erected. That foundation depends upon the rule of law. Roncarelli, he said, had suffered,

...a gross abuse of legal power expressly intended to punish
him for an act wholly irrelevant to the statute, a punishment
which inflicted on him, as it was intended to do, the destruction of his economic life as a restaurant keeper within
the province.... That . . . such a step and its consequences
are to be suffered by the victim without recourse or remedy,
that an administration according to law is to be superseded
by action dictated by and according to the arbitrary likes,
dislikes and irrelevant purposes of public officers acting
beyond their duty, would signalize the beginning of disintegration of the rule of law....

Roncarelli had a remedy in law, and the Supreme Court
reinstated the trial judge's award of damages.

The history of the Jehovah's Witnesses is relevant to
our own time. Whether or not the Witnesses' efforts brought
adherents to their cause, they established the right of minorities and dissenters to use the streets to propagate their
beliefs. The members of a free society must be able to use
the streets not only for passage but also for communication.
Public places—streets, sidewalks, squares, parks—are public
amenities, that ought to be open to the public for free
passage, recreation, and a variety of activities, including
political gatherings. Whether or not they shall be depends
on our view of fundamental freedoms. Are they basic to
our constitutional arrangements? Or are they merely a
sideline to the main purposes of legislative activity? Ivan
Rand's view held the field in Canadian law for 20 years.

But in 1978 the Supreme Court of Canada repudiated
Rand's view of the place of fundamental freedoms in Canadian constitutional law. In *Attorney-General of Quebec vs.
Dupond*, the Court, in a six to three decision, explicitly
rejected the idea that fundamental freedoms might constitute independent constitutional values. In 1969 the City
of Montreal had passed a by-law to give extraordinary
powers to the City's Executive Committee. The by-law
provided:

When there are reasonable grounds to believe that the holding of assemblies, parades or gatherings will cause tumult,

endanger safety, peace or public order or give rise to such acts, on report of the Directors of the Police Department and of the Law Department of the City that an exceptional situation warrants preventive measures to safeguard peace or public order, the Executive Committee may, by ordinance, take measures to prevent or suppress such danger by prohibiting for the period that it shall determine, at all times or at the hours it shall set, on all or part of the public domain of the City, the holding of any or all assemblies, parades or gatherings.

The police have ample powers, under the Criminal Code, to disperse unlawful assemblies. Nevertheless, the Executive Committee of the City Council, concerned that there had been a continuing series of demonstrations, and some violent behaviour, passed an ordinance prohibiting the "holding of any or all assemblies, parades or gatherings" on the public domain for 30 days. The question arose, could any municipality, pursuant to powers conferred by a province, pass such a by-law? The matter did not reach the Supreme Court until 1978.

When it did, Mr. Justice Jean Beetz, speaking for the majority, held that the by-law was designed to suppress conditions likely to favour the commission of crimes. In Canadian constitutional law this is quite different from legislating in relation to criminal law itself; it is within provincial competence since it may be said to be merely a local matter. Thus the by-law did not relate to criminal law, a federal matter, and was within provincial legislative competence. Chief Justice Bora Laskin spoke for the judges in the minority. He said that "the City of Montreal had enacted a mini-Criminal Code, dealing with apprehended breach of the peace, apprehended violence and the maintenance of public order." In his opinion, the by-law was "...so explicitly directed to breach of the peace and to the maintenance of public order as to fall squarely within exclusive federal authority in relation to criminal law." Referring to the fact that the ban applied to all assemblies, parades, and gatherings, he said:

Here, persons who might seek to associate or gather for innocent purposes are to be barred, not because of any problem as to whether certain public areas should be open at certain times or on certain days or occasions—all of which go to their ordinary regulation—but because of a desire to forestall the violent or the likely violent. This is the invocation of a doctrine which should alarm free citizens even if it were invoked and applied under the authority of the Parliament of Canada.

Mr. Justice Beetz explicitly rejected the argument that fundamental freedoms were distinct matters under Canadian constitutional law. He held that the City of Montreal, exercising powers conferred by the province, could impose restrictions on freedom of speech. Then, in a startling passage, he laid down the very narrowest definition of freedom of speech:

...Demonstrations are not a form of speech but of collective action. They are of the nature of a display of force rather than of that of an appeal to reason; their inarticulateness prevents them from becoming part of language and from reaching the level of discourse.

No doubt municipalities should have the power to grant or to withhold permits for parades, assemblies and demonstrations on public property. They must see that the streets are safe, available to all for free passage, and that public places are not given over exclusively to parades, assemblies and demonstrations. This does not, however, lead inevitably to the conclusion that municipalities should have the power to prohibit any gathering in any public place at any time or all the time, or that a province may confer such power. These observations of Beetz's constitute a repudiation of all that his great predecessor had sought to affirm twenty years before.

Mr. Justice Beetz' idea of freedom of speech is a truncated one. He severed, for constitutional purposes, some of the essential means of exercising freedom of speech: assemblies, parades, gatherings and demonstrations. Of course, parades and demonstrations are not, to many of us, agreeable ways of exercising freedom of speech and of the press. But Mr. Justice Beetz' characterization of demonstrations as "not a form of speech but of collective action" and as a display of force rather than an appeal to reason is unsound. A parade with placards is one thing. But speeches may be—and usually are—given at demonstrations. Leaflets are given out to passers-by. These are time-honoured forms of the exercise of freedom of speech in Canada. Assemblies, parades and demonstrations may be the only means available to those without easy access to the media or the means to advertise to bring their grievances to the attention of the public. Not every cause reaches the columns of the *Globe and Mail* or *Le Devoir*.

Freedom of speech should be available to persons who do not have ready access to the newspapers, radio, and television. Moreover, with the increasing concentration of the mass media in ever fewer hands, dissenters and dissent may not be adequately covered by them or, when they are, their causes may be excoriated or trivialized. Parades, assemblies and demonstrations are legitimate forms of the exercise of freedom of speech, and they are essential to an informed public, especially at times when the media publicize only one side of the question—as, for instance, when the press joined in the campaign against Japanese Canadians in 1942, or when the media became a *de facto* arm of the federal government's public relations department during the October Crisis of 1970.

The Charter of Rights guarantees freedom of conscience and religion, together with freedom of thought, belief, opinion, and expression, and freedom of peaceful assembly and freedom of association. The Charter is to be entrenched as the supreme law in Canada. Any law enacted by Parliament or the provinces that is inconsistent with the provisions of the Charter will be, to the extent of its inconsistency, without force and effect. Fundamental freedoms will be now beyond the reach of provincial (and federal) legislation. One of the happy results of the enactment of the Charter is that it will reverse the *Dupond* decision, and enshrine fundamental freedoms as independent constitutional values.

The man who did most to clarify Canadian thought about our fundamental freedoms was Mr. Justice Ivan Rand. While he may be a hero to many English-speaking Canadians, what should French-speaking Canadians think of him? Here was a series of "epoch-making decisions," as Chief Justice Jules Deschênes of the Quebec Superior Court has described them, a series of confrontations between the Supreme Court, a federal institution, and the province of Quebec. Federal power was used to strike down Quebec laws. Should Quebec not have the power to suppress religious utterances that are offensive to its Catholic majority? Should Quebec not have the power to limit the freedom of political dissenters? Some may argue that the provinces should have jurisdiction over the fundamental freedoms. No doubt, in matters of cultural and linguistic usage (subject to entrenchment of official languages and minority language educational rights), the province of Quebec is in a special position: there are reasons why Quebec should have jurisdiction over these matters, and no good reason why the other provinces should. But, in my opinion, Quebec ought to be in the same position as the other provinces with respect to fundamental freedoms. No province should have the power, nor should the federal government have the power, to take away fundamental freedoms of the citizen.

Did the confrontation between Duplessis and the Supreme Court weaken Confederation? Did it encourage separatist stirrings by limiting Quebec's legislative power? Perhaps, but I do not think it did. What would have been the consequences if the Supreme Court had failed to intervene? There would have been no protection for the rights of dissenters in Quebec. This would have diminished the prospect of release from a nearly dictatorial form of government for those seeking to liberalize Quebec life and institutions.

Professor Walter Tarnopolsky, Canada's leading scholar on civil liberties, has said:

The best testing of the standard of civil liberties in a society is the way that society treats its dissenters and minorities. Few dissenters, and no other religious minorities, have put Canada to the test quite so acutely in this century as have the Witnesses of Jehovah.

The Witnesses' clashes with authority provided the occasion for elaborating the constitutional values which undergird Canadian federalism. Freedom of speech and freedom of religion are fundamental aspects of Canadian democracy, and may be claimed by dissenters, whether or not their views affront the beliefs of the majority. No government may take away these rights, and even the highest officials may not abuse the power of their office to deprive dissenters of these rights.

SEVEN

Democracy and Terror: October, 1970

CANADIANS HAVE LONG thought of their country as the peaceable kingdom. We have never had a civil war; we have never been held in subjection by a brutal and lawless government; we are not afflicted by the random violence that disfigures political life in the United States.

The October Crisis of 1970 was, however, the end of Canadian innocence. The advent of terrorism in Quebec and the federal government's decision to treat it as incipient insurrection were an abrupt shock to Canadian complacency. Urban terrorists in Canada, like those in Latin America, were capable of kidnapping a foreign diplomat, of making off with a cabinet minister, and of murder. How should the government of the peaceable kingdom deal with such a crisis? What ought the attitude of its people to be?

The limits of political dissent had been rent by successive acts of violence. This was not a strike that had become a riot, not a demonstration that had turned ugly; it was, rather, the typical form of terrorist activity that afflicts modern democracy: imitative, isolated, and without popular support. Yet such protest may produce confusion in the state, and apprehension among the people. In such a crisis, governments may lose their nerve; and, in the war against terrorism, the fundamental freedoms of noncombatants are always at risk.

The October Crisis is now ten years and more behind us, but who can forget the high drama of that searing month: the kidnappings, the proclamation of the War Measures Act, the outlawing of the FLQ, the Canadian armed forces' occupation of Montreal and Quebec City, the arrest of hundreds of Quebecers, and the murder of

Pierre Laporte? The tension of those days gripped all Canada.

A decade is too little time to permit a completely dispassionate judgement of these events. But there can be no doubt that the crisis tested Canadian statesmen severely. Alarmed by the depredations of *Le front de libération du Québec* (FLQ), they took draconian measures to check what they said was an apprehended insurrection and, at the same time, to stifle dissent throughout Canada. They conferred extraordinary powers on the police. Hundreds of innocent persons were detained. This manifestation of an authoritarian impulse revealed much about the mind and character of our leaders. It also revealed much about ourselves. Many questions asked then still concern us today. Should the government have agreed to the FLQ's demands in order to secure the release of the captives? Was the government right to invoke the War Measures Act? Why did the police in Quebec arrest so many and charge so few? Why were Canadians loth to question the wisdom of the measures that were taken?

The FLQ had emerged in the 1960s, a turbulent decade in the province of Quebec. On March 8, 1963, Molotov cocktails had been thrown through the windows of three federal armouries in Montreal. Throughout the rest of the decade, bombings of federal armouries and Anglophone institutions in Quebec continued. Many persons were injured, and some were killed. Military equipment, dynamite, and ammunition were stolen. On February 13, 1968, a bomb planted by the FLQ at the Montreal Stock Exchange injured 27 persons. Then came more explosions during May and June, 1970.

Some of the persons responsible for these bombings had been arrested, convicted and sentenced to prison. The FLQ regarded them as political prisoners and proclaimed their intention of resorting to kidnapping and assassination to free them. In June, 1970, the Quebec provincial police discovered evidence of plots by the FLQ to kidnap the United States consul-general and the Israeli consul-general in Montreal.

On Monday morning, October 5, the FLQ kidnapped James Cross, the British trade commissioner in Montreal. Four men drove in a stolen taxi to Cross's house. They rang his doorbell, saying they had a birthday present for Cross, who had just passed his forty-ninth birthday. Once inside, one of them drew a revolver; the other produced a submachine gun. They took Cross captive, and drove off with him in the taxi; then they transferred him to another car, where they made Cross wear a gas mask that had the eyepieces painted so that he could not see where they were going. They then took him to a house where they were to keep him prisoner for the next 51 days.

At noon that day, the kidnappers telephoned a radio station and said to look for a message in a locker at the University of Quebec in Montreal. The message said that Cross was being held by the Liberation cell of the FLQ. It went on to set out the conditions for Cross's release: the FLQ manifesto had to be published in all newspapers and on French-language television; 23 "political prisoners" convicted of or facing trial for acts of terrorism must be freed and given safe passage to Algeria or Cuba; the federal government had to take back into its employ 450 truck drivers the post office had recently dismissed; half a million dollars worth of gold bullion was to be delivered to the FLQ; and the search for the kidnappers must be called off. The key demand was for the release of the "political prisoners."

For seven years, the FLQ had been engaged in acts of terror. The "political prisoners," whose freedom was demanded, had not been charged because they were dissenters; they had not been convicted because they opposed the established order in Quebec. All of them had been charged with or convicted of criminal offences of a nonpolitical character, not with sedition or conspiracy. There was no justification for calling them political prisoners, but the FLQ insisted on its demand for their release until the end.

The FLQ's demands could not be met. Any government that acquiesced in them would be renouncing its mandate to govern. Two governments were involved. The federal government was responsible for the welfare of Cross, a foreign diplomat. But Quebec was responsible for the administration of justice in the province. Some of the "political prisoners" were held in federal institutions, others were held in Quebec provincial institutions. Throughout the crisis, Ottawa had to confer with the government of Quebec, headed by Premier Robert Bourassa. On the night of October 9, after Ottawa and Quebec City had conferred, Mitchell Sharp, secretary of state for external affairs, told the House of Commons that the FLQ's demands were wholly unreasonable. Nevertheless, he hoped that some arrangement could be made for Cross's safe return and that the kidnappers would "find a way to establish communication to achieve this."

From the beginning, Prime Minister Trudeau asserted that there could be no compromise. But not everyone agreed with him. Claude Ryan, then publisher of *Le Devoir* and a figure of immense intellectual authority in Quebec, suggested that the government should be prepared to release some of the prisoners in question to save Cross's life. The federal government made one concession: the FLQ manifesto was read over the radio and television network of Radio Canada, the French-language service of the Canadian Broadcasting Corporation, on Thursday evening. The manifesto, addressed to the workers of Quebec, read in part:

The Front de Libération du Québec wants the total independence of Quebecers, united in a free society, purged forever of the clique of voracious sharks, the patronizing "big bosses" and their henchmen who have made Quebec their hunting preserve for "cheap labour" and "unscrupulous exploitation."

Workers of Quebec, start today to take back what is yours: take for yourselves what belongs to you. Only you know your factories, your machines, your hotels, your universities, your unions....

Make your own revolution in your area, in your places of work. And if you do not make it yourselves, other usurpers, technocrats and others will replace the iron fist of the cigar smokers which we know now, and all will be the same again. Only you are able to build a free society.

We must fight, not one by one, but together. We must fight until victory is ours with all the means at our disposal as did the patriots of 1837-38 (those whom your sacred Church excommunicated to sell out to the British interests)....

We are the workers of Quebec and we will go to the end. We want to replace the slave society with a free society, functioning by itself and for itself. A society open to the world.

Allowing the broadcast of this mélange was not the same thing as releasing the "political prisoners." The FLQ issued a communiqué on October 9 giving the authorities until 6 pm on October 10 to comply with its demands or Cross would be "executed." The FLQ and the nation waited for the authorities' next response. It came on October 10, half an hour before the deadline, when Jérome Choquette, Quebec minister of justice, made a speech on television in which he asked the kidnappers to release Cross. Choquette said the authorities would not release the "political prisoners," but he assured the kidnappers that the applications for parole of the prisoners already convicted would be considered "objectively" and that the cases still before the courts would be considered "with clemency." Choquette did, however, offer safe conduct out of Canada for the kidnappers themselves. Choquette's offer went beyond Trudeau's initial position of no compromise, but it went no distance toward meeting the FLQ's principal demand: the release of the "political prisoners." In fact, Choquette's statement, though it offered the kidnappers their freedom, was not likely to persuade them to yield up Cross. If they accepted Choquette's offer to leave the country, there was no prospect of the "political prisoners" leaving with them. The kidnappings would, therefore, have yielded no tangible results. Although the terrorists agreed to this proposal in the end, it was unrealistic to hope that they would accept such a proposal at this early stage.

Exchanges of imprisoned terrorists for captives had taken

place in other countries. But Ottawa and Quebec City held firm. The kidnapping of Pierre Laporte followed. But though this second kidnapping was a response by the FLQ to Choquette's refusal to release the "political prisoners," it was not an articulated response. Laporte was carried off by the Chenier cell of the FLQ, but this cell had no contact with the Liberation cell, which had kidnapped Cross. The Chenier cell, we now know, consisted in the first instance of the occupants of an automobile that was passing through the state of New York. They were two brothers, Jacques and Paul Rose, their mother, Rosa Rose, and a friend, Francis Simard. When they heard on a news broadcast that Cross had been kidnapped, they at once turned back to Canada, drawn by the crisis. Back in Montreal, they bought two rifles and a shotgun. They had already decided what they would do if Choquette rejected the FLQ's demand for the release of the "political prisoners." When, at 5:30 pm on Saturday, October 10, Choquette announced that no "political prisoners" would be released, the Rose brothers, Simard, and a friend, Bernard Lortie, set out for St. Lambert, a suburb of Montreal, to kidnap Pierre Laporte. About 6:00 pm, as Laporte left his house, two of them, armed and wearing ski masks, forced him into their car and drove away.

The kidnapping of Laporte, a powerful member of the Quebec cabinet, was quite a different matter from the kidnapping of Cross, a foreign diplomat. With this second kidnapping, a crisis which had seemed manageable became a crisis the consequences of which could not be foreseen. It might have been possible to resolve the Cross kidnapping in a calm and detached fashion, but the kidnapping of Laporte engaged the anguished attention of virtually every politician in Ottawa and Quebec City. Laporte's kidnapping affected them far more closely than had Cross's, and it threw into disarray the machinery of crisis management that Ottawa and Quebec City had established to deal with the Cross kidnapping. This time the two governments had to decide what to do with the life of one of their own at stake.

On Sunday night, Premier Bourassa received a letter in which Laporte, addressing him as "Mon cher Robert," urged him to release the "political prisoners":

> You have the power to dispose of my life. If it were only a question of that, and this sacrifice were to produce good results one could think of it, but we are facing a well-organized escalation which will only end with the release of the political prisoners. After me, there will be a third one, then a fourth, and a twentieth. If all political men are protected, they will strike elsewhere, in other classes of society.

There had already been two kidnappings. Did the FLQ have the capacity to strike again—and perhaps yet again—as Laporte in his message warned? Should the government yield? Or was it more important than ever to hold firm?

Bourassa replied that same night by a radio broadcast. The government of the province, he said, was prepared "to set up mechanisms that would guarantee, as Mr. Laporte says it will, that the release of political prisoners will surely result in the safe release of the hostages." Bourassa's statement was tantamount to a promise to release the prisoners that he had now called "political," and he may have been going further than the federal government was prepared to go. Because some of the prisoners were in federal institutions, both governments would have to be involved in any accord with the FLQ. However, if Bourassa had been able to arrange an exchange of prisoners, including those in federal custody, it would have required an extraordinary act of will by the federal government to refuse to implement it. Such a refusal would have deeply divided the two governments and, if either hostage were murdered, many would have held the federal government responsible. Bourassa's conciliatory broadcast represented the furthest point reached by either government in meeting the demands of the FLQ. Bourassa retreated from it almost at once.

In any event, Trudeau was uncompromising. On Tuesday, October 13, the CBC broadcast an interview with him, now famous, in which he declared that the federal government could never allow "a parallel power" to dictate to the duly elected government of Canada.

> I think [that] society must take every means at its disposal to defend itself against the emergence of a parallel power which defies the elected power in this country, and I think that goes to any distance. So long as there is a power in here which is challenging the elected representatives of the people, I think that power must be stopped and I think it's only...weak-kneed bleeding hearts who are afraid to take these measures.

Claude Ryan and René Lévesque, the leader of the Parti Québécois, gathered a group of prominent Quebecers, who issued a statement on Wednesday evening, October 14, calling upon Bourassa to free the "political prisoners" in exchange for Cross and Laporte. They claimed that the federal government's ascendancy over the provincial government and Trudeau's over Bourassa "risks reducing Quebec and its government to tragic impotence."

Everyone in Ottawa and Quebec City was deeply concerned by the rapid march of events. On Sunday, October 11, the *Front d'action politique* (FRAP), a group organized to oppose Montreal's Mayor Jean Drapeau in the forthcoming civic elections, had declared support for the FLQ's "objectives." It also declared that it could not always condemn those who resorted to violence against the established order. On Wednesday, October 14, the Montreal executive committee of the Confederation of National Trade Unions (CNTU) endorsed "without equivocation all the objectives of the FLQ manifesto." On the same day, Michel Chartrand, the chairman of the Montreal executive committee of the CNTU, and Robert Lemieux, a lawyer representing the FLQ, addressed a meeting of students at the University of Montreal. On the following day, Thursday, a thousand students voted to close the University of Montreal to support the release of the "political prisoners." Some 800 students at the University of Quebec at Montreal voted to go on strike. That evening, about 1,500 students marched to the Paul Sauvé Arena, where they heard a series of speeches by Pierre Vallières (author of *White Niggers of America* and regarded by many as the philosopher of the FLQ), Lemieux, Chartrand, and others.

Professor Denis Smith, in *Bleeding Hearts, Bleeding Country*, commented on the rising tension:

> ...to politicians who opposed any effective concession to the terrorists, but who were still temporizing, these contagious events could only signify a worrying disintegration of their political authority. From this perspective, it was natural that more and more desperate consideration would be given to the problem of how to reassert political authority.

Bourassa quickly abandoned the conciliatory line he had taken on Sunday night. On Wednesday, he asked that the Canadian armed forces be sent into the province of Quebec. The armed forces, which had already begun to guard prominent figures in Ottawa, now moved into Quebec to provide protection for public figures and public buildings in Quebec City and in Montreal.

On Thursday, October 15, at 9:00 pm, Bourassa broadcast an offer of safe passage out of Canada for the kidnappers of both Cross and Laporte, once they had released their captives, but he offered no other concessions. He said that he must have an answer to this offer by 3:00 am the next day. No one expected an answer, and none came. At 4:00 am on Friday, October 16, the federal government invoked the War Measures Act. At the same time, under the authority of the Act, it proclaimed the Public Order Regulations, 1970.

The federal government's official reason for invoking the War Measures Act rested on two letters to Prime Minister Trudeau, one written by Mayor Jean Drapeau of Montreal, the other by Premier Bourassa. Both letters were sent during the early hours of Friday, October 16, and both letters requested extraordinary measures. Bourassa's letter requested "...the authority to apprehend and keep in custody individuals who, the attorney-general of Quebec has valid reasons to believe, are determined to overthrow the government through violence and illegal means....We are facing a concerted effort to intimidate and overthrow the government and the democratic institutions of this province through planned and systematic illegal action, including insurrection."

Drapeau's letter was supported by a report written by Maurice St. Pierre, the director of the Montreal police department, in which it was alleged that the kidnappings,

> ...are the first stage of a seditious plan... leading directly to insurrection and the overthrow of the state.
>
> Under the circumstances, the investigations which must be carried out by police authorities must necessarily include all the activities of the various cells of this seditious organization and should not be restricted, if it is not to be doomed to failure, to a mere search for the individuals who have perpetrated the heinous kidnapping of the two (2) persons who are still being held.
>
> The slow pace of procedures and the restrictions resulting from the legal machinery and means at our disposal do not allow us to meet the situation.

Drapeau in his letter called for "the assistance of higher levels of government" against "the seditious plot and the apprehended insurrection in which the recent kidnappings were the first step."

One thing, at least, was clear. Additional powers were sought to cope with sedition and insurrection. No one claimed at the time or with any conviction thereafter that these powers were needed to track down the kidnappers. It was to meet the threat to institutions of government in Quebec that the War Measures Act was invoked. Indeed, without positing such a threat, the Act could not have been invoked.

Under the War Measures Act, the federal cabinet may assume extraordinary powers in time of "war, invasion or insurrection, real or apprehended." The Act was invoked in 1914, following its enactment during the First World War, and again, in 1939, at the outbreak of the Second

World War. In 1970, the federal government invoked the War Measures Act for the first time without the excuse of war. The proclamation of October 16 read:

> Whereas the War Measures Act provides that the issue of a proclamation under the authority of the Governor-in-Council shall be conclusive evidence that insurrection, real or apprehended, exists and has existed for any period of time therein stated and of its continuance, until by the issue of a further proclamation it is declared that the insurrection no longer exists.
>
> And whereas there is in contemporary Canadian society an element or group known as Le Front de Libération du Québec who advocate and resort to the use of force and the commission of criminal offences including murder, threat of murder and kidnapping as a means of or as an aid in accomplishing a governmental change within Canada and whose activities have given rise to a state of apprehended insurrection within the Province of Quebec.
>
> Now Know Ye that We, by and with the advice of our Privy Council for Canada, do by this Our Proclamation proclaim and declare that apprehended insurrection exists and has existed as and from the fifteenth day of October, one thousand nine hundred and seventy.

The War Measures Act gives the cabinet authority to pass whatever regulations it deems necessary for the "security, defence, peace, order and welfare of Canada," including such measures as censorship, arrest, detention, and deportation. The cabinet proceeded to do just that, approving the Public Order Regulations, 1970, at the same time that the War Measures Act was invoked.

The Public Order Regulations banned the FLQ. Section 3 of the Regulations provided that,

> The group of persons or association known as Le Front de Libération du Québec and any successor group or successor association of the said Le Front de Libération du Québec, or any group of persons or association that advocates the use of force or the commission of crime as a means of or an aid in accomplishing governmental change within Canada is declared to be an unlawful association.

The Regulations also provided that to be a member or an officer of the FLQ was an offence, and attendance at an FLQ meeting was *prima facie* evidence of membership. The owner, lessee, agent or superintendent of any premises who allowed them to be used for meetings of the FLQ was guilty of an offence.

A series of provisions conferred on the police enhanced powers of arrest. Under the Criminal Code, a police officer may, on reasonable and probable grounds, arrest a person he or she believes has committed or is about to commit an indictable offence. But, under the Regulations, a police officer was given the power to arrest anyone he or she had "reason to suspect" had committed or was about to commit a crime. Similarly, with regard to police powers of search and seizure. Ordinarily a police officer may enter premises and seize property only with a search warrant, which must be obtained from a judicial officer. The Public Order Regulations gave police officers the right to search and to seize whenever and wherever they had "reason to suspect," without their having to obtain a warrant from a judicial officer. Professor D.A. Schmeiser has said the Regulations had the effect of obviating the requirement that police officers act reasonably.

Another series of provisions abrogated due process of law, by limiting the citizen's right to *habeas corpus*, the right to bail, and the right to counsel. Under the Criminal Code, an arrested person must be brought before a justice of the peace within 24 hours, and the Crown must be ready at that time to prefer a charge. Under the new Regulations, the Crown did not have to charge an arrested person until seven days after his arrest, and the attorney-general could, before seven days passed, order the accused to be detained for a further 21 days. This power effectively disposed of the right of *habeas corpus* as we know it. A person arrested under the Criminal Code may apply to be released on bail. Under the Regulations, a prisoner could apply for bail only with the consent of the provincial attorney-general. The Regulations also permitted a prisoner to be held incommunicado, thereby denying him the right to counsel.

What, in the face of the War Measures Act and the Public Order Regulations, 1970, had become of The Canadian Bill of Rights? The Canadian Bill of Rights had been enacted in 1960 specifically to prohibit (among other things) arbitrary detention and denial of bail without just cause. These provisions had no application during the October Crisis because The Canadian Bill of Rights itself provides that it is to be inoperative in a case where the War Measures Act has been proclaimed.

On Saturday, October 17, the day after the War Measures Act had been invoked, Pierre Laporte was murdered. That evening, his body was found in an abandoned car at St. Hubert airport. James Cross was still in the hands of his captors.

The War Measures Act had been proclaimed to deal with the insurrection that was said to be imminent. The Act did not assist the police to find the kidnappers. The Act did give the police the power to intern, and this extraordinary power was used to arrest and detain hundreds of persons associated with a broad range of political dissent in the province of Quebec.

The Quebec provincial police began to take persons into custody at dawn on the morning that the federal government proclaimed the War Measures Act. Those arrested did not know of the proclamation. They were unaware that during the night their right to due process of law had been taken away while they slept. The War Measures proclamation declared that the activities of the FLQ had "given rise to a state of apprehended insurrection within Quebec." But the proclamation was not limited to Quebec: it applied throughout Canada. The same extraordinary powers were conferred on the police in every province, and the police of Halifax, Toronto, Vancouver and other cities made arrests.

On October 16, the prime minister addressed the nation on television. The government, Trudeau said, intended to "root out the cancer of an armed, revolutionary movement." Public support for the government's assumption of extraordinary powers was tremendous. Everyone seemed to be swept along by what was perceived to be the government's firmness in a confrontation with terrorists who sought the forcible overthrow of Canada's institutions.

Were the kidnappers trying to overthrow the government of Quebec? More to the point, was there a widespread conspiracy to overthrow the government of Quebec and, if so, did the conspirators have the means to attempt it? As for the kidnappers, so far as they had any conceptualized goals, no doubt they wished to secure the release of the "political prisoners" and to humiliate the government of Quebec. But did they have allies who were prepared to join with them to overthrow the government of the province? Was the cabinet's judgement sound? Was its fear of an insurrection reasonable? No one wanted such questions raised. Once the decision had been taken, there was every reason for members of the government to justify their action. No one, perhaps, went further than Jean Marchand, who declared,

> These people [the FLQ] have infiltrated every strategic place in the province of Quebec, every place where important decisions are taken....They are in a position to cause the Quebec and the Federal Governments, as well as the City of Montreal, irreparable harm, with the support of outside organizations.

Marchand never offered the slightest evidence to support this allegation.

Professor James Eayrs, who was writing a newspaper column in the Toronto *Star* at the time, tried to place the crisis in perspective. "Invoking the War Measures Act against the FLQ elevates a ragged platoon of terrorists to the status of belligerents against the realm of Canada—as if they were the Central Powers, the Axis Powers, the Communist powers." Eayrs was virtually alone in this judgement. Newspaper columnists and editorial writers throughout the nation supported the government's action. To question the propriety of invoking the War Measures Act was to side with the kidnappers.

Perhaps the most exaggerated reaction to the crisis came

in British Columbia. The provincial government there, carried along by the prevailing hysteria—indeed, swimming strongly with the current—passed an order-in-council on November 2, 1970, that declared "as public policy that no person teaching or instructing our youth in educational institutions receiving Government support shall continue in the employment of the educational institution if they advocate the policies of Le Front de Libération du Québec, or the overthrow of democratically elected governments by violent means." The language of this order-in-council illustrates the way the morbid excitement of a crisis can spread and lead to the abrogation of civil liberties, even in places far removed from the threat. For who could say what the policies of the FLQ were? Clearly, they opposed Anglophone domination of the Quebec economy. They wanted to achieve independence for Quebec. Surely teachers should have been allowed to discuss the crisis, and these goals of the FLQ—goals shared by many Quebecers—and revolutionary politics, without having to be fearful of being denounced as an ally of the FLQ? It is bad enough that the *Alliance des Professeurs de Montréal* felt obliged to warn its members that any attempt to discuss the FLQ's manifesto in relation to contemporary events might result in loss of employment. It is ludicrous that teachers in British Columbia should have found themselves in the same situation.

Was there any evidence at all that an insurrection in Quebec was imminent? Two men had been kidnapped—by two different groups who might or might not be closely linked. Public figures in Quebec, who had been making inflammatory speeches for years, were still making inflammatory speeches. There had been meetings. Students had publicly demonstrated their support for the FLQ, but it was not the first time that students in Quebec or elsewhere had supported radical or dubious causes. Did this kind of evidence justify a state of siege?

On October 23, Trudeau, in answer to questions, offered the House his justification for invoking the War Measures Act:

...The first fact was that there had been kidnappings of two very important people in Canada and that they were being held for ransom under threat of death. The second was that the government of the province of Quebec and the authorities of the City of Montreal asked the federal government to permit the use of exceptional measures because, in their own words, a state of apprehended insurrection existed. The third reason was our assessment of all the surrounding facts, which are known to the country by now —the state of confusion that existed in the province of Quebec in regard to these matters.

That was the evidence that the head of the government, in a considered answer, relied upon. Trudeau referred as well to the fact that "a great quantity of dynamite has been stolen in Quebec during the last year and not recovered, that there is a great quantity . . . of rifles and small arms that have disappeared." Trudeau cannot be accused of withholding evidence. "The facts that are known to the House," he said, "are the facts on which we acted and it is on that that we stand." The evidence that has come to light since 1970 supports Trudeau's contention that the House had all the information available to the government at the time. The disclosures made since 1970 about some of the activities of the RCMP, while disturbing, do not appear to have been known to the federal cabinet in 1970.

There had been an insurrection against the regime at Quebec City in the past—a real insurrection. In 1837, Louis-Joseph Papineau had inspired an armed uprising against the government of Lower Canada, and there were armed clashes between the rebels and British troops. At St. Charles and St. Eustache, the rebels had been defeated. There were many casualties. One of the rebels who was killed was Dr. Jean Chenier. Thousands were imprisoned. Martial law was declared. The rebellion was renewed in 1838, and crushed again. There were grounds for extraordinary measures then. But the FLQ, unlike Papineau, Chenier, and the rebels of 1837-38, had no organized popular following, no rational scheme for establishing a new order in Quebec, and no intention of engaging the Canadian armed forces or the police in open conflict.

There was no basis for claiming that an insurrection was imminent in 1970. Robert Stanfield, leader of the Conservative party during the October Crisis, supported the government then. But, in June, 1979, he wrote that events in Quebec at the time "did not amount to the apprehended insurrection against which the Federal Government was invoking the War Measures Act and the use of extraordinary powers." Few would argue with this verdict. Why, then, would anyone, considering the evidence, have reached any other conclusion in 1970?

Clearly, Trudeau and his colleagues felt that they had to do something. But when every allowance has been made for the difficulties they had in assessing what was really happening—given the two kidnappings, the fiery statements of Quebec radicals, and the personal dilemma the Laporte kidnapping presented for many of them—it is impossible to avoid the conclusion that, given "the state of confusion that existed in the province of Quebec," Trudeau and his colleagues decided to assert the federal power and authority in a definitive way. Terrorists and terrorism would not shake them. The strength of the state had to be demonstrated.

Pierre Laporte's death on the day following the proclamation of the War Measures Act greatly strengthened Trudeau's hand. The anger that Canadians felt at this murder constituted a moment of political exaltation for Trudeau, his apotheosis. But the mood could not last. As October passed, the siege mentality and the public's willingness to suspend judgement also began to pass. There were no further kidnappings, no further acts of violence. People began to realize that a firm stand against kidnappers was one thing; the proclamation of the War Measures Act was quite another. A few protests began to be heard. Some political commentators and editorial writers began to question whether or not the apprehended insurrection, if there had ever been one, could be said still to exist.

The difficulty the federal government had in persisting in its contention that an insurrection, imminent on October

16, was still about to occur began to be felt. On November 2, 1970, the federal government introduced in Parliament new legislation, the Public Order (Temporary Measures) Act, 1970. The new legislation, assented to on December 3, revoked the proclamation of the War Measures Act. But extraordinary measures were to remain in force. The preamble to the new legislation said that public order in Canada was still endangered by the FLQ. Under this new Act, a person arrested had to be brought before a justice within three days, rather than seven; and the attorney-general of a province could extend a period of arrest to a maximum of seven days, rather than 21. But even when a prisoner had appeared before a justice of the peace, the attorney-general's consent was still required for anyone thus detained to be released on bail. There was a special provision in the Act that it was to override the provisions of the Canadian Bill of Rights prohibiting arbitrary detention or imprisonment and denial of bail without just cause. (The new legislation expired on April 30, 1971, and with it the extraordinary measures called forth by the October Crisis lapsed.)

The extraordinary powers conferred on the police pursuant to the War Measures Act and the Public Order (Temporary Measures) Act did not assist in freeing James Cross or in tracking down Pierre Laporte's killers. Bernard Lortie, a member of the Chenier cell, was arrested on November 6. In December, the other members of that cell, Paul and Jacques Rose and Francis Simard, surrendered to the police in a basement outside Montreal. That same month, the government struck a deal with Cross's kidnappers, the members of the Liberation cell. Cross was released by his captors on December 4, the day after final passage of the Public Order (Temporary Measures) Act, in exchange for safe passage to Cuba.

Paul Rose was convicted and sentenced to life imprisonment for the murder of Pierre Laporte; so was Francis Simard; Bernard Lortie was convicted of kidnapping Pierre Laporte and sentenced to 20 years; Jacques Rose was convicted as an accessory in Laporte's kidnapping and was sentenced to eight years. Two of Cross's kidnappers, tired of exile in Cuba and then in France, returned to Canada in 1978 to plead guilty, and they were sentenced to two years' less a day imprisonment. Another returned in 1979 and was sentenced to three years. Still another returned in 1981. One remains in France.

The negotiations with the kidnappers and the proclamation of the War Measures Act should be examined separately. I think it is possible to pass judgement on each aspect of the crisis.

The acts of terrorists, dramatizing grievances that are shared by a class or even by a whole people, may achieve widespread sympathy. It cannot be doubted that in Quebec many who deplored the kidnappings nevertheless felt a kind of admiration for the audacity of the kidnappers and for their dedication, no matter how abhorrent the means they used, to the cause of Quebec independence.

But there are terrorists and terrorists. The FLQ were not guerillas forced to use violence against a regime that would not allow the expression of any form of dissent. Far from it. Just a few months earlier, the Parti Québécois, espousing Quebec independence, had elected seven members to the Quebec National Assembly. This was not a case where a desperate people, crushed by institutionalized violence, had no means of protest except terror. Terrorism in the liberal democracies cannot be made legitimate by arguments that, in other countries and under other regimes, may be persuasive. The means chosen by the FLQ were utterly disproportionate to the gravity of their cause. In such a case it is the terrorist, not the regime, who represents arbitrary force and wilful violence. To have released the "political prisoners," as the FLQ demanded, would have been wrong.

Where Trudeau and his advisors can be called to account is in the proclamation of the War Measures Act without sufficient cause, in the stringency of the measures taken under the authority of the Act, and in the perpetuation of those measures by the enactment of the Public Order (Temporary Measures) Act. On the strength of powers conferred by these measures, the police in Quebec detained hundreds of their fellow citizens who constituted no threat to the province or to Canada, who had not committed criminal acts of any kind, and who were not in any way connected with the FLQ. On proclamation of the War Measures Act on October 16, 1970, the Quebec provincial police and the Montreal city police arrested hundreds of persons; they were subjected to interrogation, many of their homes were searched, sometimes repeatedly. Four hundred and ninety-seven persons were arrested in Quebec. Of all those arrested, only 62 persons were ever charged. Of this number, only 18, less than one-third, were convicted. The ones who were convicted were, of course, primarily those responsible for the kidnappings and the murder of Pierre Laporte. Only two of these convictions were for offences under the Public Order Regulations and the Public Order Act. Two convictions out of nearly 500 arrests is not by any standards a great haul of insurrectionists. Over 450 persons were either never charged or were acquitted. The conclusion is inescapable that these arrests were made arbitrarily, and that the interrogation of all of these people did not reveal any evidence that an insurrection was imminent. The whole exercise reveals how unwise it is to have such extraordinary power easily available to any government.

In 1958, Trudeau had written in *Vrai*, a Quebec political journal:

> Tomorrow morning, preferably in the small hours, any one of you may be arrested....You find that bizarre? You think I am exaggerating? Far from it....We are indignant to think that in the days of absolute monarchy a *lettre de cachet* could send free men to penal servitude with no other form of trial. But does it appal us...that similar things continue to happen in the democratic society we live in?

What Trudeau had regarded as an outrage during the dark days of the Duplessis era had become, when he was prime minister in 1970, a state necessity.

The saddest aspect of this story was the indifference of the people of Canada to the arbitrary arrests of fellow citizens in the province of Quebec. Trudeau had also written in *Vrai* in 1958, "Few men are aroused by injustice when they are sure of not being its victims...when authority in any form bullies a man unfairly, all other men are guilty; for it is their tacit assent that allows authority to commit the abuse." That assent was forthcoming in October, 1970. Robert Stanfield, in the revised edition of *Rumours of War* (1978), described the indifference of the great public:

> The plain truth is that most Canadians did not care whether or not there really was an apprehended insurrection. They did not like what was going on in Quebec and they approved of their federal Government taking strong measures to deal with the situation; if the Government had no tools other than the War Measures Act, then by all means let the Government use it. To many if not most Canadians any questioning of the invocation of the Act was unpatriotic even before the murder of Pierre Laporte.
>
> What is most significant and revealing is not that the government of the day resorted to such a measure—another government might have done that, too—but that in a state of concern the public enthusiastically approved the measure, and since then has never wanted any accounting for either the claims of an apprehended insurrection or the behaviour of security and police forces towards the citizens whose basic legal rights were suspended.

Many politicians—together with other citizens—believe that, in a political crisis, the ordinary rules of debate must be suspended, and those who seek to take advantage of the right to criticize must be treated as if they wished to accomplish the destruction of the state. All doubts about the wisdom of government action must be vanquished if the enemies of the state are to be vanquished.

It is not, however, upon the assumption of extraordinary governmental powers that the safety of the state depends, but upon the conviction of the people that the right to dissent is essential to the life and health of the state. Firmness is better shown—and often greater courage is required to show firmness—in the defence of civil liberties, by reminding the electorate of the need to distinguish between sedition and dissent, and of the difference between criminal acts established by evidence and guilt by association.

The proclamation by Trudeau's government of the War Measures Act was an affirmation of the will to govern against an attempt by terrorists to prove that our institutions are impotent. The use of terrorism is lamentably widespread. By acts of terrorism, terrorists try to shake the will of those who govern—to make the state tremble. Against this threat, Trudeau affirmed the federal government's determination to deal decisively with subversive activities. But was it necessary to turn two kidnappings into a seditious conspiracy, a conspiracy of proportions so threatening that it could be checked only by the abrogation of civil liberties throughout Canada? Would not a resolute and uncompromising defence of civil liberties have served the nation better? The government certainly had, and should have assured the public that it knew it had, ample power and the necessary means to capture the kidnappers. I think that such actions would have demonstrated the strength of the nation and of its Constitution more surely than the abrogation of the citizen's rights. Our leaders should have called for patience and restraint, not for extraordinary measures to augment the already formidable powers of the government and the police.

At the time, few urged prudence and calm. The media constituted themselves a cheering section for Trudeau and his government. Robert Stanfield, a thoughtful and liberal man, did not feel that he, as leader of the Conservative party, could oppose the use of the War Measures Act or the Public Order Act. The NDP opposed the Public Order Act, as they had earlier opposed the government's motion that the House approve the invoking of the War Measures Act, but they did so at an enormous political cost, a cost so prohibitive that they were not prepared to vote against the Act when it came up for third reading. Only David MacDonald, a Conservative MP from Prince Edward Island and a minister of the United Church, stood to vote against it then. It is astonishing that in a House of Commons abundantly provided with lawyers, not one of them was prepared to vote against the abrogation of due process on this occasion. But should we be astonished? After all, in 1942, when anti-Japanese sentiment had overwhelmed the country, the only voice raised in Parliament in defence of the Japanese Canadians was that of Angus MacInnis. The lawyers were silent on that occasion, too.

The police were emboldened to arrest hundreds of persons connected in one way or another with political dissent in Quebec. They raided the offices of the New Democratic Party in Montreal. They even searched the home of Gérard Pelletier, secretary of state in the federal government. Others, still free, not only in Quebec but also in other provinces, who may have opposed the invoking of the War Measures Act, were inhibited in their public statements, and they exercised their right to criticize the government and its actions only at the risk of arrest. I speak now not about criticism in Parliament or in the legislatures, which is protected from prosecution, but about criticism voiced in the streets, in public demonstrations, in the holding of meetings, and in the distribution of pamphlets. With the press, radio, and television serving as guardians, not of free speech but of the government's reputation, it was more imporant than ever to preserve freedom of speech in public meetings and in the streets. Yet, because of the Regulations passed under the War Measures Act, the exercise of such freedom was placed in jeopardy.

In a sense, the proclamation of the War Measures Act achieved exactly what the FLQ had sought. At a stroke, the terrorists of the FLQ had succeeded in establishing themselves as a parallel power. They had seized a diplomat and a politician, they had seen the War Measures Act proclaimed, and a police state established in Quebec. Gérard Pelletier has argued, in *The October Crisis*, his apologia for the federal government's actions, that the FLQ knew their activities would lead to repression. He holds that the FLQ were, therefore, the authors of the War Measures Act. The logic of his argument suggests that the federal government is not autonomous and that it is not finally responsible for what it does. According to Pelletier, the government simply responded in the way that the FLQ wanted it to respond. This is hardly a defence.

Yet the gains should not be overlooked. Only one life was lost. The government did not succumb to the FLQ's principal demand, that the "political prisoners" be freed. There were no further kidnappings. Indeed, during the 1970s, there were no further acts of terrorism in Quebec. Perhaps the emergence of the Parti Québécois and its steady advance toward power provided a lawful channel whereby the whole spectrum of nationalist causes in Quebec, including those that had resorted to terror in the 1960s, could find expression. It may also be argued that the proclamation of the War Measures Act was the main reason for the disappearance of terrorist activity. But no one can be certain. My own conviction is that a firm stand by the federal government in support of civil liberties would have achieved the same end. A refusal by the government to yield to the temptation to use the instruments of legal oppression—restraints on freedom of speech and of association, searches and seizures without cause, and the denial of due process—would have thwarted the FLQ as surely as the proclamation of the War Measures Act.

Professor Noel Lyon, writing in the *McGill Law Journal*, has suggested that the cabinet's use of the executive powers delegated to it constituted a usurpation of the judicial function. The cabinet's decree, in the Public Order Regulations, that the FLQ was an association that advocated the use of force or the commission of crime as a means of accomplishing governmental change within Canada and declaring it to be an unlawful association, was nothing less than a judgement by the executive that the FLQ was a seditious conspiracy, and its members and supporters parties to the conspiracy. This is a judgement that should have been left to the courts, applying the ordinary law of sedition. According to Professor Lyon, the Public Order Regulations set up a criminal class action, and the judiciary was "reduced to the role of timekeeper, keeping track of who attended what meetings and spoke or communicated what statements." Guilt, he said, "was determined by executive decree."

The courts have not agreed with Professor Lyon's characterization of the Regulations, and they have not been held to be unconstitutional on that ground. Nevertheless, his argument is—and it ought to be—unsettling. The Public Order Regulations were, the courts held, measures that the federal executive had authority to pass. In the legal sense, their enactment was not in violation of the rule of law. But, in a broader sense, it was. They were executive decrees to limit freedom of speech and freedom of association and to make certain kinds of speech and association unlawful. It may be argued that this power is fundamental to national security. But no authority except Parliament should be able to wield such power, and Parliament itself should not be able to take up these powers without profound and convincing cause.

Study of the October Crisis demonstrates that a prime minister, whose earlier career had been devoted to defending the rights of dissenters, could himself become the instrument of large-scale arrests and the repression of dissent, simply because the powers to do so are available to the persons elected to govern us. Our Constitution should reflect a faith in laws, not in those who govern; it should reflect a faith in fundamental freedoms, not a willingness to give the persons who govern us the power to repeal them.

Pierre Trudeau, before he entered Parliament, provided compelling arguments for the entrenchment of fundamental freedoms and for placing limits on police power. In high office, in October, 1970, he provided compelling evidence why these freedoms should be entrenched. But it was not just Pierre Trudeau, it was all of us. The October Crisis was a crucible. During that period, unnamed fears that lie just beneath our conscious minds were suddenly fused into one clear certainty to which everyone clung. For a moment, Canadians banished all their uncertainties related in one way or another to the crisis by exorcising the FLQ. Questions about the rights of all kinds of dissenters,

French or English, were ignored in a glorious act of self-indulgent wrath. Canadian unity had never been more fervently felt nor more stridently upheld by so many.

The October Crisis brought us to a condition that prevails in many countries whose methods we reject. In them, conformity to an arbitrary and elusive norm may be insisted upon. In them, the stifling of political dissent inevitably stifles social and cultural creativity as well. Fundamental freedoms must, therefore, be entrenched in the Constitution, and they must be entrenched beyond the easy reach of the War Measures Act. Would this disarm the federal government when faced with some new threat of terrorism? Of course not. The Criminal Code provides the means for the police to deal with terrorism, as the October Crisis itself demonstrated.

The government's proclamation of the War Measures Act, issued at 4:00 am on Friday, October 16, asserted that the FLQ had resorted to murder, threats of murder, and kidnapping. Should not the government have had the power to act in such a case? Of course it should, and it already had the power. Persons alleged to have committed such crimes should be charged under the Criminal Code. The FLQ terrorists were charged—and they were convicted—under the Code, just as their predecessors throughout the 1960s had been charged and convicted. If the FLQ had constituted a treasonous conspiracy to overthrow the government by force, its members could still have been charged and proceeded against under the Criminal Code.

Arguments for the necessity to expand police power were spurious in 1970 and they are spurious today. Enhanced police powers did not save Pierre Laporte; they did not make society, nor did they make any one of us, the slightest bit safer. They did arbitrarily interrupt the lives of hundreds of citizens to no purpose—and any one of us might have been one of those citizens.

Of course, though hundreds were arrested and interned by the police, none were held, as Cross was, in a state of uncertainty as to whether he would be allowed to live.

Neither were any of them murdered, as Laporte was. But Cross was kidnapped, and Laporte murdered by terrorists. It is hardly to be expected that the terrorists would be governed by the rule of law or evince any respect for due process. The FLQ did not act in the name of the state; they were not exercising powers conferred by Parliament. The police were; thus the advisability of conferring such power, and the manner in which the police exercised it, are subjects of legitimate concern to citizens of a country which believes in the rule of law. We try to deter kidnapping and murder, and we prosecute and punish those who commit such acts. At the same time, we should be vigilant to see that powers exercised on our behalf are not abused.

The War Measures Act was enacted to provide the federal government with the power to mobilize the nation against external enemies and to extinguish internal rebellion. It was intended to provide for the case of a domestic insurrection with coherent objectives and mass support, an insurrection representing a contending theory of the way in which the state should be organized or its wealth distributed, and presenting a challenge to the armed forces of the state. But social protest in the urban, industrialized nations may manifest itself in an assault on the life or the home of a prominent politician, diplomat, or industrialist. The War Measures Act as an instrument for combatting this form of terrorism is quite unsuitable. Terrorism is not war; nor is it insurrection.

The federal government must have the power to act, and to act swiftly, in defence of the nation in times of war or of national emergency. The armed forces may have to be deployed. Economic restraints may have to be imposed. The federal government must have the power to arrest and detain persons who, there are reasonable grounds to believe, may commit acts, or have committed acts, that are in violation of the Criminal Code. But federal powers must stop there. Nothing in our history justifies going further. The power to round up minorities and dissenters merely because they espouse radical political or religious beliefs, or merely because their race or their language is different from that of the majority, without evidence of any breaches of the Criminal Code, must be denied to those who govern us.

Robert Stanfield, in the introduction to the revised edition of *Rumours of War*, wrote:

> Civil liberties in Canada will therefore continue to depend basically upon the importance Canadians attach to them and upon our willingness to defend them even in times of stress. In our search for protection from violence we must recognize that arbitrary abrogation of individual rights weakens rather than strengthens social order.

Under the Charter of Rights and Freedoms the cabinet will not have the exclusive power to determine whether or not there is an apprehended insurrection. By Section 1 of the Charter any infringement of the fundamental freedoms guaranteed by the Charter must be "demonstrably justified." The courts are not bound automatically to accept the opinion of the cabinet; they will have to determine whether or not the abrogation of fundamental freedoms is justified each time the government claims that an emergency makes it necessary. Thus some constraints are placed on the federal emergency power. But only after the fact. The cabinet still has the power to invoke the War Measures Act. Nor is there any need to seek parliamentary sanction before doing so. Any challenge in the courts to a proclamation that an insurrection exists can only be brought thereafter. The courts will undoubtedly be reluctant to interfere in what is essentially a matter for political judgement.

The question remains, what measures will the police call for in another crisis? To what extent will those who govern feel obliged to act accordingly? How far will the public acquiesce? Will those who govern feel inhibited, when demands are made for restrictions on due process, by a deep sense that civil liberties are precious in Canada, that the Charter of Rights and Freedoms ought to be respected, that fundamental freedoms ought to be maintained even during a crisis? The enactment of the Charter of Rights, the symbolic value it will have for the nation, the extent to which Canadians perceive that it embodies the ideals of citizenship—all these will be more meaningful than the pure legal effect of the Charter in securing the protection of fundamental freedoms even when gravest cause is thought to be seen for their attenuation.

EIGHT

The Nishga Indians and Aboriginal Rights

THE ISSUE OF aboriginal rights is the oldest question of human rights in Canada. At the same time it is also the most recent, for it is only in the last decade that it has entered our consciousness and our political bloodstream. It began with the White occupation of a continent already inhabited by another race, a race with its own cultures, its own languages, its own institutions, and its own way of life. Today the members of that race are advancing claims to the lands they once occupied and calling for self-determination and self-government. These claims give rise to fundamental issues, and we have come to understand that these issues are somehow bound up with what happened long ago. And they are: for the claims of the present day are founded on aboriginal rights.

Aboriginal rights are simply the rights to which Native peoples are entitled because they are the original peoples of Canada. Until recently, the idea of aboriginal rights seemed irrelevant to Canadian concerns. But during the 1970s we began to realize that aboriginal rights are the axis upon which our relations with the Native peoples revolve. To recognize aboriginal rights is to understand the truth of our own history, while, for the Native peoples, such recognition is the means by which they may achieve a distinct and contemporary place in Canadian life.

The emergence of Native peoples as a political force in the 1970s occurred because of initiatives that Indians, Inuit and Metis all over Canada have taken themselves. One thing is common to all of these initiatives: the idea of aboriginal rights. The Native peoples own idea of themselves has acquired a sharper focus. At the same time, our own ideas about Native peoples are undergoing a great change: once thought to be peoples on the margins of our history and irrelevant to present-day concerns, they are now seen by a growing number of Canadians as having a moral, indeed, a constitutional right to fashion a future of their own.

The history of White-Native relations in Canada may be epitomized in the history of relations between the Whites and the Indians of British Columbia. There the Native protest over the loss of their lands has been more audible than elsewhere, and the Indian land question has agitated the province for more than a century. One tribe, the Nishgas, has been in the forefront of this controversy. The story of the Nishga Indians illustrates the quest of all Canadian Indians for legal recognition of their aboriginal rights. Their story takes us back to the beginnings of European colonization of North America, and it brings us forward to the very centre of the present conflict over land claims, Indian self-determination, and the concept of Indian government.

The Nishgas are one of the tribes of the northwest coast. Here the sea and the forest have always offered a good life and, before the Whites arrived, the Indian population along the northwest coast was one of the densest in North America. Here the Nishgas had their settlements, fishing places and hunting grounds. They regarded the Nass River valley as their own. They defended it before the White man came, and they have defended it since. Today they have four villages in the Nass valley: Kincolith, Greenville, Canyon City and New Aiyansh. They say that they, as the people who have occupied this valley since time immemorial, are entitled to claim it as their own today.

In claiming aboriginal title, the Nishgas are no different from Indians elsewhere in Canada. When the Europeans discovered, then began to colonize North America, the Indians regarded themselves as the rightful owners of the land. They were the original occupants of the land, and each tribe traditionally held its own tribal territory, a territory that other tribes also recognized.

The European nations asserted sovereignty over the New World by virtue of the principle of discovery. They waged wars among themselves when one nation sought to wrest newly discovered territory from another, and the results of these wars always left one European nation or another holding dominion over the territory in dispute. There was never any question in the minds of the Europeans that the Indians might retain sovereignty over the lands that had been theirs. The Europeans based their assumption of power over the Indians on the supposed moral superiority of European culture and religion over those of the Indians and on the undoubted superiority of European arms. Nevertheless, the European powers did acknowledge that the Indians retained an interest—a legal interest—in their lands because they had been the original occupants. This legal interest came to be known as aboriginal title, or Indian title.

Having acknowledged that the Indians had a legal interest in their lands, the Europeans had to consider how the Indians could be persuaded to give it up. So treaties were made with the Indians providing for the surrender of their title. In the United States, when the government could not acquire land by negotiation, it acquired it by war. Yet each time the United States government subjugated an Indian tribe, it made a treaty to obtain the surrender of Indian title. In Canada, although few treaties were made in the Atlantic provinces and in Quebec, the British, by the mid-eighteenth century, had established a policy of treating with the Indians for their land. This policy was enshrined in the Royal Proclamation of 1763. Thus, by 1850, treaties had been made with the Indians for the surrender of virtually the whole of southern Ontario; as settlement proceeded westward across the prairies, treaties were made (beginning in the 1870s) with the Indians there to enable the construction of the Canadian Pacific Railway to proceed, opening the country to agriculture. Treaties were also made to open up natural resources on the frontier. The prospect of extracting oil from the Athabaska tar sands, first mooted in the 1880s, led to a treaty with the Stonies in 1899, and in 1921 treaties were made with some of the northern tribes as a consequence of the discovery of oil at Fort Norman in the Northwest Territories. In 1974, the Cree and Naskapi Indians and the Inuit of northern Quebec signed the James Bay Agreement, whereby they surrendered aboriginal title to their lands, so that the James Bay Project, a vast hydroelectrical development, could proceed. All of these treaties were intended to achieve one main purpose: to extinguish the aboriginal title of the Native peoples so that agricultural or industrial development could go ahead.

But in British Columbia very little of the province is covered by treaties, even to this day. The British navy reached the northwest coast only late in the eighteenth century when, in 1778, Captain Cook landed at Nootka on Vancouver Island. In 1841, the Hudson's Bay Company established Fort Victoria on Vancouver Island, but settlement began to grow only after 1849, when Vancouver Island was made a Crown colony. The Hudson's Bay Company dominated the colony for some time, largely through its chief factor, James Douglas, who was also, after 1851, governor of the colony. He had had a long experience of Indian affairs, and indeed had married a Half-breed woman "after the custom of the country." Between 1849 and 1854, Douglas made a series of treaties with the Indians of southern Vancouver Island by which they surrendered their lands to the Company in return for blankets and small amounts of money. But these treaties also provided for reserves for the Indians, in the face of encroaching White settlement, and the Indians retained the right to hunt and fish over the lands they had surrendered until these lands were taken up for settlement. Douglas insisted that only after aboriginal title had been extinguished by treaty could settlement proceed.

After 1854, Douglas was unable to maintain this policy. The Colonial Office in London urged him to continue to make treaties with the Indians, but it would not provide the funds to enable him to do so. The settlers denied that it was their responsibility, and they would not vote funds for the purpose. The colony's house of assembly had at first acknowledged aboriginal title, but when the house realized that the money for the extinguishment of aboriginal title would have to be provided locally, it began to insist there was no such thing as aboriginal title and that there was no obligation to compensate the Indians for their land. The mainland colony of British Columbia, established in 1858, also adopted this policy. When the two colonies were united in 1866, the policy continued. In 1867, Joseph Trutch, chief commissioner of lands and works of the newly united colony, wrote:

> The Indians have really no right to the lands they claim, nor are they of any actual value or utility to them, and I cannot see why they should either retain these lands to the prejudice of the general interests of the Colony, or be allowed to make a market of them either to the Government or to Individuals.

Although British Columbia did not recognize aboriginal title, the authorities did agree that the Indians had to live somewhere, and reserves were, therefore, set aside for them. When he was governor of Vancouver Island, Douglas had directed the chief commissioner of lands and works to be guided by the Indians themselves in determining the location of reserves and in setting their boundaries. But after Douglas retired in 1864 this policy, like his earlier insistence upon treaties being made to extinguish the Indian title, was repudiated, and reserves were laid out without consultation with the Indians.

History books tell us that British Columbia entered Confederation in 1871 because John A. Macdonald had promised to build a railway to the Pacific. That promise, and the delays in implementing it, were a continuing source of conflict between Ottawa and British Columbia. Equally acrimonious was their continuing dispute over Indian title and Indian reserves. Under the British North America Act, "Indians and Lands Reserved for the Indians" come under federal jurisdiction. By the Terms of Union of 1871 (the terms under which British Columbia entered Confederation) the federal government assumed responsibility for the Indians and "the trusteeship and management of the lands reserved for their use and benefit." The Terms of Union also stated that the federal government, in discharging its responsibilities to the Indians, was to follow a policy "as liberal as that hitherto pursued by the British Columbia Government," but no specific provision was made for settlement of the Indian land question. Given the decidedly illiberal policy that the government of the colony had followed, the words of the Terms of Union were either altogether cynical on the part of the federal government or agreed to in a state of complete absentmindedness. In any event, as the Terms of Union stated that all public lands were to be the property of the provincial government, how was the federal government to acquire the necessary lands to complete the laying out of reserves for the Indians of the province? All that the Terms of Union said on this point was that the province was to convey to the federal government "tracts of land of such extent as it had hitherto been the practice of the British Columbia Government to appropriate for that purpose."

The question of reserves had to be tackled at once, because reserves had not yet been set aside for all of the Indians. The question of what size a reserve should be to be adequate was a difficult one. The province allowed Whites to pre-empt 320 acres of land for a homestead. What provision should be made for the Indians? In 1873, the federal government recommended that every Indian family of five persons be given 80 acres of land. The province would agree to only 20 acres. In 1874, the federal government disallowed the Land Act passed in that year by the British Columbia government relating to the disposition of Crown lands because the Act made no provision for Indian reserves. Only after the province had agreed to the establishment of a procedure for the selection and allotment of reserves was the statute approved.

The question of aboriginal rights was another matter. Although the province was, albeit reluctantly, prepared to provide land for Indian reserves, it was unwilling, just as the old Colony of British Columbia had been, to acknowledge any obligation to provide compensation for Indian lands taken for settlement. The province intended to survey its territory and to issue Crown grants without making any more treaties.

John A. Macdonald was not unsympathetic to British Columbia's position. In 1872 Trutch, by now lieutenant-governor of the province, wrote to Macdonald, addressing him as "Dear John":

> If you now commence to buy out Indian title to the lands of B.C. you would go back on all that has been done here for 30 years past and would be equitably bound to compensate the tribes who inhabited the districts now settled [and] farmed by white people equally with those in the more remote and uncultivated portions....

But in 1873 Macdonald was thrown out of office as a result of the Pacific Scandal. He was succeeded by a Liberal, Alexander Mackenzie. To the Liberals the claims of the Indians were not a purely academic question. Télesphore Fournier, Mackenzie's minister of justice, raised the question of aboriginal rights in British Columbia in the opinion he wrote recommending disallowance of the province's 1874 Land Act:

> ...with one slight exception as to land in Vancouver Island surrendered to the Hudson Bay Company, which makes the absence of others the more remarkable, no surrender of lands in that province has ever been obtained from the Indian tribes inhabiting it, and that any reservations which have been made, have been arbitrary on the part of the government, and without the assent of the Indians themselves, and though the policy of obtaining surrenders at this lapse of time and under the altered circumstances of the province, may be questionable, yet the undersigned feels it is his duty to assert such legal or equitable claim as may be found to exist on the part of the Indians.

Then, referring to the policy exemplified by the Royal Proclamation of 1763, he said,

> There is not a shadow of doubt, that from the earliest times,

England has always felt it imperative to meet the Indians in council, and to obtain surrenders of tracts of Canada, as from time to time such were required for the purposes of settlement.

He concluded with a devastating indictment of provincial policy.

Considering, then, these several features of the case, that no surrender or cession of their territorial rights, whether the same be of a legal or equitable nature, has been forever executed by the Indian tribes of the province—that they alledge that the reservations of land made by the Government for their use, have been arbitrarily so made, and are totally inadequate to their support and requirements, and without their assent—that they are not averse to hostilities in order to enforce rights which it is impossible to deny them, and that the Act under consideration not only ignores those rights, but expressly prohibits the Indians from enjoying the rights of recording or pre-empting lands, except by consent of the Lieutenant-Governor;—the undersigned feels that he cannot do otherwise than advise that the Act in question is objectionable, as tending to deal with lands which are assumed to be the absolute property of the province, an assumption which completely ignores, as applicable to the Indians of British Columbia, the honour and good faith with which the Crown has, in all other cases, since its sovereignty of the territories in North America, dealt with their various Indian tribes.

The matter was one which Mackenzie's government regarded as fundamental to the legitimacy of occupation and settlement of the province. Lord Dufferin, the governor-general, travelled to British Columbia in 1876, where he made a speech urging the settlement of the Indian land question:

Now, we must all admit that the condition of the Indian question in British Columbia is not satisfactory. Most unfortunately, as I think, there has been an initial error ever since Sir James Douglas quitted office in the Government of British Columbia neglecting to recognize what is known as the Indian title. In Canada this has always been done;

no Government, whether provincial or central, has failed to acknowledge that the original title to the land existed in the Indian tribes and communities that hunted or wandered over them. Before we touch an acre we make a treaty with the chief representing the bands we are dealing with, and having agreed upon and paid the stipulated price, often-times arrived at after a great deal of haggling and difficulty, we enter into possession, but not until then do we consider that we are entitled to deal with an acre. The result has been that in Canada our Indians are contented, well affected to the white man, and amenable to the laws and govern-ment. At this very moment the Lieutenant-Governor of Manitoba has gone on a distant expedition in order to make a treaty with the tribes to the northward of the Saskatch-ewan. Last year he made two treaties with the Chippewas and Crees; next year it has been arranged that he should make a treaty with the Black feet, and when this is done the British Crown will have acquired a title to every acre that lies between Lake Superior and the top of the Rocky Mountains.

But Mackenzie and Dufferin were no more successful than Douglas had been in persuading the government of British Columbia to modify its position. The White settlers of the province and their government regarded the Indians as an obstruction to progress. In any event, like Lieutenant-Governor Trutch, they had persuaded themselves that the Indians had been treated fairly. Trutch had told John A. Macdonald that "Our Indians are sufficiently satisfied and had better be left alone.... "

Trutch was wrong. The Indians were not satisfied. During the 1860s and during the 1870s, some persons feared an Indian war. Indeed, there had been armed clashes; in one of these, the Chilcotin uprising in 1864, 13 Whites had been killed. There was, however, no Indian war: the Indian people submitted to the White invaders. But their feeling of loss, their sense of intolerable grievance, persists to this day.

Mackenzie's government had attempted to obtain a set-tlement of their claims for the Indians of British Columbia, but it failed because there was no constitutional obligation requiring the province to make a settlement. The province held the public lands. How could there be a land settlement unless it agreed? Mackenzie's Liberal administration was defeated in 1878. With Macdonald's return to office, Ottawa adopted a more conciliatory attitude toward British Columbia's stand on the Indian land question. After that year, the federal government became less and less willing to intervene in provincial affairs to protect the rights of the Indians.

Examination of the correspondence that passed between Ottawa and British Columbia offers some insight into the nature of federal-provincial conflicts. The Indians them-selves, however, do not speak to us through these docu-ments. We know they felt anger and bitter resentment. But what, in fact, was happening to them? How were their lives affected by the progressive loss of their lands and by their confinement to reserves?

When the White fur traders arrived, the Indians of the northwest coast already had a sophisticated culture, a cul-ture that was at first enriched and refined by contact with the Whites. Chisels and axes, for instance, made possible great advances in the carving of totem poles. Claude Lévi-Strauss, the great French anthropologist, has described the Indian culture of the northwest coast as one of the great efflorescences of mankind, and the Indians themselves as fit to be compared with the ancient Greeks and Romans. The collapse of that culture is seen by many as one of the great tragedies of modern times. How did it happen?

The Indians were indispensable partners in the fur trade. They collected the furs and brought them to the forts. All that changed with the abandonment of the fur trade and the advance of settlement. Under the new dispensation Indian labour was not needed. What was wanted was In-dian land. As White settlement encroached on Indian land, Indian society and the Indian economy were transformed. Hunting and fishing continued to be the base of the Indian economy, but the Indians were prepared to enter other occupations. Some became farm labourers. Others were seasonally employed in logging camps and sawmills, in road and railway construction, and on fishing boats and in fish canneries. But the extent to which Indians could adapt to the new circumstances was limited: when they left their reserves, they encountered many forms of prejudice, barriers that made it difficult for them to adapt, and impossible to adapt completely.

Indian society was unstable for other reasons, too. The Indians were defenceless against the diseases brought by the Europeans. Smallpox and tuberculosis took an enormous toll of lives. Alcohol became a manifestation of, and contributed to disintegration and decay. By 1900, the Indian population of the northwest coast, which at mid-century had stood at about 50,000, was reduced to 10,000, many of whom were enfeebled by disease. The appalling decline in the Indian population led to the conclusion, widely held among Whites, that the Indians were a people condemned by history, who would soon become extinct. Any sense of urgency about coming to grips with the question of aboriginal title diminished year by year.

The Indians were not completely excluded from various forms of wage labour, and their hunting and fishing activities were not totally prohibited or curtailed, but Indian unemployment and underemployment, their dependence on reserves, and their economic deprivation stem from this period. Perhaps even more damaging to the Indians than these losses was the denigration of their way of life that was implicit in every relation they had with White society, from the abolition of the potlatch to the refusal to allow them to vote. (The Indians, along with the Chinese and the Japanese, were denied the right to vote in British Columbia in 1895. They did not get it back until 1949. It is astonishing to think that Indians in Canada did not receive the right to vote in federal elections until 1960, when John Diefenbaker was prime minister.) The White presence, from the fur trade and the missions, to the advent of agriculture and industrial development, to the proliferation of government institutions, has dominated and it continues to dominate Indian society. There is an intrinsic relationship between this domination and the cluster of social pathologies and economic difficulties that afflict Indian communities today.

White attitudes common in British Columbia a century ago persist even today. The policies we pursued in the past were designed to suppress Indian languages, Indian culture, and the Indian economy. During the nineteenth century, we believed—and many persons still believe—that the Indian economy and, indeed, Indian society, was moribund, that Indian culture was at best a colourful reminder of the past and that what we see of it today is only a pathetic remnant of an age now gone.

Nevertheless, in the midst of these hammer blows, the Indians of the northwest coast continued to cling to their beliefs and to their own idea of themselves. And they remained determined to insist upon their aboriginal rights. In 1887, the provincial government appointed a royal commission "To Enquire into the Conditions of the Indians of the Northwest Coast." When the commission visited the Nass valley, the Nishga chiefs raised the question of aboriginal rights. David Mackay, one of the chiefs, summed up the Nishga point of view:

> What we don't like about the Government is their saying this: "We will give you this much land." How can they give it when it is our own? We cannot understand it. They have never bought it from us or our forefathers. They have never fought and conquered our people and taken the land in that way, and yet they say now that they will give us so much land—our own land. These chiefs do not talk foolishly, they know the land is their own; our forefathers for generations and generations past had their land here all around us; chiefs have had their own hunting grounds, their salmon streams, and places where they got their berries; it has always been so. It is not only during the last four or five years that we have seen the land; we have always seen and owned it; it is no new thing, it has been ours for generations. If we had only seen it for twenty years and claimed it as our own, it would have been foolish, but it has been ours for thousands of years.

Nevertheless, White encroachment on Indian lands continued. In 1885 the completion of the Canadian Pacific Railway had brought a rush of new immigrants. British Columbia, formerly easily accessible only by sea, could now be reached by rail from the east. By the turn of the century, the province's White population had greatly increased, and the resource industries and the road and rail networks had been greatly extended. These developments further limited the territory on which the Indians could hunt and fish. As early as 1895, the federal department of fisheries began to restrict the Indian food fishery, that is, the right of Indians to fish for food for themselves and their families, and by 1915 Indian hunting and trapping was brought under provincial regulation.

The Indians still had their reserves, of course. But these, too, came under attack after the turn of the century. Since 1874, the federal and provincial authorities had jointly laid out new Indian reserves, but in 1908 the province refused to lay out any more. The province insisted, instead, that the existing reserves must be reduced in size and that lands already held by the Indians must be made available for agricultural and commercial uses.

All this time, the Indians continued to press for recognition of their aboriginal title. In 1906 and again in 1909, delegations of Indian chiefs from British Columbia went to London to present their demands to the king himself. But the Imperial government was powerless to intervene, even if it were disposed to do so. In any event, the province would not change its position. In 1909, the premier, Richard McBride, said, "Of course it would be madness to think of conceding to the Indians' demands. It is too late to discuss the equity of dispossessing the Red man in America." McBride believed that the question of aboriginal title would never have been raised were it not for the "pernicious advice of some unscrupulous whites." This theme recurs again and again in our dealings with the Native peoples. Many Canadians have found it convenient to believe that Native peoples would not have thought of asserting their claims to the land, if it were not for the influence of subversive Whites. Thus historians have argued that the Metis would not have advanced a claim to aboriginal title in 1816, if they had not been put up to it by the Nor'Westers; while in the 1970s White radicals were supposed to have persuaded the Dene who, it was said, would not themselves have advanced such a position, to insist upon a settlement of their land claims before a pipeline could be built along the Mackenzie valley.

In 1910, Prime Minister Wilfrid Laurier met representatives of the Indians at Prince Rupert. "The only way," he told them, "to settle this question that you have agitated for years is by a decision [of the Privy Council], and I will take steps to help you." The federal government then prepared a list of questions, to which the Indians agreed, to be submitted to the Privy Council. But Premier McBride rejected the whole idea. He would never agree, he asserted, to any adjudication of the question of aboriginal title.

On April 26, 1911, a deputation of the Indian chiefs of the northwest coast again met with Laurier at Prince Rupert. Laurier told them,

> The matter for us to immediately consider is whether we can bring the Government of British Columbia into Court with us. We think it is our duty to have the matter inquired into. The Government of British Columbia may be right or wrong in their assertion that the Indians have no claim whatever. Courts of law are just for that purpose—where a man asserts a claim and it is denied by another. But we do not know if we can force a government into court. If we can find a way, I may say we shall surely do so....The Indians will continue to believe they have a grievance until it has been settled by the court that they have a claim, or that they have no claim.

But in the autumn of 1911, Laurier's government was defeated. His successors, Conservative and Liberal, refused for the next 50 years to consider the question of aboriginal claims in British Columbia and refused to intercede on the Indians' behalf with the province's intransigent politicians. Only in 1969 were the Indians finally able to force the government of British Columbia into court to have the question of aboriginal title adjudicated.

When Premier McBride continued to demand reductions in the size of reserves in the province, the federal government appointed Dr. J.A.J. McKenna of Winnipeg to negotiate the question with him. McKenna's discussions with McBride led to the McKenna-McBride Agreement, whereby the two governments agreed to establish a joint royal commission to make a final and complete allotment of Indian lands in British Columbia. The agreement's initial terms of reference included the question of aboriginal title, but McBride adamantly refused to deal with that subject. McKenna agreed to drop it and to investigate only the question of reserves.

From 1912 to 1916, the McKenna-McBride Commission (as the royal commission was known) travelled throughout the province to take evidence. In 1915, its members visited the Nass valley, where Gideon Minesque spoke for the Nishgas:

> We haven't got any ill feelings in our hearts but we are just waiting for this thing to be settled and we have been waiting for the last five years—it is not only a short time that we have lived here; we have been living here from time immemorial—it has been handed down in legends from the old people and that is what hurts us very much because the white people have come along and taken this land away from us. I myself am an old man and as long as I have lived, my people have been telling me stories about the flood and they did not tell me that I was only to live here on this land for a short time. We have heard that some white men, it must have been in Ottawa; this white man said that [the Nishgas] must be dreaming when they say they own the land upon which they live. It is not a dream— we are certain that this land belongs to us. Right up to this day the government never made any treaty, not even to our grandfathers or our great-grandfathers.

To Gideon Minesque, the facts were plain enough. The Nishgas were the original inhabitants of the valley. They had lived there from time immemorial. They had no doubt that the land belonged to them. "It is not a dream—we are certain.. ." Gideon Minesque was addressing the larger question of Indian title. The Commission, however, re-stricted itself to the allotment of land for reserves. In British Columbia as a whole the commission confirmed some of the existing reserves, and it added about 87,000 acres of new reserve land. But the commission removed from the reserves some 47,000 acres of land the Indians held. These "cut-off" lands were far more valuable than the lands given to the Indians to replace them.

The commission's four-volume report was published in 1916. Both the federal government and the province believed that the Indian land question in British Columbia had finally been settled—even though the report had not touched on the question of aboriginal title. Nor had the commission dealt with Indian grievances over hunting and fishing rights, timber rights and water rights. What, in summary, the commission had done was to remove from the reserves good land that Whites wanted and to replace it with poor land.

In 1913, the Nishgas formed the Nishga Land Committee. They sent a petition to Ottawa seeking an adjudication of their claim. Soon they had allies. In 1916, other tribes on the coast and in the interior of the province joined the Nishgas in seeking an adjudication of the question of Indian title. Together, they formed the Allied Tribes of British Columbia. The Allied Tribes rejected the report of the McKenna-McBride Commission and, for a decade, they held meetings, raised funds, and sent petitions to Ottawa, pressing the government to submit the question to the Privy Council.

The federal government refused to take this step, but in 1926 it did appoint a Special Joint Committee of the Senate and House of Commons to examine the question. The Allied Tribes at first regarded the appointment of the Parliamentary Committee as a signal success, but when the Committee met in haste in 1927, near the end of the parliamentary session, the Indians' spokesmen were treated with discourtesy and their claims were treated as trivial. The recommendations that the Committee made constituted a rejection of the Indians' claim that they had been unjustly treated. According to the Committee, the Indians of British Columbia had been treated at least as generously as Indians in Ontario and the west with whom treaties had been made. However, in lieu of treaty payments, the Committee recommended a grant amounting to $100,000 annually, over and above the normal costs of federal administration of Indian affairs in the province, to be spent by the Indian Affairs branch for the Indians' benefit. The Indians were treated, not as a people with a claim deserving of fair and honourable consideration, but as mendicants.

The ideas of Télesphore Fournier, of Lord Dufferin, and of Wilfrid Laurier seemed to have faded into nothingness. Aboriginal title, which federal authorities had recognized during the nineteenth century, the title the Indians insisted the province should recognize now, was officially regarded as belonging to a world of the past. Determined that this question should never be raised again, Parliament included a provision in the Indian Act of 1927 that made it an offence punishable by law to raise funds for the purpose of pursuing any claim of aboriginal title.

The Allied Tribes of British Columbia disbanded. Although the Indian land question was no longer a public issue, the Indian people did not—could not—regard the matter as finally settled. During the 1950s, it arose again. In 1959, Peter Kelly, a Haida Indian leader who had addressed the Parliamentary Joint Committee in 1927, argued before another Parliamentary Joint Committee that the question of aboriginal title should be taken to the Supreme Court of Canada:

> But, gentlemen, so long as that title question is not dealt with, every Indian in British Columbia feels that he has been tricked, and he never will be satisfied. I want to say to this committee, in all seriousness, that you will do a good service to the country if you in some way see to it that this is dealt with. Let us say that it be dealt with by the Supreme Court of Canada. That is as far as we can go now. We used to go to the Privy Council, but that is not possible now. Once again, I want to say this: if that is done,

it would show the good faith of the government and it will convince the Indians of British Columbia today that the government is anxious to do what is considered just and fair for the Indians of B.C. If the case is lost, that would be settled once and for all: if we win, then you will have to deal with us.

In 1967, the Nishga Indians brought a suit before the Supreme Court of British Columbia. Their claim was a simple one. Indian title, they alleged, had never been extinguished in British Columbia. Their suit was brought against the province. In 1911, the Laurier government had not been able to devise a way of getting the province into court. The law said that no one could sue the province to recover an interest in land. To do that it was necessary to obtain the consent of the provincial government. That was out of the question: the provincial government would never consent. So the Nishgas simply asked the court for a declaration that their aboriginal title had never been lawfully extinguished; they weren't asking for an order restoring their interest in the land. A fine distinction, but a vital one if they were to have their claim adjudicated. Peter Kelly had said, "If we win, then you will have to deal with us."

In April, 1969, the trial of the Nishga Indians' claim opened in the Supreme Court of British Columbia before Mr. Justice J.G. Gould. Frank Calder, President of the Nishga Tribal Council, told the court that,

> ...from time immemorial the Nishgas have used the Nass River and all its tributaries within the boundaries so submitted, the lands in Observatory Inlet, the lands in Portland Canal, and part of Portland Inlet. We still hunt within those lands and fish in the waters, streams and rivers, we still do, as in time past, have our campsites in these areas and we go there periodically, seasonally, according to the game and the fishing season, and we will maintain these sites and as far as we know, they have been there as far back as we can remember.
>
> We still roam these territories, we still pitch our tents there whenever it is required according to our livelihood and we use the land as in times past, we bury our dead

within the territory so defined and we still exercise the privilege of free men within the territory so defined.

Counsel for the province of British Columbia argued that aboriginal title was a concept unknown to the law and that, even if such title had existed, it had been extinguished by the old Colony of British Columbia before it entered Confederation as a province in 1871. (Once British Columbia had entered Confederation, only the federal government could extinguish Indian title. It was conceded that the federal government had not taken any legal action since Confederation to extinguish aboriginal title in British Columbia.)

Calder and the other members of the Nishga Tribal Council, representing each of the four Nishga villages, gave evidence. Calder's evidence is typical. He testified as follows:

Q. Are you on the band list?
A. I am.
Q. Would you tell his lordship where you were born?
A. I was born in Nass Bay, near the mouth of the Nass River.
Q. Where were you raised?
A. I was raised at Nass Bay and mostly at Greenville.
Q. Were your parents members of the Greenville Indian Band?
A. Yes they are.
Q. Going back beyond your own parents, are you able to say whether your forefathers lived on the Nass River?
A. Yes, they did.
Q. Now, Mr. Calder, are you a member of the Nishga Tribe?
A. Yes, I am.
Q. What Indians compose the Nishga Tribe?
A. The Nishga Indians that live in the four villages of the Nass River.
Q. What are the names of the four villages?
A. Kincolith...
Q. Kincolith?
A. That's correct, Greenville, Canyon City and [New] Aiyansh.

Q. Can you tell his lordship, Mr. Calder, whether all of the Indians who live in the four communities on the Nass River are members of the Nishga Tribe?

A. Yes, they are members of the Nishga Tribe.

Q. Do you include not only the men and women but the children as well?

A. Yes.

Q. What language do the members of the Nishga Tribe speak?

A. They speak Nishga, known as Nishga today.

Q. Is that language related to any other languages that are spoken on the North Pacific Coast?

A. It is not the exact—our neighbouring two tribes, we more or less understand each other, but Nishga itself is in the Nass River, and there is no other neighbouring tribe that has that language.

Q. What are the names of the two neighbouring tribes who have a limited understanding of your language?

A. Gitskan and Tsimshian.

Q. Do you regard yourself as a member of the Nishga Tribe?

A. Yes, I do.

Q. Do you know if the Indian people who are members of the four Indian bands on the Nass River regard themselves as members of the Nishga Tribe?

A. Yes, they do.

Q. Apart from their language, do they share anything else in common?

A. Besides the language they share our whole way of life.

Q. Now, Mr. Calder, I am showing you...a map. Does the territory outlined in the map constitute the ancient territory of the Nishga people?

A. Yes, it does.

Q. Have the Nishga people ever signed any document or treaty surrendering their aboriginal title to the territory outlined in the map?

A. The Nishgas have not signed any treaty or any document that would indicate extinguishment of the title.

The evidence of Professor Wilson Duff, an anthropologist from the University of British Columbia, and the leading scholar in the province on the northwest coast Indians' ideas of aboriginal title, linked the past to the present. He had prepared for the court a map showing the extent of the tribal territory of the Nishgas. He testified as follows:

Q. Did you, Professor Duff, in fact prepare for counsel the map that has been marked exhibit 2 in this case?

A. Yes, I did.

Q. Are you familiar with the anthropological history of the Indian people who inhabited the area delineated in the map and the surrounding areas?

A. Yes, I am.

Q. Who has, since time immemorial, inhabited the area delineated on the map?

A. The Nishga Indians.

Q. Can you tell the court what position the Indians in the areas adjacent to that delineated on the map took regarding the occupancy by the Nishga Tribe of that area?

A. All of the surrounding tribes knew the Nishga as the homogeneous group of Indians occupying the area delineated on the map. They knew of them collectively under the term Nishga. They knew that they spoke their own dialect, that they occupied and were owners of that territory and they respected these tribal boundaries of the territory.

Duff described the culture of the northwest coast Indians and the concept of Indian title as understood by the Indians themselves. A number of passages from his book *The Indian History of British Columbia* were read to demonstrate these points.

Q. Now in your book you say:
"At the time of contact the Indians of this area were among the world's most distinctive peoples. Fully one-third of the native population of Canada lived here. They were concentrated most heavily along the coast-line and the main western rivers, and in these areas they developed their cultures to higher peaks, in many respects, than in any other part of the continent north of Mexico. Here, too, was the greatest linguistic diversity in the country, with two dozen languages spoken, belonging to seven of the eleven language families

represented in Canada. The coastal Indians were, in some ways, different from all other American Indians. Their languages, true enough, were members of American families, and physically they were American Indians, though with decided traits of similarity to the peoples of Northeastern Asia. Their cultures, however, had a pronounced Asiatic tinge, evidence of basic kinship and long continued contact with the peoples around the North Pacific rim. Most of all, their cultures were distinguished by a local richness and originality, the product of vigorous and inventive people in a rich environment."

Would that paragraph apply to the people who inhabited the area delineated on the map (i.e., the Nishgas)?

A. Yes.

Q. The next paragraph reads:

"It is not correct to say that the Indians did not own the land but only roamed over the face of it and used it. The patterns of ownership and utilization which they imposed upon the lands and waters were different from those recognized by our system of law, but were nonetheless clearly defined and mutually respected. Even if they didn't subdivide and cultivate the land, they did recognize ownership of plots used for village sites, fishing places, berry and root patches, and similar purposes. Even if they didn't subject the forests to wholesale logging, they did establish ownership of tracts used for hunting, trapping and food gathering. Even if they didn't sink mine shafts into the mountains, they did own peaks and valleys for mountain goat hunting and as sources of raw materials. Except for barren and inaccessible areas which are not utilized even today, every part of the province was formerly within the owned and recognized territory of one or other of the Indian Tribes."

Does that paragraph apply to the people who inhabited the area delineated on the map?

A. Yes, it does.

Q. Does it apply to the Nishga Tribe?

A. Yes, it does.

Q. To what extent would the use and exploitation of the

resources of the Nishga territory have extended in terms of that territory? Would it have extended only through a limited part of the territory or through the whole territory?

A.   To a greater or lesser degree of intensity it would extend through a whole territory except for the most barren and inaccessible parts, which were not used or wanted by anyone. But the ownership of an entire drainage basin marked out by the mountain peaks would be recognized as resting within one or other groups of Nishga Indians and these boundaries, this ownership would be respected by others.

The case for the province rested on a series of ordinances passed during the pre-Confederation era by the Crown colony of Vancouver Island and the colony of British Columbia, which provided for the Crown grants and other forms of tenure. The contention of the province was that this exercise of legislative power had operated to extinguish whatever interest the Indians may have had in the lands comprising the province, albeit without compensation. After all, how could it be said that Indian title still subsisted, when the pre-Confederation governments had assumed the power to dispose of the very lands the Indians claimed.

The trial judge, Mr. Justice Gould, accepted this argument and dismissed the Nishga Indians' claim. He held that, if aboriginal title had existed, it had been extinguished by the ordinances passed by the old colonial governments of Vancouver Island and British Columbia.

The Nishgas carried their case to the British Columbia Court of Appeal. There they suffered another setback. Mr. Justice Gould had not determined whether or not there is such a thing as aboriginal title. He had simply held that, if there were such a title, it had been extinguished before the colony had entered Confederation. He left to the higher courts the determination of whether or not aboriginal title is a concept recognized by Canadian law. The British Columbia Court of Appeal was ready to address the question. The judges of that court held that the law had never acknowledged any such concept as aboriginal title, that while governments might choose as a matter of policy to deal with Indians as if they did have a legal interest in land, there was, in reality, no such legal interest—no Indian title—and there never had been. Thus the Nishga Indians had never had aboriginal title. They went on to say that, if they had had such a title, it had been extinguished during the pre-Confederation era (as Mr. Justice Gould had held). Chief Justice H. W. Davey demonstrated the attitude of the court. Observing the Nishgas across an ethnographic gulf, he declined to believe that the Nishgas had their own ideas of land ownership, saying, "They were undoubtedly at the time of settlement a very primitive people with few of the institutions of civilized society, and none at all of our notions of private property."

It has been difficult to convince lawyers and judges that the Native peoples of Canada have certain rights based on the indisputable fact that they occupied vast areas if not the whole of this continent before the Europeans discovered, then colonized it. They had their own cultures, their own social institutions, their own laws. But of this lawyers and judges remained unaware. Chief Justice Davey was one of British Columbia's finest judges: he was patient, scholarly, and upright. Yet he could not understand that Native peoples had sophisticated concepts of legal relations and legal rights. He could not accept that people without a written language can, nevertheless, have an elaborated legal system of their own. And, as for their aboriginal title, how could the court acknowledge it? It was ill defined, it was not recorded in a system of title deeds, and it was not a form of private property but property held communally by the tribe.

Chief Justice Davey's inability to comprehend the true nature of Native culture and Native claims is widely shared. It results in an attitude toward Native people that infuriates them. This attitude is sometimes manifested in an attempt to preserve Native culture and sometimes in an attempt to eradicate it, but it is always manifested in a patronizing way. It assumes that Native culture cannot be viable in a contemporary context, that it cannot have a place in an urban, industrial society. This is the crux of the matter. Native peoples insist that their culture is still a vital force in their own lives, that it informs their own view of themselves, of the world about them, and of the dominant White society. We too easily assume that Native culture is static and unchanging. We see the Native peoples as locked into their past. Such an assumption may become self-fulfilling: by refusing to give Native people the means to deal with present problems in their own terms, their culture may, in fact, become static. But they are not locked into the past: we are excluding them from the present.

The culture of Native peoples amounts to more than crafts and carvings, dancing and drinking. Their tradition of decision-making by consensus, their respect for the wisdom of their elders, their concept of the extended family, their belief in a special relationship with the land, their respect for the environment, their willingness to share— all of these values persist in one way or another among them today, despite unremitting pressure to abandon them.

Thus Indian culture is not moribund. Indian ideas about their relationship with the land are the foundation of aboriginal title. But the Nishgas could not persuade the British Columbia Court of Appeal that they had ever in their long past had title to the Nass valley, or that they could assert any title in the present. Neither could the Nishgas nor any other of the Native peoples of Canada persuade the federal government to recognize aboriginal title. *The Statement of the Government of Canada on Indian Policy*, 1969, declared:

> Aboriginal claims to land...are so general and undefined that it is not realistic to think of them as specific claims capable of remedy except through a policy and programme that will end injustice to Indians as members of the Canadian community.

Prime Minister Trudeau, speaking on this subject in Vancouver on August 8, 1969, said, "Our answer is no. We can't recognize aboriginal rights because no society can be built on historical 'might have beens'." So there was no relief to be had in the courts, and no acknowledgment of their claims by the federal government.

But the Native peoples' conviction that their future must lie in the assertion of their common identity and in the defence of their common interests has proved stronger than anyone could have anticipated. Government policy was overthrown by the determination of the Native peoples to reject it. And the Nishga Indians' appeal to the Supreme Court of Canada was one of the principal instruments of that overthrow.

But wasn't Trudeau right? Shouldn't Native peoples be treated as any other minority? Why should there be a special place for them in Canadian life? The reason is simple. To refuse to acknowledge a special status for the Natives is to repudiate Canada's constitutional history. In the British North America Act, the Fathers of Confederation provided that Parliament should have exclusive legislative jurisdiction over the Native peoples of Canada. Why should the Native peoples be given special consideration? No such provision was made for the Ukrainians, the Swedes, the Italians, or for any other ethnic group or nationality. The Indians, the Inuit and the Metis did not immigrate to Canada as individuals or families who expected to be assimilated. Immigrants chose to come here and to submit to Canadians laws and institutions; their choices were individual choices. The Indians, the Inuit and the Metis were already here: they have been forced to submit to the laws and institutions, be they Anglophone or Francophone, of the dominant White society. And they have never relinquished their claim to be treated as distinct peoples in our midst.

To affirm the simple reality of this ancient truth—that the Native peoples are the aboriginal peoples of Canada and therefore have aboriginal rights—the Nishgas appealed to the Supreme Court of Canada. They urged the federal government to intervene on their behalf in the proceedings in the Supreme Court. Here at last was the opportunity, sought since Laurier's day, to bring the province of British Columbia before the Supreme Court of Canada and to resolve the question of Indian title in British Columbia. Jean Chrétien, then minister of Indian affairs and northern development, although personally sympathetic to the Nishgas' cause, declined to intervene, because he felt constrained by the federal policy enunciated in 1969 to refuse recognition of aboriginal rights.

The chiefs of the four villages in the Nass valley, together with village elders wearing their traditional sashes, travelled to Ottawa for the hearing in November, 1971. Seven judges of the Supreme Court of Canada sat on the case. The argument of the appeal took five days. The judges of the Supreme Court reserved their decision for fourteen months. When finally the court handed down its judgement in February, 1973, the Nishgas appeared to have lost, four to three. At last they had reached the end of the road. But careful study of the reasoning of the seven judges who heard the case soon made clear that, although technically the Nishgas had lost their case, they had in fact won a moral victory. Moral victories are not usually of any tangible value, but this victory had a great deal to do with bringing about a fundamental change in federal government policy.

Mr. Justice Wilfred Judson, speaking for three judges, found that the Nishgas, before the coming of the White man, had aboriginal title, a title recognized under English law. But, he went on to say, this title had been extinguished by pre-Confederation enactments of the old colony of British Columbia. Mr. Justice Emmett Hall, speaking for three judges, found that the Nishgas, before the coming of the White man, had aboriginal title, that it had never been lawfully extinguished, and that this title could be asserted even today. On this reckoning, the court was tied.

Mr. Justice Louis-Philippe Pigeon, the seventh judge, expressed no opinion on the main issue. He held against the Nishgas on the ground that they had proceeded by issuing a writ against the province of British Columbia. They should, he said, have proceeded by way of a petition of right, a procedure which was unavailable to them since it was necessary to have the consent of the province to issue a petition of right against the province. Mr. Justice Pigeon's vote meant that the Nishgas had lost, four to three.

Here is the crucial point. All of the six judges who had addressed the main question supported the view that English law in force in British Columbia when colonization began had recognized Indian title to the land. Here, for the first time, Canada's highest court had unequivocally affirmed the concept of aboriginal title. Mr. Justice Judson, in describing the nature of Indian title, relied on the passages from Professor Duff's *The Indian History of British Columbia* that were quoted above. He concluded,

> The fact is that when the settlers came the Indians were there, organized in societies and occupying the land as their forefathers had done for centuries. This is what Indian title means....What they are asserting in this action is that they had a right to continue to live on their lands as their forefathers had lived and that this right has never been lawfully extinguished.

Mr. Justice Judson went on to hold that the old colony of British Columbia had effectively extinguished the aboriginal title of the Nishga Indians. But he had no doubt that there is such a thing as aboriginal title.

Mr. Justice Hall, speaking for the three judges who were prepared to uphold the Nishgas' claim, urged that the court should adopt a contemporary view and not be bound by past and mistaken notions about Indians and Indian culture. In the judgement of Mr. Justice Hall you will find that sense of humanity—that stretch of the mind and heart— that enabled him to look at the idea of aboriginal rights and to see it as the Indian people see it. This required some idea of the place of Indian history in our own history. He suggested that Chief Justice Davey, in asserting that the Nishgas were at the time of settlement "a very primitive people with few of the institutions of civilized society, and none at all of our notions of private property," had assessed the Indian culture of 1858 by the same standards that the Europeans applied to the Indians of North America two or more centuries before. Mr. Justice Hall rejected this approach:

> The assessment and interpretation of the historical documents and enactments tendered in evidence must be approached in the light of present-day research and knowledge disregarding ancient concepts formulated when understanding of the customs and culture of our original people was rudimentary and incomplete and when they were thought to be wholly without cohesion, laws or culture, in effect a subhuman species. This concept of the original inhabitants of America led Chief Justice Marshall in his otherwise enlightened judgement in *Johnson vs. McIntosh* (1823) 8 Wheaton 543, which is the outstanding judicial pronouncement on the subject of Indian rights, to say: "But the tribes of Indians inhabiting this country were fierce savages whose occupation was war...." We now know that that assessment was ill-founded. The Indians did in fact at times engage in some tribal wars but war was not their vocation and it can be said that their pre-occupation with war pales into insignificance when compared to the religious and dynastic wars of "civilized" Europe of the 16th and 17th centuries.

Mr. Justice Hall concluded that the Nishgas had their own concept of aboriginal title before the coming of the White man and were still entitled to assert it today. He said:

> What emerges from the...evidence is that the Nishgas in fact are and were from time immemorial a distinctive cultural entity with concepts of ownership indigenous to their culture and capable of articulation under the common law, having "developed their cultures to higher peaks in many respects than in any other part of the continent north of Mexico."

Emmett Hall's contributions to Canadian life are numerous. But none is more important than his strong and stirring judgement in the Nishgas' case. For he held that the Nishgas' title could be asserted today. No matter that the province would be faced with innumerable legal tangles. What was right was right.

The Supreme Court's judgement, although it was not

handed down until fourteen months after the hearing in
the case, came at a propitious moment. The election of
1972 had returned the Liberals to power, but as a minority
government. To remain in office, the Liberals depended
on the good will of the opposition parties. The Nishga
decision now catapulted the question of aboriginal title
into the political arena. In Parliament, both the Conservatives and the New Democrats insisted that the federal
government must recognize its obligation to settle Native
claims. The all-party Standing Committee on Indian and
Northern Affairs passed a motion that approved the principle that a settlement of Native claims should be made in
regions where treaties had not already extinguished aboriginal title. On August 8, 1973, Jean Chrétien announced
that the federal government intended to settle Native land
claims in all parts of Canada where no treaties had yet
been made. Mr. Justice Hall's judgement can now be seen
to be the basis for the assertion today of Native land claims
throughout Canada.

Of course the Nishgas were not alone in effecting this
fundamental change in federal government policy. The
National Indian Brotherhood and many provincial and territorial Native organizations had worked steadily toward
the same end—but the Nishga case was a crucial development in the long process.

The land claims movement has given rise to a call among
the Native people for self-determination. After years of
poor achievement in our schools, after years of living on
the fringes of an economy that too often has no place for
them as workers and no need of them as consumers, and
without the political power to change these things, the
Native peoples have decided that they want to substitute
self-determination for enforced dependency.

The Nishga Indians, like the rest of Canada's Native
peoples, are re-entering Canadian history. They are not
some ghostly rabble whose former presence had left too
faint a mark to catch the attention of our political leaders
today. For more than two centuries, the history of Canada
was the history of an encounter between the French and

the Native peoples, then of an encounter between the English and the Native peoples. Only during the last century and a half have the Native peoples been relegated to a place off centre stage. Now they are returning from the wings to demand a speaking part again.

But what about the provinces? The federal government has agreed to settle aboriginal claims. But, unless the provinces are obligated by the Constitution to negotiate a settlement of Native claims, the provincial governments will no doubt continue to deny, as they have in the past, the existence of aboriginal rights or of any obligation to negotiate a settlement of aboriginal claims.

On December 15, 1980, the Nishgas appeared before the Special Joint Committee of the Senate and the House of Commons on the Constitution. Sixty-five years after Gideon Minesque had told the McKenna-McBride Commission that the Nishgas' claim to the Nass valley was "not a dream—we are certain that this land belongs to us," the President of the Nishga Tribal Council, James Gosnell, told the committee:

> The history of our people since the first white contact is the history of our struggle for recognition of aboriginal title to our lands. Our people are resolved to carry this struggle on until the Canadian nation, your Parliament, the Courts, and your people, see fit to justly settle our claim to the ownership of our lands.

On January 29, 1981, the Joint Committee agreed to recommend an amendment to the new Constitution, which provides:

> The aboriginal rights and treaty rights of the aboriginal peoples of Canada are hereby recognized and confirmed.

These words appear now in the Constitution. They will be binding not only on the federal government, but also on the provinces. They may provide the means by which the provinces will be brought to negotiations.

In the past, we sought to make the Native peoples over

in our own image. These efforts towards assimilation have failed. The Indians, the Inuit and the Metis survive, determined to be themselves. In the past their refusal to assimilate was usually passive, even covert. Today, this refusal is plain and unmistakable, a fact of national life that cannot be ignored. And now there is a constitutional provision which will give the Native peoples the means to enforce their right to a distinct place in Canadian life.

But what will it all mean, in practical terms? What measures may be required to define this distinct place for them? How can Natives who wish to do so defend their traditional economy while others, who wish to do so, find a place in the industrial economy of the dominant society? How can they defend their language, their art, their history? How can they be enabled to defend their right to a future of their own? These questions lie at the heart of Native claims.

No one can say how this new era will turn out. Will the provinces be recalcitrant? Will the courts be capable of grappling with the questions of "myth, legend, history and law" which aboriginal claims present? Will the politicians seek to limit the scope of any settlement so as to leave unanswered the very question of the structure of the relations between the dominant society and the Native peoples—the question that will await us no matter how long we seek to avoid it?

Native claims, whether founded on aboriginal rights or treaty rights, begin with the land; but they do not end there. They extend to renewable and non-renewable resources, education, health and social services, public order and, over-arching all of these, the future shape and composition of political institutions. The proposals that Native people are making are, many of them, far-reaching. They should not, however, be regarded as a threat to established institutions, but as an opportunity to affirm our commitment to the human rights of indigenous minorities. When all is said and done, the question of Native rights is a question of human rights. We must not make the mistake of underestimating the commitment that men and women have to those who share their own identity and their own past. It is more powerful than any ideology.

Settlement of their claims ought to offer the Native peoples a whole range of opportunities. In some cases priority should be given to local renewable resource activities—not because such activities are universally desirable, but because they are on a scale appropriate to many Native communities. These are activities that local people can undertake, that are amenable to local management and control, and that are related to traditional values. Development need not be defined exclusively in terms of large-scale, capital-intensive technology. But there is no reason why Native peoples should not have access as well to the economy of the dominant society where large-scale technology predominates. The settlement of Native claims ought to provide the means to enable Native peoples to thrive, and Native cultures to develop, in ways denied them in the past. They can become hunters, trappers, fishermen, lawyers, loggers, doctors, nurses, teachers, workers in the oil and gas fields, or in the sawmills and the stores. But most important of all, the collective fabric of Native life will be affirmed and strengthened. The sense of identity of individual Native people—their very well-being—depends upon it.

The Native peoples do not want to recreate a world that has vanished. They do, however, want to find a place in the world that we have forced upon them. Indian treaties, Indian reserves, the Indian Act—these are all institutions that we have devised to manage the Native peoples primarily for our own convenience. Now they want to develop institutions of their own fashioning; they are eager to see their cultures grow and change in directions they have chosen for themselves. They do not wish to be objects of sentimentality. They do not want Native culture, Native communities and the Native economy to be preserved in amber for the amusement and edification of others. They do not want to return to live in tents and igloos. Like us, they are residents of the twentieth century. They, too, live in a world in which progress has an industrial and technological definition. However, because the Native peoples use the technology of the dominant society, that fact does not mean that they should study only English or French in school, that they should learn no history except ours, or that they should be governed by our institutions alone.

It will take time for the Native peoples to limn their claims, for their claims are not limited to land and resources. They wish to achieve a measure of self-determination and self-government, and they see their claims as the means by which these things will be achieved. They are already undertaking to define their claims in the fields of education, health and social services—claims as significant to the urban Native as the rural Native. For instance, Native people complain that in school their children are told about the kings and queens of England and about the brave band of settlers who established the colony of New France on the shores of the St. Lawrence River. All that, they say, is your history. What about our history? They want schools in which their children can study Native history, Native languages, Native lore, and Native rights. Of course they also want their children to speak English or French, as the case may be, to understand the history of our European antecedents and their expansion into the New World, and to study mathematics, natural sciences, and everything else a person needs to know to function in the dominant society. But they must have schools in which they can learn about who they are as well as who we are. The Nishga Indians now have their own school district; it is one of the first in Canada to embrace a predominantly Native population. In June, 1979, ten years after the trial of their land claim before the Supreme Court of British Columbia, the first class graduated from the Nishga Secondary School.

If, in working out settlements of Native claims, we try to force Native development into moulds that we have cast, the whole process will end in failure. No tidy, bureaucratic chart will be of any use; and no governmental policy or program can succeed unless it takes into account the Native peoples' determination to remain themselves— Indian, Inuit or Metis. For this reason, the Native peoples must have distinct social, economic and political institutions. At the same time, they must have access to the social, economic and political institutions of the dominant society. When we are devising such arrangements, it is important to understand precisely what we are talking about. We are not talking about apartheid. In South Africa, the Blacks have been confined to *bantustans;* they have no right to live, to vote, or to work in South Africa except on sufferance. What Native peoples in Canada are asking for is the right to their own institutions, to the extent that they require them to preserve their culture and their sense of collective identity, and access to the institutions of the dominant society. Only if we were to deny them such access could our policy be said to be one of apartheid.

Canada is committed to a fair settlement of Native claims. This has come about because our institutions have offered the means for redress, and our tradition of tolerance has demanded that redress be made. Of course, this is only a beginning. But it offers to Canada an opportunity to make a contribution to human rights for indigenous peoples everywhere. Pierre Trudeau has suggested that,

> Canada could become the envied seat of a form of federalism that belongs to tomorrow's world....Canada could offer an example to all those new Asian and African states who must discover how to govern their polyethnic populations with proper regard for justice and liberty....Canadian federalism is an experiment of major proportions; it could become a brilliant prototype for the moulding of tomorrow's civilization.

It is all very well to say that Canadian institutional arrangements may speak to the emerging nations of Asia and Africa. But why not to our own hemisphere? There are 50 million Native people in North and South America, almost everywhere dispossessed, everywhere poor, everywhere powerless. In the past they refused to die; today they will not be assimilated. They insist that we must address the issues that have pursued us for almost 500 years, since Columbus set foot in the New World. How can we work out a just relationship between the dominant societies established by the white Europeans and the indigenous peoples of North and South America? In Canada this can be achieved through a fair settlement of Native claims. The settlement of these claims may, therefore, be important to men and women in many countries, truly a "prototype for tomorrow's civilization."

Epilogue: Towards the Regime of Tolerance

THIS BOOK HAS told the story of minorities and dissenters. Yet their story is a story that affects us all. All of us are conscious, in one way or another, of limitations to our freedom, even at its furthest periphery, and we may feel inhibited by them. Who can tell when the periphery will cease to be the periphery? When does a limitation of freedom at the periphery cut into the blood and bone of a free society? In matters related to civil liberty, an attack on the periphery is as serious as an attack on the heartland. As F. R. Scott has said, "No citizen's right can be greater than that of the least protected group."

The confrontations between the institutions of the state and minorities and dissenters reveal the true face of Canadian democracy. They have shown that we must establish safeguards—stronger than those that have existed in the past—to protect minorities and the rights of dissenters. The new Constitution, together with the Charter of Rights and Freedoms, provides these safeguards. Of course, they are not complete safeguards. No Constitution can completely resolve the great issues of human rights and fundamental freedoms raised in this book. To those who crave certainty in these matters, this will be a disappointment. But these issues are in a sense never resolved. They will continue to be the subject of inquiry, debate, and controversy. In the future, there will be doubts expressed, on grounds not so far considered, about the adequacy of our institutions; there will be protests, in language that will sometimes threaten or dismay, on behalf of causes only faintly discerned as yet; there will be cries for the curtailment of due process; there will be demands by newly emerging minorities; and conflicts here at home and overseas will give rise to calls for the suppression of minorities on grounds of racial, religious, linguistic or cultural differences. We shall have to remember that our belief in the free marketplace of ideas and our willingness to live according to this belief are the foundations of our stability and strength. The Constitution and the Charter will buttress these foundations.

I believe in the uses of democratic institutions. Representative government, due process, trial by jury, free trade unions—all of these are the means to the dispersal of political and economic power. All of these, it seems to me, will be strengthened by the Constitution and Charter which offer those who are under attack a place to stand, ground to defend, and the means for others to come to their aid.

The constitutional debate itself has had its uses. It is important that we reflect on the strengths and weaknesses of the institutions by which we are governed, and even more important, that we reflect on the idea of Canada. Why do we believe in Canada? What are the things that are most important in our shared history? Why is Canada worth preserving in the 1980s? Here we are, in the 115th year of Confederation, twenty-four million souls scattered among the snow and scenery. Canada has persisted. Why? And why should its survival matter?

Some believe that the Canadian achievement lies in the utilization of our natural resources—the establishment of the fishery, the gathering of fur, the development of the grain trade, the building of an empire in timber, and now the exploitation of oil and gas and minerals on our frontiers and beyond. Here lies the Canadian achievement, in the conquest of our cold and distant landscapes and seascapes. These common tasks, it is said, are what unite us all.

But isn't there more to it than that? Isn't there a distinctive Canadian intellectual contribution to the legal and political order, a product of the encounter between the English and the French in North America, yet distinctive because it represents something essentially Canadian?

We are two distinct societies—two nations, if you will. It would be a mistake to pretend otherwise. Yet we are mixed up together, and we have chosen to stay together. There are a million or more Native people in our midst, claiming a measure of self-determination. And there are millions of new Canadians, immigrants of every ethnic and racial background, and every political and religious persuasion. Thus diversity is in a sense the essence of the Canadian experience; and the Constitution and the Charter reflect this diversity.

Some argue that we will be left with a constitutional hodge-podge: protection for languages here, over there guarantees for aboriginal peoples, here an affirmation of multiculturalism. But surely these represent the logical outcome of our history, surely they reflect the strengths of our nation. Our two languages, English and French, represent the two great European civilizations that established the Canadian polity. In some provinces both languages will be official languages; under the Constitution minority language educational rights will be entrenched in all provinces and territories. The Native peoples, who were here before the French or the English, will be assured of a special status, and their aboriginal rights recognized. But the designation of two official languages, the entrenchment of minority language educational rights, and the recognition of the special place of the Native peoples—none of these are to stand in the way of immigrants continuing to use their own languages and adhering to their customs as a matter of private choice. It is provided that the Charter shall be interpreted in a manner consistent with the preservation and enhancement of the multicultural heritage of Canadians. Whatever their race, national or ethnic origin, colour or religion, Canadians are to be equal under the law and entitled to the equal protection of the law.

Canada can, perhaps, develop ways whereby men and women of different races, religions, languages and culture can live together. Woodrow Wilson's ideal of the nation-state has proved impossible of achievement. Even Great Britain and France are now contending with the questions with which the presence of minorities confronts them. Even if Quebec were to achieve independence, she would at once be faced with the very questions that now confront Canadians: the rights of a great linguistic minority, the claims of the Native peoples, and the place of numerous ethnic and racial groups.

A strong nation will nurture diversity; a strong nation can abide dissent. Perhaps the French-Canadian presence will not survive in the Anglophone strongholds, but it will be a diminished Canada that denies French-Canadian minorities the opportunity to survive, indeed to flourish. The voice of dissent in Canada may be stopped, but it will be a fearful and irresolute people who do it. We may reject the claims of the Native peoples, but if we do, we shall be turning our backs on the truth of our beginnings as a nation.

Many have suggested that the Constitution and the Charter are fundamentally flawed because they are not the product of consensus between the federal government and the provinces. They were adopted pursuant to a joint resolution of Parliament; there were no concurrent resolutions of all the provinces or even of a majority of the provinces. Indeed, except for Ontario and New Brunswick, the provinces were opposed. The Supreme Court of Canada has determined that there is no legal requirement for the concurrence of all the provinces or even a consensus of the provinces. Given that, after many years, a consensus with the provinces could not be achieved, it is difficult to argue that, if Canada were ever to patriate its Constitution, the federal government, having submitted a resolution to Parliament, should not have proceeded on its own to Westminster.

Some argue that the unilateral patriation of the Constitution will set a precedent, giving the federal government the power to act on its own whenever it sees the need to amend the Constitution—that unilateral patriation will thus undermine the very essence of the federal structure of the nation. I don't think it will. The Constitution can in future be amended only by Parliament and a certain combination of provinces, or by national referendum. The amending formula is weighted according to population. Quebec and Ontario both have a veto. So do the four western provinces, and so do the four Atlantic provinces. I do not see how it could be otherwise. Does anyone suggest that every province should have a veto? Or that no province should have a veto? But, point out those who fear the new Constitution will give the federal government too much power, a provincial veto can be overcome by a national referendum vote. Will this really mean that the federal government can win every referendum by choosing the right question to ask? I do not think so. The Quebec government spent four years trying to think of a question to ask Quebecers that would yield the answer it wanted. In the end it failed; the electorate will perceive the true issue to be determined. Is a vote on a constitutional amendment inconsistent with the idea of federalism? I do not think so. The inventors of federalism, the Founding Fathers of the United States of America, included such a provision in the Constitution of the United States. In an imperfect world, these provisions will do.

Has the federal government's insistence that Parliament should act alone divided the country, as those who reject the Constitution and the Charter allege? We have had twelve months and more of contention since the Trudeau proposals were introduced in September, 1980. Quebec, it is said, will never accept the Constitution and the Charter; neither will the western provinces.

Quebec voted for federalism in 1980; I find it difficult to believe Quebecers will reject it because the Constitution is being brought home. Has the west been alienated? In a sense, the west has always been alienated; there is a western tradition of protest. There has always been tension between Ottawa and some of the provinces. There have been advocates of separation from time to time throughout Canadian history, and not only in Quebec. In 1878, the Legislature of British Columbia passed a resolution to secede from Confederation, on the ground that there had been undue delay in the construction of the promised railway to the Pacific coast. I think the prairie protest movements of the 1920s and 1930s were far more significant indicators of western alienation than the cries of disaffection that we hear today.

Once the Constitution is brought home, what changes will it mean in the existing distribution of powers between the federal government and the provinces? The federal government will continue as our national government. What about the provinces? They are powerful today. Some of them have enormous revenues and resources, and they will continue to possess them under the new Constitution. In fact, their reach over resources and revenue will be extended by the Constitution, a measure that will be to the advantage of the resource-rich provinces. At the same time, equalization—the means by which the provinces that are not as well endowed are sustained by sharing the revenue generated in the richer provinces—will be entrenched in the Constitution. Each province will have the legal tools to execute the political will of the people of the province; of that I have no doubt.

The Constitution will, however, place some limitations on provincial powers. It will place these limitations equally on federal powers. It will do so with respect to language rights and fundamental freedoms. It is here that the views of opponents of the Charter in Quebec and the western provinces converge. They reject the view that language rights should be entrenched; and they also insist that the provinces are the appropriate guardians of fundamental freedoms. It seems to me the questions involved here are basic. If we cannot agree on entrenchment of Francophone rights in the English-speaking provinces and of Anglophone rights in Quebec, then it seems to me there is no commonality of views about the values that should undergird Canadian federalism. Similarly with fundamental freedoms. If every Canadian is not to enjoy freedom of conscience, of speech, of religion, of association and assembly, as necessary incidents of citizenship in the Canadian state, if the social contract between the citizens and the federal state to which they owe allegiance does not include express provisions for the safeguarding of fundamental freedoms throughout Canada, freedoms common to every citizen in every province and enforceable equally in every province, then what is the point of our remaining together? What is the common bond—what are the common values—that hold us together?

Of course, the entrenchment of minority rights will limit the powers of Parliament and of the provinces. This is the whole point. These rights should never be subjected to the will of the majority. They are *minority* rights. The use of the War Measures Act in the First World War and the Second World War to suppress political and religious dissent; its use in peacetime in 1946 to banish the Japanese Canadians and in 1970 to curtail due process; the extension of police power to harass some Canadians and to spy on thousands of others—these illustrate abuses of federal legislative powers over human rights and fundamental freedoms. But on this issue, I want to make myself quite clear. I do not believe diversity is—or dissent is—nor have they ever been, coextensive with provincial rights. Too often, we have seen one province or another insisting upon conformity to some prevailing orthodoxy. When in the 1890s, schools were taken away from French Canadians in Manitoba, it was by the province. In 1912, it was the province of Ontario that passed Regulation 17 to limit the use of French in the Franco-Ontarians' separate schools. In the late 1930s, it was the province of Alberta that passed legislation to limit freedom of the press. When, in the 1940s, Japanese Canadians were removed from their homes on the Pacific coast and interned, the province of British Columbia, far from trying to protect its citizens, led the attacks against them. It was the province of Alberta that passed legislation to restrict the sale of land to Hutterites in 1944 (and, it should be said, that repealed the legislation in 1972). When, in 1969, the federal government proposed to sever the constitutional link between Ottawa and the Native peoples, the federal government found that the Native peoples had no wish to be left to the exclusive jurisdiction of the provinces. Thus, under existing constitutional arrangements, the Native peoples of the north oppose provincial status for Yukon Territory and the Northwest Territories. In 1970, when the federal government invoked the War Measures Act, it was the provincial authorities in Quebec that immediately imprisoned hundreds of its citizens as political dissenters. In the 1970s it has been the province of Quebec that has tried to deny English-speaking Canadians migrating to that province the right to educate their children in their own language.

Many argue that the entrenchment of human rights and fundamental freedoms, placing them beyond the reach of Parliament and the provinces, will diminish the powers of our elected representatives and enhance the powers of the courts. And, of course, it will do precisely that. In a federal state, the courts interpret the provisions of the Constitution that divide legislative powers. Why should they not also have the task of interpreting the nature and scope of the rights that belong to all the people and lie beyond the reach of legislative authority? Judges may not always be wiser than politicians, but they should be able to stand more firmly against angry winds blowing in the streets.

Canadians are the heirs of two great European civilizations. From England, we have the legacy of parliamentary institutions and the rule of law. From France, we have inherited egalitarian ideals and our notions about the rights of man. Can we not build on these foundations a structure of freedom in which the place of minorities and the rights of dissenters are secure?

This exercise in Constitution-making should enable us to know ourselves, to discover who we are and what we may become, to realize the uses of diversity and dissent. This is what the Canadian experience is all about: to see if people who are different can live together and work together, to learn to regard diversity not with suspicion, but as a cause for celebration—to realize Laurier's regime of tolerance in the life of the nation.

Chapter Notes

Much of my professional life has been spent considering questions of human rights and dissent. When I decided to write about them in their historical, cultural, and legal context in Canada, I was fortunate to be able to draw upon the work of Canada's historians, not only that of giants such as Arthur Lower, Donald Creighton and Harold Innis, but also of the current generation of Canadian historians, who have explored and revealed much about every aspect of the Canadian experience.

Most of these historians have travelled the main highway of Canadian history. It is from them that we have learned who we are and how we got here. My own journey has taken me from Port Royal to the Nass valley. But I have tried to give an account of some of the people and some of the issues forgotten along the way. Of course, I have not dealt with them all. This book does not tell of the expulsion of the Protestant, English-speaking farmers from the Eastern Townships of Quebec at the turn of the century. Neither is there an account of the enactment of Robert Borden's War Time Elections Act of 1917, disenfranchising naturalized immigrants from the countries of Central and Eastern Europe, legislation founded on principles of ethnic discrimination. I have devoted a chapter to the Jehovah's Witnesses, but not to the Mennonites, the Hutterites or the Doukhobours. Nor have I discussed the legislation passed in Alberta in the late 1930s to restrict freedom of the press. Nor the struggle led by Thérèse Casgrain for votes for women in Quebec. A book that tried to cover all of the ground would be very much longer than this one.

Anyone reading about human rights and fundamental freedoms in Canada realizes that much of the ground has been traversed by F. R. Scott and Pierre Trudeau. I have taken the liberty of quoting from the writings of both, since no two Canadians have pondered questions of human rights and cultural conflict as deeply as they have. Scott's life and work has recently been celebrated. His *Essays on the Constitution: Aspects of Canadian Law and Politics* (University of Toronto Press, 1977) is a remarkable testament to his lifelong vision of a Canada that exemplifies tolerance and social justice. Pierre Trudeau, before entering politics, wrote extensively about relations between Canada's two founding peoples, especially about language policy, and about civil liberties. Many of these pieces have been collected in *Federalism and the French Canadians* (Macmillan of Canada, 1968); in them Trudeau worked out the idea of Canada that he has pursued throughout his political career.

I have not tried to impose a single, unqualified meaning on such words as "nation," "society," and "people." I think, however, that where each appears, the meaning intended is plain.

André Siegfried, discussing relations between English and French, called his book *The Race Question in Canada* (Eveleigh Nash, London, 1907, reprinted in The Carleton Library, McClelland and Stewart Limited, 1966). In 1907 that was the accepted term. Today the issue is linguistic and cultural, and should be described as such. I have, in Chapters 2 and 8, used the expression "White" to denote the dominant society and culture of Canada, which, though not wholly White, is thought of as such by Native peoples. At any rate, this kind of usage leaves "ethnic" with a fairly precise meaning (which occasionally overlaps with "race").

It is impossible to list all of the books that I turned to in tracing the development of ideas of human rights and dissent in Canada. The following, by no means complete, list includes some that I found especially helpful. Virtually all of the quotations in the text are to be found in *Hansard*, other official sources, or the standard textbooks. Where a quotation would not be easily available, I have given the citation in these notes. I have included citations for the legal cases referred to. Most of the statutes referred to are cited in the cases. The judgement of the Supreme Court of Canada, concerning the propriety of the federal government resolution to patriate the Constitution and entrench a Charter of Rights and Freedoms was handed down on September 28, 1981.

Chapter 1: The Acadians: Expulsion and Return

The best short history, in English, of the Acadians is by Professor Naomi Griffiths, *The Acadians: Creation of a People* (McGraw-Hill Ryerson Limited, 1973). My references to the population of Acadia are taken from her book, as she has taken great care in her estimates. Estimates of the number who lived in Acadia at the time of the expulsion range from 7,000 to 18,000, and of those expelled from 6,000 to 10,000. In *The Acadian Deportation: Deliberate Perfidy or Cruel Necessity* (Copp Clark Ltd., 1969), Professor

Griffiths has assembled many of the documents regarding the deportation as well as the various views of writers and historians.

In Marcel Trudel's *The Beginnings of New France, 1524-1663*, translated by Patricia Claxton (The Canadian Centenary Series, McClelland and Stewart Limited, 1973), there is a detailed account of the early French settlements in North America. Carl O. Sauer in *Seventeenth Century North America* (Turtle Island: Berkeley, 1980) has provided a good account of the life of the first French settlers at Port Royal. The standard work on Acadia is John Bartlett Brebner's *New England's Outpost: Acadia Before the Conquest of Canada* (Meridian Books, The World Publishing Company, 1927). *Canada Before Confederation* by R. Cole Harris and John Warkentin (Oxford University Press, 1974), a fine study in historical geography, includes a most helpful discussion of Acadian farming.

I have tried to write about Acadia without becoming entangled in an account of the rivalry between Charles d'Aulnay and Charles de la Tour in the 1730s and 1740s. It is fascinating, but beside the point I wish to make. This may be unjust to de la Tour, who has been described as the father of Acadia. Mine may also be the first account of Acadian history that makes no reference to Longfellow's "Evangeline."

The history of denominational schools in the Maritime provinces is discussed at length in *Book II, Education,* of the *Report of the Royal Commission on Bilingualism and Biculturalism* (Queen's Printer, Ottawa, 1968). The judgement of the New Brunswick Supreme Court in *Ex parte Renaud* is reported in (1873) 14 N.B.R. 273. The Privy Council expressed its approval of *Ex parte Renaud* in *Maher vs. Town of Portland* (1874) 2 Cart. 486.

Professor Alfred G. Bailey's paper read to the Humanities Research Council of Canada may be found in G. A. Rawlyk, ed., *Historical Essays on the Atlantic Provinces* (The Carleton Library, McClelland and Stewart Limited, 1967). I think Professor Bailey's views were representative of Anglophone opinion at the time.

Under the Charter of Rights, the right of citizens to have their children educated in a minority language applies only wherever in a province the number of children "is sufficient to warrant the provision to them out of public funds of minority language instruction." Whether or not such instruction is received in minority language schools (as opposed to classrooms in majority language schools) will depend on the interpretation that may be given to the expression "minority language educational facilities." The resolution of these issues lies in the future. I refer to them in Chapter 3.

I have not made any reference to the government of New Brunswick's bill, introduced in 1981, which promises the Acadians "distinct social, educational, and cultural institutions," as it is not yet clear what the final form of the legislation will be.

Chapter 2: Louis Riel and the New Nation

In this chapter I have not accented the word "Metis," as the Metis do not do so in their publications.

More books have been written about Louis Riel than about any other figure in Canadian history. G. F. G. Stanley's biography, *Louis Riel* (Ryerson Press, 1963) is the standard work. Stanley also discussed both Riel uprisings in *The Birth of Western Canada* (published in 1936, reissued by University of Toronto Press in 1961). Stanley advanced the theory in this book that the two insurrections constituted a stand by the Metis against the coming of White settlement, agriculture, commerce and industry to Manitoba and Saskatchewan, and should not be seen as primarily a clash between English-speaking Protestants and French-speaking Catholics. Stanley and the late Professor W. L. Morton (in *Manitoba: A History*, University of Toronto Press, 1957, Second Edition, 1967) each regarded the Metis as dupes of the Nor'Westers during the Pemmican War. It was in an essay entitled "The Bias of Prairie Politics," which appeared in Donald Swainson, ed., *Historical Essays on the Prairie Provinces* (The Carleton Library, McClelland and Stewart Limited, 1970) that Morton suggested that Riel and the Metis were the forerunners of Prairie protest movements.

Some excellent pieces may be found in *The West and the Nation, Essays in Honour of W. L. Morton*, edited by Carl Berger and Ramsay Cook (McClelland and Stewart Limited, 1976), particularly "The Anglican Church and the Disintegration of Red River Society, 1818-1870" by Frits Pannekoek, and "French Quebec and the Métis Question, 1869-1885" by Arthur Silver. Doug Owram, in *Promise of Eden, The Canadian Expansion Movement and the Idea of the West 1856-1900* (University of Toronto Press, 1980) has shown how the west was transformed in the minds of Ontarians from a sub-Arctic wilderness to a land suitable to large-scale agricultural settlement.

Desmond Morton, in his introduction to *The Queen vs. Louis Riel* (University of Toronto Press, 1974) has examined sympathetically Macdonald's decision to allow Riel to hang, useful as a contrast to most accounts. George Woodcock has explored the relationship between Riel and Dumont in *Gabriel Dumont, The Métis Chief and His Lost World* (Hurtig, 1975).

The Metis of Manitoba, by Joe Sawchuck (Peter Martin Associates, 1978), is an excellent little book about the emergence of the New Nation and its present-day manifestations. *Native Rights in Canada* (Second Edition, General Publishing, 1972), by Professor Peter Cumming and Neil Mickenberg, contains a very good historical account of Metis claims and the policies adopted by the federal government in relation to those claims. There is an excellent chapter on the same subject in H. W. Daniels' *Native People and the Constitution of Canada* (Mutual Press, 1981), the Report of the Metis and Non-Status Indian Constitutional Review Commission. I have not tried to indicate the form that a settlement of Metis claims might take. That lies in the future. What I have tried to do is to address the question of constitutional recognition for the Metis as an aboriginal people.

Chapter 3: Laurier and The Separate Schools

The quotation that opens the chapter and the penultimate quotation are both from *The Heirs of Lord Durham (Manifesto of a Vanishing People)* (Burns and MacEachern, Limited, 1978). In this book, The French Canadians outside Quebec state their case today.

Laurier's career and the school crises in Manitoba and Ontario are fully covered in O. D. Skelton's *Life and Letters of Sir Wilfrid Laurier* (2 volumes, The Carleton Library, McClelland and Stewart Limited, 1965). John W. Dafoe wrote a useful impression of Laurier's career in *Laurier, A Study in Canadian Politics* (Thomas Allen & Son Ltd., 1922, reprinted in The Carleton Library, McClelland and Stewart Limited, 1963). Joseph Schull in his *Laurier* (Macmillan of Canada, 1965) has some good chapters touching on the school question. See also Professor Blair Neatby's *Laurier and a Liberal Quebec* (McClelland and Stewart Limited, 1973). The leading work, in English, on *The French Canadians: 1760-1967*, is by Mason Wade (Macmillan of Canada, 1968).

Book II, *Education*, of *The Report of the Royal Commission on Bilingualism and Biculturalism* (Queen's Printer, Ottawa, 1968), contains an excellent history of French-language education in the English-speaking provinces. Professor D. A. Schmeiser in *Civil Liberties in Canada* (Oxford University Press, 1964), has discussed at length the legal history of conflicts in Canada relating to denominational education. See particularly Chapter IV, "Denominational Education."

The school crisis in Manitoba is dealt with in W. L. Morton's *History of Manitoba* (University of Toronto Press, 1966). It is the subject of a full-length treatment in *Priests and Politicians, Manitoba Schools and the Election of 1896*, by Paul Crunican (University of Toronto Press, 1973). In Chapter 9, Crunican has attempted to assess the true extent of clerical involvement in the election of 1896. An excellent book of essays on the school crises in Manitoba and the west, and in Ontario, is Craig R. Brown, ed., *Minorities, Schools and Politics* (University of Toronto Press, 1969). The contributors are D. G. Creighton, W. L. Morton, Ramsay Cook, Manoly R. Lupul, Marilyn Barber and Margaret Prang.

Barrett vs. City of Winnipeg is reported in (1892) 19 S.C.R. 374 (Supreme Court of Canada) and (1892) A.C. 445 (Privy Council). *Brophy vs. Attorney-General of Manitoba* is reported in (1893) 22 S.C.R. 577 (Supreme Court of Canada) and (1895) A.C. 202 (Privy Council). I have not discussed at length the complicated legal arguments regarding the interpretation of Section 22 of the Manitoba Act that account for the turnabout of the Privy Council in *Brophy vs. A. G. of Man.* Schmeiser has done this in *Civil Liberties in Canada*, pp. 163-4. The judgements of the courts in *Ottawa Separate School Trustees vs. Mackell* are reported in 32 D.L.R. 245 (Ontario High Court); 24 D.L.R. 475 (Ontario Court of Appeal) 32; (1917) A.C. 62 (Privy Council) and see *Attorney General of Manitoba vs. Forest* (1979) 2 S.C.R. 1032.

Chapter 4: The Banished Canadians: Mackenzie King and the Japanese Canadians

Ken Adachi's book *The Enemy That Never Was: A History of the Japanese Canadians* (McClelland and Stewart Limited, 1976) is the essential account of the history of the Japanese Canadians. It is authoritative and complete. Barry Broadfoot's collection of interviews, *Years of Sorrow, Years of Shame: The Japanese Canadians in World War II* (Doubleday Canada Limited, 1977) is a useful companion to Adachi's book. The Japanese Canadians themselves have published a moving and beautifully illustrated history of their life in Canada, entitled *The Japanese-Canadians, A Dream of Riches, 1877-1977*, published by the Japanese-Canadians Centennial Committee, Vancouver, 1978.

F. E. La Violette produced the first survey of *The Canadian Japanese in World War Two* (Toronto, Canadian Institute of International Affairs, 1948). Professor W. Peter Ward has written an excellent scholarly analysis of the nature, origin and persistence of anti-Asiatic feeling in British Columbia, *White Canada Forever* (McGill-Queen's University Press, 1978). It includes a thorough discussion of the measures taken against the Japanese Canadians in British Columbia. Ward elaborated on the subject in "Class and Race in the Social Structure of British Columbia, 1870-1939" (*British Columbia Studies*, No. 45, Spring, 1980). Professor H. F. Angus wrote about discrimination against Orientals in British Columbia in (1931) IX *Canadian Bar Review* 5 and (1942) IX *Canadian Journal of Economics and Political Science* 506, and see Patricia E. Roy, "The Oriental Menace in British Columbia," in *Historical Essays on British Columbia*, ed. J. Friesen and H. K. Ralston (McClelland and Stewart Limited, 1976).

The Report of the Special Committee on Orientals in British Columbia, December, 1940, prepared by three senior public servants, indicated that the principal danger to the Japanese Canadians, particularly those who might enlist, lay in the hostile attitude of Whites towards them. The Committee, therefore, recommended that Japanese Canadians should not be called up for military training. This did not, however, constitute a justification for evacuation and internment.

A good history of the Japanese Americans is Frank F. Chuman's *The Bamboo People: The Law and Japanese Americans* (Publisher's Inc., Del Mar, California, 1976).

The judgement of the Supreme Court of British Columbia (*en banc*) in *Cunningham vs. Tomey Homma* is reported in (1899-1900) 7 B.C.R. 36, and the judgement of the Privy Council in the same case is reported at (1903) A.C. 151. The judgment of the Supreme Court of Canada in *Reference re Deportation of the Japanese Canadians* is reported in (1946) S.C.R. 248, of the Privy Council in (1947) A.C. 87. In discussing the litigation I have referred to the issue of deportation as bearing upon the powers of the Canadian government over Canadian citizens. At the time Canadians were classified as British subjects, there being no Canadian Citizenship Act until 1950. My own usage is intended to avoid confusion.

In 1947, a Commission of Inquiry, under Mr. Justice R. I. Bird of the Supreme Court of British Columbia, was appointed to investigate the claims of Japanese Canadians that they had suffered pecuniary loss. It was found that some properties had been sold below fair market value, and additional payments were recommended. As a result, Japanese Canadians received a further $1,222,929. But many Japanese Canadians found that they were not eligible for compensation, and many others chose not to bring their claims before the Commission in view of its limited terms of reference. The Commission's recommendations and the limited compensation paid as a result of them are not regarded by the Japanese Canadians as having concluded the matter. The Japanese Canadian Citizens Association has suggested that compensation today might take the form of government support for a foundation dedicated to the preservation and enhancement of Japanese-Canadian history and culture.

In this chapter, I have referred to the problems of enacting legislation to curb hate propaganda. Canada enacted amendments to the Criminal Code outlawing hate propaganda in 1969, pursuant to the recommendations of the Special Committee on Hate Propaganda, 1966, chaired by Professor Maxwell Cohen. These amendments make it an offence, punishable by imprisonment for five years, to advocate genocide, that is, to advocate the destruction of any group distinguished by colour, race, religion or ethnic origin. No prosecution has ever been brought under this section. Other provisions make it an offence to incite hatred of any such group where such incitement is likely to lead to a breach of the peace. It is also an offence wilfully to promote hatred against any such group. There has been only one prosecution under these latter provisions. The charge was one of promoting hatred against French Canadians in Essex County. A conviction at trial was reversed on appeal: *R. V. Buzzanga and Durocher* (1979) 49 C.C.C. 2d 369 (Ont. C.A.). The case is bizarre, and no guide to the usefulness of the legislation, because the literature in question was distributed by two young French Canadians with a view to generating militancy among their own people. There are also provisions for the confiscation of hate propaganda, but these have not been used. Some of the provinces have enacted or are considering similar legislation. The British Columbia legislation was enacted pursuant to a report written by John D. McAlpine, Q. C., for the provincial government. It contains as convincing an argument for such legislation as we are likely to have: *Report Arising Out of the Activities of the*

Ku Klux Klan in British Columbia (Queen's Printer, Victoria, 1981). The legislation in British Columbia and Saskatchewan is too recent for any conclusions to be drawn regarding its effectiveness.

Chapter 5: The Communist Party and the Limits of Dissent

Professor Ivan Avakumovic has written the authoritative history of the Communist party, entitled *The Communist Party in Canada* (McClelland and Stewart Limited, 1975).

The recollections of Tim Buck have been published posthumously under the title *Yours in the Struggle: Reminiscences of Tim Buck*, ed., Bill Beeching and Phyllis Clarke (NC Press, 1977). Buck wrote *Canada and the Russian Revolution* (Progress Books, 1967). Oscar Ryan has written an adulatory biography, *Tim Buck: A Conscience for Canada* (Progress Books, 1975). These books discuss the work of the Communist party in Canada from a Communist point of view.

David J. Bercuson, in *Fools and Wise Men, The Rise and Fall of One Big Union* (McGraw-Hill Ryerson Limited, 1978) has written an excellent account of the One Big Union and the Western Labour Conference held in Calgary in 1919. D. C. Masters has written the standard account of *The Winnipeg General Strike* (University of Toronto Press, 1973). Professor Donald Avery, in *Dangerous Foreigners, European Immigrant Workers and Labour Radicalism in Canada, 1896-1932* (McClelland and Stewart Limited, 1979), has documented the way in which the Communist party in the 1920s was a movement of social and political protest for non-English-speaking workers, especially in the western provinces.

Two excellent books which discuss the Communist role in the trade-union movement in Canada are Gad Horowitz, *Canadian Labour in Politics* (University of Toronto Press, 1968), and Irving M. Abella, *Nationalism, Communism, and Canadian Labour* (University of Toronto Press, 1973). Abella has documented the contribution the Communist party made to the organization of industrial unionism in Canada in the 1930s and 1940s. The history of the Communist party and the trade-union movement in British Columbia is recounted in Paul Phillips, *No Power Greater* (Boag Foundation, Vancouver, 1967); see especially Chapter 9.

The assertion that a member or members of King's cabinet met with representatives of the LPP to co-ordinate electoral strategy appears in a number of authoritative works, e.g. Avakumovik, at p. 161. The statement by Robin Bourne appeared in *The Globe and Mail*, June 24, 1981.

R. *vs. Buck* is reported in (1932) 57 Can. C.C. 290 (Ont. C.A.). *Smith and Rhulands Ltd. vs. The Queen* is reported in (1953) 2 S.C.R. 95. The decision of the Benchers in *Martin vs. Law Society of B. C.* is reported in (1949) 1 D.L.R. 105, and of the British Columbia Court of Appeal in (1950) 3 D.L.R. 173. *Switzman vs. Elbling* (the Padlock Act case) is reported in (1957) S.C.R. 285. I have not overlooked the fact that the notion that freedom of speech is entrenched in the BNA Act as a concomitant of parliamentary institutions was first put forward by Chief Justice Lyman Duff and Mr. Justice Cannon in *Reference re Alberta Legislation* (1938) S.C.R. 100. But Mr. Justice Rand gave the concept forceful and unique expression in the series of judgments referred to in Chapters 5 and 6. Professor McWhinney's description of Mr. Justice Rand as a legal philosopher is found in his *Judicial Review in the English-Speaking World*, (Second Edition, University of Toronto Press, 1960, p. 216).

Chapter 6: *Jehovah's Witnesses: Church, State, and Religious Dissent*

Professor M. J. Penton of the University of Lethbridge, himself a Witness, has written the definitive history of the *Jehovah's Witnesses in Canada: Champions of Freedom of Speech and Religion* (Macmillan of Canada, 1976). I have relied upon his account, the only complete one, of the treatment of the Witnesses during the First World War, their conflicts with the broadcasting authorities between the wars, and their treatment during the Second World War. Professor Walter Tarnopolsky's review of Professor Penton's book appeared in (1978), 59 *Canadian Historical Review,* 259.

Pierre Trudeau in *Federalism and the French Canadians* (Macmillan of Canada, 1968) and André Laurendeau in *Witness for Quebec* (Macmillan of Canada, 1973) discussed the great issues that preoccupied Quebec intellectuals in the Duplessis years.

Kenneth McRoberts and Dale Postgate in *Quebec: Social Change and Political Crisis* (Revised Edition, McClelland and Stewart Limited, 1980) have reviewed the origins of the Quiet Revolution and the significance of the changes it brought. Marcel Rioux's *Quebec in Question* (James Lorimer & Company, 1978) is an excellent short history of Quebec, written by an *Indépendantiste*. And see *Ideologies in Quebec: The Historical Development* by Denis

Monière, translated by Richard Howard (University of Toronto Press, 1981).

Boucher vs. The King is reported in (1951) S.C.R. 265. *Saumer vs. Quebec* is reported in (1953) 2 S.C.R. 299, (1953) 4 D.L.R. 641. *Attorney-General vs. Dupond* is reported in (1978) 2 S.C.R. 770. *Roncarelli vs. Duplessis* is reported in (1959) S.C.R. 121. I have already discussed the *Dupond* case in (1980) 1 Supreme Court L.R. 503.

Chapter 7: Democracy and Terror: October, 1970

William Kilbourn, relying upon a phrase of Northrop Frye's, entitled his 1970 anthology *Canada: A Guide to the Peaceable Kingdom* (Macmillan of Canada, 1970). The book appeared not too long before the October Crisis.

Professor Denis Smith in 1971 published a critique of Trudeau's handling of the October Crisis, *Bleeding Hearts, Bleeding Country: Canada and the Quebec Crisis* (Hurtig, 1971). He was severely critical of Trudeau, both as regards his dealings with the kidnappers and his invoking of the War Measures Act. Smith's book contains an especially good analysis of the political goals of the FLQ. In *Rumours of War* (James Lorimer & Company, 1971), Aubrey Golden and Ron Haggart provide a day-by-day account of the events of the October Crisis. Their book is the work of two dedicated civil libertarians, and they have constructed it to illuminate the civil liberties issues which arose. The second edition, published in 1978, contains a thoughtful introduction by Robert Stanfield. James Eayrs' columns, written at the time of the October Crisis, are reproduced in *Greenpeace and Her Enemies* (House of Anansi, 1973). A group of articles about the events of the October Crisis, which originally appeared in *Canadian Forum*, was published in *Power Corrupted*, edited by Abraham Rotstein (New Press, 1971). The contributors are, to say the least, critical of Trudeau and his government. Indeed, Trudeau has few defenders. Virtually no one has sought in a scholarly way to defend him. Gérard Pelletier, however, in *The October Crisis* (McClelland and Stewart Limited, 1971) offered an apologia for the federal government's handling of the October Crisis. John Gellner wrote a study of the urban guerrilla in *Bayonets in the Streets* (Collier-Macmillan Canada Ltd., 1974), which includes a useful analysis of the October Crisis. An even-handed examination of the crisis is found in Richard Gwyn, *The Northern Magus* (McClelland and Stewart Limited, 1980).

The quotes from Trudeau's early writings are to be found in Chapter 4, "The just man must go to prison," in *Pierre Elliott Trudeau: Approaches to Politics*, a collection of articles Trudeau wrote for Jacques Hébert's *Vrai*, translated by I.M. Owen (Oxford University Press, 1970).

There is a good deal of legal literature dealing with the October Crisis. Professor Walter Tarnopolsky, in *The Canadian Bill of Rights* (Second Revised Edition, The Carleton Library, McClelland and Stewart Limited, 1976), has included an excellent discussion of the civil liberties issues. My figures regarding the arrests made in Quebec are taken from his book. Professor Noel Lyon's argument regarding the validity of the Public Order Regulations, 1970, appeared in the *McGill Law Journal*, Vol. 18, No. 1, p. 1361; it was rejected by the Quebec Court of Appeal in *Gagnon and Vallières vs. The Queen*, CRNS, Vol. 14, p. 132. The order-in-council passed in British Columbia was discussed in *Jamieson* vs. *A.G.B.C.* (1971) 5 W.W.R. 600 (it was repealed in 1972). Professor Herbert Marx has written a number of articles about the October Crisis: "The Apprehended Insurrection, of October 1970 and the Judicial Function" (*University of British Columbia Law Review*, Vol. 7, p. 6). And see his "Human Rights and Emergency Powers," in R. St. J. Macdonald and John P. Humphrey, eds., *The Practice of Freedom, Canadian Essays on Human Rights and Fundamental Freedoms* (Butterworth and Co. (Canada) Ltd., 1979). The McDonald Commission's findings appear in *Commission of Enquiry Concerning Certain Activities of the Royal Canadian Mounted Police* (Queen's Printer, Ottawa, August, 1981).

Chapter 8: The Nishga Indians and Aboriginal Rights

As I represented the Nishgas before the courts in the Nishga Indians case, I have relied primarily upon my own notes and recollection of the case and events connected with it.

Professor Douglas Sanders has written an account of the legal and political background to the Nishgas' case in *British Columbia Studies*, No. 19, Autumn, 1973, p. 1. The Nishga Indians case is known as *Calder vs. Attorney-General of British Columbia* and is reported in (1969) 8 D.L.R. (3d) 59; 71 W.W.R. 81 (Supreme Court of British Columbia); (1970) 13 D.L.R. (3d) 64; 74 W.W.R. 481 (British Columbia Court of Appeal), and (1973) S.C.R. 313, 34 D.L.R. (3d) 145, (1973) 4 W.W.R. 1 (Supreme Court of Canada).

For an authoritative and insightful discussion of White-Native relations in North America from the earliest times, see J.E.

Chamberlin, *The Harrowing of Eden, White Attitudes Toward Native Americans* (Seabury Press, 1975). The legal and constitutional issues relating to aboriginal title are authoritatively covered (even though publication preceded the judgement in the Supreme Court of Canada in *Calder*) in *Native Rights in Canada*, Peter Cumming and Neil Mickenberg (Second edition, General Publishing Co. Limited, 1972).

The 14 treaties made on southern Vancouver Island between 1850 and 1854 may be found in *Papers Connected with the Indian Land Question 1850-1875* (Queen's Printer, Victoria, 1875). *Indians of British Columbia*, by Professors H. Hawthorn, C. Belshaw and S. Jamieson (University of British Columbia Press, 1965), offers an overview of Indian history and the Indian condition in British Columbia. *The Struggle for Survival*, F.E. La Violette (University of Toronto Press, 1961, reprinted with additions, 1973), is a discussion of Indian cultures and the Protestant ethic in British Columbia. George Manuel, with Peter Posluns, has written, in *The Fourth World* (Collier-Macmillan of Canada Ltd., 1974) of his own struggle and that of the Indian organizations in British Columbia to secure reforms under the Indian Act and of the beginnings of the revival of land claims as a public issue in the 1960s. The Nishgas have asserted their position most recently in *Submission of the Nishga Tribal Council to the Special Joint Committee of the Senate and House of Commons on the Constitution of Canada*, December 15, 1980. In August, 1981, the federal government appointed a representative to negotiate with the Nishgas on their claim. The province of British Columbia has not agreed to participate in these negotiations, though it has undertaken to participate with the federal government in negotiating a settlement of the question of the "cut-off" lands with the Indians of British Columbia.

Two books are especially good. Wilson Duff's *The Indian History of British Columbia, Volume 1, the Impact of the White Man* (Queen's Printer, Victoria, 1965) was intended to be the first of a series, but the series was never completed, owing to Duff's untimely death. Duff's work is original and outstanding. R.E. Cail's *Land, Man and the Law* (University of British Columbia Press, 1974) is a discussion of the disposal of Crown lands in British Columbia from 1871 to 1913. Cail's work is perhaps the leading work in the field. His account of the development of provincial policy in relation to Native title is excellent. Allan Smith, in an article on "The Writing of British Columbia History" (*British Columbia*

Studies, No. 45, Spring, 1980), reveals the failure of British Columbia historians until recently to regard the Indians as anything except peripheral to the province's history. Now see Robin Fisher's *Contact and Conflict*, subtitled *Indian-European Relations in British Columbia, 1774-1880* (University of British Columbia Press, 1978). Rolf Knight's *Indians at Work* (New Star Books, 1978) is an informal history of Native Indian labour in British Columbia, 1858-1930. (There is a useful review of Knight's book by Reuben Ware in *British Columbia Studies*, No. 46, Summer, 1980, at p.99).

In this chapter, I have used some phrases that appeared in *Northern Frontier, Northern Homeland, Report of the Mackenzie Valley Pipeline Enquiry* (Queen's Printer, Ottawa, 1977) because I think they are still apt. The words "myth, legend, history, and law" are taken from the judgement of Mr. Justice Brian Dickson in *R. vs Sutherland* (1980) S. C. C. D. 6187-01.

Appendix

CONSTITUTION ACT, 1981

PART I
CANADIAN CHARTER OF RIGHTS AND FREEDOMS

Whereas Canada is founded upon principles that recognize the supremacy of God and the rule of law:

Guarantee of Rights and Freedoms

1. The *Canadian Charter of Rights and Freedoms* guarantees the rights and freedoms set out in it subject only to such reasonable limits prescribed by law as can be demonstrably justified in a free and democratic society.

Fundamental Freedoms

2. Everyone has the following fundamental freedoms:

(a) freedom of conscience and religion;

(b) freedom of thought, belief, opinion and expression, including freedom of the press and other media of communication;

(c) freedom of peaceful assembly; and

(d) freedom of association.

Democratic Rights

3. Every citizen of Canada has the right to vote in an election of members of the House of Commons or of a legislative assembly and to be qualified for membership therein.

4. (1) No House of Commons and no legislative assembly shall continue for longer than five years from the date fixed for the return of the writs at a general election of its members.

(2) In time of real or apprehended war, invasion or insurrection, a House of Commons may be continued by Parliament and a legislative assembly may be continued by the legislature beyond five years if such continuation is not opposed by the votes of more than one-third of the members of the House of Commons or the legislative assembly, as the case may be.

5. There shall be a sitting of Parliament and of each legislature at least once every twelve months.

Mobility Rights

6. (1) Every citizen of Canada has the right to enter, remain in and leave Canada.

(2) Every citizen of Canada and every person who has the status of a permanent resident of Canada has the right

(a) to move to and take up residence in any province; and

(b) to pursue the gaining of a livelihood in any province.

(3) The rights specified in subsection (2) are subject to

(a) any laws or practices of general application in force in a province other than those that discriminate among persons primarily on the basis of province of present or previous residence; and

(b) any laws providing for reasonable residency requirements as a qualification for the receipt of publicly provided social services.

Legal Rights

7. Everyone has the right to life, liberty and security of the person and the right not to be deprived thereof except in accordance with the principles of fundamental justice.

8. Everyone has the right to be secure against unreasonable search or seizure.

9. Everyone has the right not to be arbitrarily detained or imprisoned.

10. Everyone has the right on arrest or detention

(a) to be informed promptly of the reasons therefor;

(b) to retain and instruct counsel without delay and to be informed of that right; and

(c) to have the validity of the detention determined by way of *habeas corpus* and to be released if the detention is not lawful.

11. Any person charged with an offence has the right

(a) to be informed without unreasonable delay of the specific offence;

(b) to be tried within a reasonable time;

(c) not to be compelled to be a witness in proceedings against that person in respect of the offence;

(d) to be presumed innocent until proven guilty according to law in a fair and public hearing by an independent and impartial tribunal;

(e) not to be denied reasonable bail without just cause;

(f) except in the case of an offence under military law tried before a military tribunal, to the benefit of trial by jury where the maximum punishment for the offence is imprisonment for five years or a more severe punishment;

(g) not to be found guilty on account of any act or omission unless, at the time of the act or omission, it constituted an offence under Canadian or international law or was criminal according to the general principles of law recognized by the community of nations;

(h) if finally acquitted of the offence, not to be tried for it again and, if finally found guilty and punished for the offence, not to be tried or punished for it again; and

(i) if found guilty of the offence and if the punishment for the offence has been varied between the time of commission and the time of sentencing, to the benefit of the lesser punishment.

12. Everyone has the right not to be subjected to any cruel and unusual treatment or punishment.

13. A witness who testifies in any proceedings has the right not to have any incriminating evidence so given used to incriminate that witness in any other proceedings, except in a prosecution for perjury or for the giving of contradictory evidence.

14. A party or witness in any proceedings who does not understand or speak the language in which the proceedings are conducted or who is deaf has the right to the assistance of an interpreter.

Equality Rights

15. (1) Every individual is equal before and under the law and has the right to the equal protection and equal benefit of the law without discrimination and, in particular, without discrimination based on race, national or ethnic origin, colour, religion, sex, age or mental or physical disability.

(2) Subsection (1) does not preclude any law, program or activity that has as its object the amelioration of conditions of disadvantaged individuals or groups including those that are

disadvantaged because of race, national or ethnic origin, colour, religion, sex, age or mental or physical disability.

Official Languages of Canada

16. (1) English and French are the official languages of Canada and have equality of status and equal rights and privileges as to their use in all institutions of the Parliament and government of Canada.

(2) English and French are the official languages of New Brunswick and have equality of status and equal rights and privileges as to their use in all institutions of the legislature and government of New Brunswick.

(3) Nothing in this Charter limits the authority of Parliament or a legislature to advance the equality of status or use of English and French.

17. (1) Everyone has the right to use English or French in any debates and other proceedings of Parliament.

(2) Everyone has the right to use English or French in any debates and other proceedings of the legislature of New Brunswick.

18. (1) The statutes, records and journals of Parliament shall be printed and published in English and French and both language versions are equally authoritative.

(2) The statutes, records and journals of the legislature of New Brunswick shall be printed and published in English and French and both language versions are equally authoritative.

19. (1) Either English or French may be used by any person in, or in any pleading in or process issuing from, any court established by Parliament.

(2) Either English or French may be used by any person in, or in any pleading in or process issuing from, any court of New Brunswick.

20. (1) Any member of the public in Canada has the right to communicate with, and to receive available services from, any head or central office of an institution of the Parliament or government of Canada in English or French, and has the same right with respect to any other office of any such institution where

(a) there is a significant demand for communications with and services from that office in such language; or

(b) due to the nature of the office, it is reasonable that communications with and services from that office be available in both English and French.

(2) Any member of the public in New Brunswick has the right to communicate with, and to receive available services from, any office of an institution of the legislature or government of New Brunswick in English or French.

21. Nothing in sections 16 to 20 abrogates or derogates from any right, privilege or obligation with respect to the English and French languages, or either of them, that exists or is continued by virtue of any other provision of the Constitution of Canada.

22. Nothing in sections 16 to 20 abrogates or derogates from any legal or customary right or privilege acquired or enjoyed either before or after the coming into force of this Charter with respect to any language that is not English or French.

Minority Language Educational Rights

23. (1) Citizens of Canada
(a) whose first language learned and still understood is that of the English or French linguistic minority population of the province in which they reside, or
(b) who have received their primary school instruction in Canada in English or French and reside in a province where the language in which they received that instruction is the language of the English or French linguistic minority population of the province,
have the right to have their children receive primary and secondary school instruction in that language in that province.

(2) Citizens of Canada of whom any child has received or is receiving primary or secondary school instruction in English or French in Canada, have the right to have all their children receive primary and secondary school instruction in the same language.

(3) The right of citizens of Canada under subsections (1) and (2) to have their children receive primary and secondary school instruction in the language of the English or French linguistic minority population of a province
(a) applies wherever in the province the number of children of citizens who have such a right is sufficient to warrant the provision to them out of public funds of minority language instruction; and

(b) includes, where the number of those children so warrants, the right to have them receive that instruction in minority language educational facilities provided out of public funds.

Enforcement

24. (1) Anyone whose rights or freedoms, as guaranteed by this Charter, have been infringed or denied may apply to a court of competent jurisdiction to obtain such remedy as the court considers appropriate and just in the circumstances.

(2) Where, in proceedings under subsection (1), a court concludes that evidence was obtained in a manner that infringed or denied any rights or freedoms guaranteed by this Charter, the evidence shall be excluded if it is established that, having regard to all the circumstances, the admission of it in the proceedings would bring the administration of justice into disrepute.

General

25. The guarantee in this Charter of certain rights and freedoms shall not be construed so as to abrogate or derogate from any aboriginal, treaty or other rights or freedoms that pertain to the aboriginal peoples of Canada including

(a) any rights or freedoms that have been recognized by the Royal Proclamation of October 7, 1763; and

(b) any rights or freedoms that may be acquired by the aboriginal peoples of Canada by way of land claims settlement.

26. The guarantee in this Charter of certain rights and freedoms shall not be construed as denying the existence of any other rights or freedoms that exist in Canada.

27. This Charter shall be interpreted in a manner consistent with the preservation and enhancement of the multicultural heritage of Canadians.

28. Notwithstanding anything in this Charter, the rights and freedoms referred to in it are guaranteed equally to male and female persons.

29. Nothing in this Charter abrogates or derogates from any rights or privileges guaranteed by or under the Constitution of Canada in respect of denominational, separate or dissentient schools.

30. A reference in this Charter to a province or to the legislative assembly or legislature of a province shall be deemed to include a reference to the Yukon Territory and the Northwest Territories, or to the appropriate legislative authority thereof, as the case may be.

31. Nothing in this Charter extends the legislative powers of any body or authority.

Application of Charter

32. (1) This Charter applies

(a) to the Parliament and government of Canada and to all matters within the authority of Parliament including all matters relating to the Yukon Territory and Northwest Territories; and

(b) to the legislature and government of each province and to all matters within the authority of the legislature of each province.

(2) Notwithstanding subsection (1), section 15 shall not have effect until three years after this Act, except Part VI, comes into force.

Citation

33. This Part may be cited as the *Canadian Charter of Rights and Freedoms*.

PART II
RIGHTS OF THE ABORIGINAL PEOPLES OF CANADA

34. (1) The aboriginal and treaty rights of the aboriginal peoples of Canada are hereby recognized and affirmed.

(2) In this Act, "aboriginal peoples of Canada" includes the Indian, Inuit and Métis peoples of Canada.

•   •   •

PART VIII
GENERAL

59. (1) The Constitution of Canada is the supreme law of Canada, and any law that is inconsistent with the provisions of the Constitution is, to the extent of the inconsistency, of no force or effect.

Index

Abella, Prof. Irving, 140, 149
  historian of labour movement in
    Canada, 140, 149
Aboriginal rights
  in Constitution Act, 1981, 53, 249,
    257
  Indian claims to, 30-1, 47, 51-2, 53-4,
    55, 219-50 *passim*
  Metis claims to, 30-1, 47, 51-2, 53-4,
    55, 231-2, 244
  origin of concept, 30-1
  present-day definition, 53, 219
  recognition by Supreme Court of
    Canada, 244-8
Aboriginal title. *See* Aboriginal rights
Acadia and Acadians, 1-25
  and Charter of Rights and
    Freedoms, 24, 90
  culture of, 17, 23-4
  and denominational schools, 18, 20-
    1, 60, 63, 65, 69
  expansion of, 5, 7-9
  expulsion of, 1, 11-15, 16, 109, 125
  founding of, 1, 2-5
  French-English disputes over, 1, 5-6,
    8, 9-11, 15
  and minority rights, 1, 24-5
  population of, 3, 6, 7, 8-9, 11, 18
  return of, 16-17
  sense of collective identity, 21-4, 29
  struggle for survival, 23-5
  way of life, 1, 6, 7-8, 18, 23-4
Adachi, Ken, 104
All-Canadian Congress of Labour, 142
Allied Tribes of British Columbia, 234,
  235
Anglophones, in Quebec, 58, 66, 76,
  90, 258, 261. *See also* English-
  speaking minority, in Quebec
  hostility towards, 191, 261
  opposed by FLQ, 204
Angus, Professor H. F., 98, 105
Archibald, Adams G., 39, 40, 41
Assiniboia, District of, 30, 36, 39, 42.
  See also Red River Settlement
Atlantic Charter, 111, 113

Attorney-General of Quebec vs. Dupond,
  184, 187
Avery, Prof. Donald, 135

BNA Act. *See* British North America
  Act
Bailey, Prof. Alfred C., 22, 23
Banks, Hal, 151
Barrett, John, 69
Barrett vs. Winnipeg, 69, 71
Battle of Seven Oaks, 30, 31, 33
Beetz, Justice Jean
  judgement in *Dupond* case, 185, 186
Bell, J. K., 152
Benchers of the Law Society of British
  Columbia (Benchers), 155, 156
Bennett, Prime Minister R. B., 169
Biencourt, Charles de, 4
Big Bear, Chief, 49, 50
Bill of Rights. *See* Canadian Bill of
  Rights, The
Boilermakers' Union, 142, 143
Bond Head, Sir Francis, 129
Borden, Prime Minister Robert, 84, 87,
  132
Boucher, Aimé, 175, 176, 177, 178, 179
Bourassa, Henri, 77, 78, 83, 84, 85, 90
Bourassa, Premier Robert, and October
  Crisis, 193, 196-7, 198
Bourne, Robin, 160
Bowell, Prime Minister Mackenzie, 71,
  72
Brebner, John Bartlet, 6
British Columbia, 224, 232
  and Indian land claims, 222-41, 249
  and Japanese Canadians, 93-122, 262
  and October Crisis (1970), 204
British North America Act (1867), 64,
  68, 76, 90, 157. *See also*
  Confederation
  federal power of disallowance, 20-1,
    59, 61, 71, 77, 96
  and federal system, 58-9, 60-2, 87
  and immigration, 96
  and Indians, 223-4, 244